EMILY DICKINSON
and Her Contemporaries

Women's Verse in America, 1820–1885

Elizabeth A. Petrino

University Press of New England
Hanover and London

University Press of New England, Hanover, NH 03755
© 1998 by University Press of New England
All rights reserved
Printed in the United States of America
5 4 3 2 1
CIP data appear at the end of the book

For My Parents

With Love

Contents

Acknowledgments

In writing this book, I have received help from a number of people, whom I would like to mention. Joel Porte gave early and lasting advice about directions the argument was to take; Dorothy Mermin turned an attentive eye to my prose style and reading of Dickinson's poems; and Debra Fried, whose graduate seminar first introduced me to Dickinson's poetry, taught me how to read the poet carefully and like the others, embodied the highest commitment to the craft of teaching. I am permanently indebted to their example. Cheryl Walker, Martha Nell Smith, and Barton Levi St. Armand provided lengthy and generous critiques that were instrumental in revising the final manuscript. Only the author of a book and experts in the field know the value of such detailed commentary. Paula Bennett and Christanne Miller offered thoughtful criticisms, provided encouragement, and underscored for me the intellectual generosity that I have come to appreciate among Dickinson critics. Several colleagues, including Mary DeShazer, Allen Mandelbaum, and Elizabeth Phillips, read the manuscript in whole or in part and contributed to my rethinking of the project in its early stages of revision. My editor, Phyllis Deutsch, offered strong support, enthusiasm, and a determination to ensure that the book would see the light of day. I owe my largest debt to my parents and to my brother, John, whose continued interest in and support of this project have contributed to my well-being and sustained me in immeasurable ways.

Grateful acknowledgment is given to the staff and reference librarians at the following libraries who have provided congenial assistance and a clean, well-lighted place to work: the Houghton Library, Harvard University; Schlesinger Library, Radcliffe College; Jones Library, Amherst, Massachusetts; British Art Gallery and the Art and Architecture Library, and Beinecke, Yale University; Division of Rare and Manuscript Collections, Olin Library, and Hortorium Collection at Mann Library, Cornell University; Rare Books and Special Collections, Duke University; and Davis Library, University of North Carolina, Chapel Hill. I am also grateful to Wake Forest University for awarding me an Archie Grant to travel to several of the aforementioned collections and the Seguiv I. Hadari Research Leave in 1995, during which time I completed the manuscript. Parts of chapter 3 were published in *Tulsa Studies in Women's Literature* 13, no. 5 (Fall 1994): 317–38.

Finally, this book has benefited enormously from the contributions of other scholars, including those mentioned and others unnamed, who have created their own legacy—a heritage of criticism and scholarship about a poet whose affinities with other writers of her time are becoming clear.

E.A.P.

Abbreviations

Letters *The Letters of Emily Dickinson*, ed., Thomas H. Johnson and Theodora Ward, 3 vols. Cambridge: Harvard University Press, 1958.

J *The Poems of Emily Dickinson*, ed. Thomas H. Johnson, 3 vols. Cambridge, Mass.: Harvard University Press, 1953.

Leyda Leyda, Jay. *The Years and Hours of Emily Dickinson*, 2 vols. New Haven: Yale University Press, 1960.

Sewall Sewall, Richard B. *The Life of Emily Dickinson*, 2 vols. New York: Farrar, Straus and Giroux, 1974.

"PUBLICATION—IS THE AUCTION"

Chapter 1

Introduction

A Heritage of Poets and the Literary Tradition

> Music coming from under a window has many times been enhanced by its
> separateness; and though to converse athwart a door is not usual, it seems
> more un-useful to discuss such a preference than it would be to analyze the
> beam of light that brings personality, even in death, out of seclusion.
> —Marianne Moore, "Emily Dickinson" (1933)[1]

In her 1933 review of Mabel Loomis Todd's edition of selected *Letters of
Emily Dickinson*, Marianne Moore comments about the general view of the
artist: "One resents the cavil that makes idiosyncrasy out of individuality, asking why Emily Dickinson should sit in the dim hall to listen to Mrs. Todd's
music" (222). That Dickinson often addressed visitors from behind a door or
listened to music being played in the parlor from her upstairs bedroom, for
Moore, reaches beyond the mere assigning of "idiosyncrasy" as a motive. The
ambiguity of Dickinson's physical situation with respect to the music she describes aptly figures the poet's relationship to her audience. If the music comes
"from under a window," is she inside listening to the music being played in her
yard, or relegated to the outdoors? Moore's description dismisses forty years
of criticism that portrayed Dickinson as an isolated eccentric, a girl, or a spinster. Rather than endorse the prevailing view of Dickinson as a shy recluse,
Moore normalizes her willful refusal to be easily understood. In fact, the opac-
ity and resistance of Moore's own writing question the judgment among Dickinson's heirs that the Amherst poet was socially and stylistically isolated. Not
only does Dickinson literally speak "athwart a door" by standing on one side
speaking to a listener on the other, but her "separateness" also contradicts any
expectations concerning the transparency of literary language. The challenge
to the critic, then, is to draw out and to enhance the artist's "personality" and
style, almost as if they were a "beam of light" shining "out of seclusion" from
her age into our own.

Focusing on the conventional attitudes of the nineteenth-century publishing world toward readers and writers, in private and in print, I wish to widen the "beam of light" that shines from Dickinson's inspired and original verse out of the dark chamber of tradition. Still the most significant fact of Dickinson's literary biography is her decision not to publish—a defiant act that rejected the standards for women writers in this period. Nevertheless, she was fully saturated in women's literary culture and shaped by what I call the "limits of expression"—the topics for women delimited by editors and critics. As Joanne Dobson has argued, Dickinson participated in a "community of expression" in which women writers used silence, deferral, and coded rhetorical gestures, and responded with her own self-protective linguistic style: "Her 'slant' expressive strategy, non-publication, and frequent use of conventional feminine images allow Dickinson a poetics in which personal disclosure is screened through a series of fail-safe devices designed to allay anxiety about nonconforming articulation."[2] Similarly, Jane Donahue Eberwein argues that Dickinson employs social and linguistic strategies of limitation in order to test the boundaries of existence.[3] Viewed against the shared culture and literary tradition of other nineteenth-century women writers, Dickinson creates a new, powerful means of expression within the prescribed limits. Rejecting the sentimentality of most women's verse, she mines the duplicity of the female writer's position in relation to her friends and family in order to undercut popular pieties about death and the afterlife, marriage and motherhood, and the power and function of consolatory verse. Having internalized feminine constraints, she still wrote lyrics that revise, parody, mimic, and explode the conventions of women's poetry and the limits of their personal lives.

In broadening the literary and cultural contexts in which Dickinson has been read, I have borrowed the techniques of cultural history and literary criticism. I have also participated in the recovery of a neglected tradition in American women's poetry, only now becoming recognized both for the light it sheds on major authors and for its intrinsic value. Nineteenth-century American women writers often manifest their discomfort with poetic norms while adopting them. As critics such as Tompkins, Fetterley, Zagarell, and others have shown, their novels and short stories reveal this discomfort in disruptions of all types—fissures, ruptures, and narrative inconsistencies.[4] Although the poetry is by and large more conservative than the fiction, I argue that many women poets also resisted the dictates of the publishing world. Negotiating between the prescribed means of expression and the desire to express themselves freely, nineteenth-century American women poets subtly altered the predominant image of women as pious and self-effacing. These writers range from conservative to moderate, working class to upper middle class, regional to urban, and they all demonstrate a reluctance to confront the restrictions of the publishing world head-on.

Although poetry by both British and American women influenced Dickinson's own, I have chosen to focus on the American poets who are much less frequently discussed than their British contemporaries. There is a bewildering array of collections, anthologies, gift books, floral handbooks, and memorial volumes for the scholar to draw from, and I have therefore chosen to focus on a representative sampling of poets and popular generic forms. In the magazines and newspapers read in Dickinson's household, such as *The Springfield Republican*, *The Atlantic Monthly*, *Scribner's*, *The Amherst Record*, and *The Hampshire and Franklin Express*, Helen Hunt Jackson, Lydia Sigourney, Louisa May Alcott, Julia Ward Howe, Maria Lowell, as well as Emily Brontë, Elizabeth Barrett Browning, Christina Rossetti, and countless others, made their way into the poet's conscious life. These poets create a kind of cultural palimpsest, writing and rewriting central tropes about death, femininity, and motherhood that are barely visible under the erasures of literary history. Set against a new and recently recovered tradition of female verse writing, Dickinson's central place in the canon and her position as a consummate artist are clearly affirmed. Although even as a girl she spurned the tearful emotions of much women's verse, she found a variety of sentimental poems, stories, and novels worthy of mention to her friends. Fully conversant in the popular literature of the day, Dickinson drew eclectically from a wide range of contemporary literature including novels, articles, tracts, hymn books, and poems, against which she sounded her more rebellious brand of hymnody. A list of popular literature by women either found in her library (now housed at Harvard) or referred to in her letters reveals that she read a range of popular writers: Rebecca Harding Davis's *Life in the Iron Mills* (1861); Frances Hodgson Burnett's *The Fair Barbarian* (1881), which Dickinson had read with amusement in *Scribner's* and which made such an impression on her Amherst friends and neighbors that it was staged in 1883 with Mabel Loomis Todd in the starring role (Sewall, 172), Ann Manning's *The Maiden and Married Life of Mary Powell* (1852); and Elizabeth Stuart Phelps's (A. Trusta) *The Last Leaf from Sunny Side* (1854). About other books, she could hardly contain her enthusiasm. Writing in 1848 at Mount Holyoke to her friend Abiah Root, she notes that "while at home I had a feast in the reading line" (*Letters* 1, 66), mentioning a veritable smorgasbord of popular literature: Marcella Bute Smedley's *The Maiden Aunt* (1849), Henry Wadsworth Longfellow's *Evangeline* (1847), Thomas Moore's *The Epicurean* (1835), and Martin Tupper's *The Twins* and *The Heart* (1845). In 1845, in a letter to Abiah Root, she praised a poem of the type popular in newspapers of the period by a now-forgotten author, Florence Vane: "Have you seen a beautiful piece of poetry which has been going through the papers lately? *Are we almost there?* is the title of it . . ." (*Letters* 1, 34). Like her contemporaries, Dickinson praised such "effusions," as they were called, for their heightened expression and pathetic sentiment.

Since women writers were guided by the rhetorical styles of editors and publishers, I begin with an overview of the literary marketplace and discuss its impact on Dickinson's decision not to publish. From 1820 to 1880, editors who assembled collections of female verse frequently referred to the poems as "effusions," or emotional outpourings, which they then "fathered" by publishing them under their names. Reviewers in this era often characterized women's verse as more affective and less intellectual than men's, more "natural" and unpremeditated in composition. Women were considered closer to emotions than men, and apt to express pious sentiments almost without conscious thought. Critics regularly compared women's poetic voice to a child's or to birdsong. By contending that women's poetry emerges naturally from the sentiments and the emotions, sanctioned only by publication, they prepare us to understand Dickinson's refusal to allow the bulk of her poems to be printed, lest publication reduce her "Human Spirit / To Disgrace of Price—" (J, 709). Each subsequent chapter sets Dickinson's verse in relation to one or more nineteenth-century American woman poets.

The poetry and culture of mourning, among the most common subjects for nineteenth-century American women poets, is discussed in the second section of this book. While Dickinson partook of the popular cultural myths and fictions concerning death and the afterlife, she found the premises of mid-nineteenth-century America deeply questionable. Sentimental poetry portrays women and children who embody the ideals of evangelism and education. Influenced by the vast numbers of children's deaths in this period, popular writers, such as Louisa May Alcott, Henry Wadsworth Longfellow, Thomas Hood, and Lydia Sigourney, wrote tributes on the deaths of infants, children, and adolescents. Situating Dickinson's poems in relation to those of contemporaries both dramatizes the way she transformed the elegy and promotes a profound understanding of how they adapted the tenets underlying elegiac meditations to their own advantages. A popular infant elegist, for instance, Sigourney often highlights a mother's death in childbirth by juxtaposing a mother's funeral with her infant's christening; Sigourney's elegies suggest that the mother's death returns her to an infant-like state and that her son substitutes for her on earth. Taken together, her poems maintain a pious exterior, while still expanding what a woman could express in a popular and accepted verse genre. Dickinson, however, in exploring the pain and anxiety that both adults and children suffer, rejects the prospect of a blissful gathering of the family circle after death; she suggests that such a reunion is only a fiction in the minds of the mourning family.

The representation of death in extraliterary materials—posthumous portraits, funerary sculpture, the "rural cemetery" movement, and other mourning artifacts—renders more explicit fear and anxiety about death in the culture at large. The prevalence of the motif of the huge dead child, posed against more minute backgrounds, points to the breakdown in nineteenth-century consolatory fictions that was already underway in the early 1800s. Dickinson uses epitaphs to play on the absence implicit in the act of writing and reverses the expected roles of mourner and mourned to shorten our distance from the dead. Drawing on funerary iconography and epitaphic inscriptions, her poetry readjusts perspective, either from the vantage point of the dead, who encourage the living to join them, or from the living, who are so accustomed to remembering the dead that they seem more dead than alive.

The third section of this book explores how Dickinson adapts two common female discourses, floral language and geographic imagery, to reconstruct the popular conception of femininity and its rhetorical possibilities. Dickinson's habit of presenting flowers with poems falls within the context of the language of flowers, which constructed a nonverbal system of communication based on a series of codes. Floral dictionaries proliferated in England and America, including Frances Sargent Osgood's *The Poetry of Flowers, and Flowers of Poetry* (1841), Sara Josepha Hale's *Flora's Interpreter; or, The American Book of Flowers and Sentiments* (1833), and Dorothea Dix's *The Garland Of Flora* (1829). The language of flowers afforded women, who were frequently depicted as flowers and encouraged to shy away from the harsh light of self-revelation and public scrutiny, a way to express their thoughts. Dickinson uses floral lyrics to express emotions that were deemed unacceptable for women. Adapting the divine and secular resonances of floral images as used by more conservative writers like Osgood, she undercuts the pious image of woman and instead privileges secrets, silence, and deferral over actual communication.

Nineteenth-century American women poets often used extreme geographical settings—tropical jungles and arctic locales—to convey women's isolation in their domestic lives, and Dickinson adopts the vocabulary of "zones" and "solstices" that arises in the art and poetry of this period. A popular poet, short story writer, and novelist, Helen Hunt Jackson frequently describes alienation, anger, and sarcasm and portrays an intensity of feeling that is wrenchingly physical. A friend and correspondent of Dickinson's, Jackson also defines the limits of expression to which a female author had to conform and the degree to which she could question those strictures. Betsy Erkkila argues in *The Wicked Sisters: Women Poets, Literary History & Discord* (1992) that Dickinson's and Jackson's relationship showed the constraints on women's works in publishing, and a reading of their correspondence and poems shows that Dickinson refused to submit her verse to the rigors and rewards of the literary marketplace.[5] Conversely, Jackson's poetry reveals the degree to which a woman might adopt the conventional imagery of the period and still portray women's lives as unhappy and unfulfilled. Dickinson's use of tropical and arctic settings, her evocation of Emersonian nature worship as an alternative to normative Christianity, her critique of women's roles, and of the need to suppress passion are expressed in her nature poems and perhaps in her most radical symbol—the volcano.

In the final chapter, I consider the impact on the classroom and scholarship of reading Dickinson's verse against that of other nineteenth-century American women poets. Examining critics who argue for the importance of women's poetry from two different perspectives—aesthetic achievement and social context—I contend that the emergent field of nineteenth-century American women's poetry can radically change our perspective on the artistic, intellectual, and social milieux in which Dickinson and others wrote. What comes of this repositioning of Dickinson against her female contemporaries is, I believe, a fuller historical contextualizing of a consummate poet who drew richly from a wide range of contemporary sources, both high and low. With the exception of Barton Levi St. Armand's masterful study of the poet's relation to Victorian culture and Judith Farr's discussion of Dickinson's artistic and literary sensibilities, few have placed her poems in their cultural and intellectual contexts.[6] I augment these studies by grounding Dickinson's poems in their native territory and searching for parallels among poets whose names were as familiar to her as the wildflowers and plants with which their verses were often compared. Examining conventional poetic genres and literary discourses that were more or less the province of women, such as the child elegy and the flower poem, I broach unexplored critical territory and emphasize gender and culture more strongly than previous critics.

Although critics have argued that placing Dickinson against other women writers makes her originality all the more apparent, most have only gestured at the possible directions such a study might take or its feminist implications. The recovery of neglected works by nineteenth-century American women writers has aided many scholars in reconstructing the literary tradition in America.[7] But I also wish to suggest that exploring the culture and poetry of nineteenth-century women significantly complicates our understanding both of Dickinson's "individuality," in Moore's assessment, and of the other writers' achievement. Rather than view Dickinson as the capstone of a particular theory of women's literature, I wish to explore how her "separateness," in Moore's phrase, nevertheless throws into bold relief a profound connection with the underlying topics of women's verse and allows us to see both her and her female contemporaries differently. In *The Madwoman in the Attic* (1979), Sandra Gilbert and Susan Gubar argue the poet dramatizes and enacts within her lyrics personae whose life histories share features with the lives of romantic heroines in British and American fiction. They trace a line of descent that begins with Jane Austen, who maintains an ironic detachment toward the lives of her characters, and ends with the Brontës and George Eliot, who increasingly identify their heroines' lives with their own. They claim that Dickinson dramatically enacts in her poems her own life story, "an extended fiction whose subject is the life of that supposed person who was originally called Emily Dickinson."[8] Yet Dickinson speaks to the difficulty of making such connections between life and art. She writes to Higginson in 1862, "When I state myself, as the Representative of the Verse—it does not mean—me—but a supposed person" (*Letters* 2, 412). Her remark cautions us about conflating her art and her life, the poetic model of which is more appropriately, as Elizabeth Phillips notes, the dramatic monologue than a self-referential enactment of her life.[9] If we take Moore's defense of Dickinson's behavior as a commentary on her relationship to literary convention, then we might profitably explore her most immediate relationship to a neglected female literary tradition. After receiving a copy of J. E. Cross's *The Life of George Eliot* from Thomas Wentworth Higginson in 1885, she wrote to thank him and noted, "Biography first convinces us of the fleeing of the Biographied—" (*Letters* 3, 864). As Dickinson hints concerning Eliot, biographical treatments of the lives of nineteenth-century women writers often accompanied their deaths but failed to capture their lively selves.

Although Gilbert and Gubar's approach has been instrumental in defining a female literary tradition, I would argue that we need to investigate Dickinson's poetry more fully with respect to the literary achievements of her sister poets.[10] Viewed against the backdrop of a shared cultural and literary milieu, Dickinson's poetry challenges assumptions about women's lives. Other women poets had already begun to resist publishing constraints, consolatory fictions, parental roles, and floral associations in verses, so often maligned, that subtly reflect the adaptation of traditional feminine poetic discourses. In *Stealing the Language: The Emergence of Women's Poetry in America*, Alicia Suskin Ostriker argues that women poets before the modern age contradict their outward appearance. Among all the poets she mentions, Dickinson is the most self-conscious and artful in her manipulation. Able to sustain both the conventional and radical meanings through her use of ambiguity, Dickinson is exemplary among nineteenth-century poets who betray a double-sided adherence to, and subversion of, the dictates of femininity that she terms "duplicitous."[11] According to Ostriker, the constraints of subject matter led to an overdose of sentimental rhetoric in women's poetry and a corresponding diminution of artistic power:

It is also evident that the sentimentality is a result of authors' pretending not to know, not to feel, what they do know and feel. Inflated, exclamatory rhetoric is a device employed when a poet is supposed to seem natural and impulsive but is obliged to repress awareness of her body and her ego. Flights to sublimity arrive at banality when the actual world of men, women, and manners is restricted material. Soporific meters without prosodic experimentation arise when the intention is to please and soothe. (33)

Ostriker's characterization of sentimental poetry clearly stems from an awareness that nineteenth-century American female poets had to constrain their verses to accepted modes. Ostriker mentions that sentimentality arises precisely when the author is "pretending not to know" what is perfectly obvious, and her definition underscores the way nineteenth-century female poets felt the dual responsibility to maintain respectability and to articulate concerns of national importance. Although Christian evangelism, womanhood, and the home were frequent subjects, public poetry provided a forum for their deepest concerns, such as temperance, abolition, women's rights, and Native-American activism. Under the guise of sentimentality, women wielded emotional power that had national ramifications. For all the talk of "separate spheres" in the political and social lives of men and women, nineteenth-century female poets were clearly as engaged as their male counterparts in issues of national importance. Furthermore, "flights to sublimity" that "arrive at banality" appear in some of Longfellow's (and even Whitman's) most majestic and long-winded phrases, as in "The Song of Hiawatha": "As he bore the red deer homeward, / And Iagoo and Nokomis / Hailed his coming with applauses."[12] Certainly, Whittier and Bryant at times might be accused of "soporific meters." Longfellow, too. And Frances Osgood discusses "the actual world of men, women, and manners" in her witty and irreverent poems about romantic courtship, and her most sexually charged poems, such as "The Cocoa-Nut Tree," demonstrate women's erotic selves were alive and kicking.

In her benchmark study of nineteenth-century American women's poetry, *The Nightingale's Burden: Women Poets and American Culture before 1900*, Cheryl Walker explores the generic structure of women's poetry but avoids discussing their conventional topics, such as religion and the deaths of children, in order to focus on the relation between women and the patriarchal determinants of social order. In reconstructing the social, psychological, and historical milieux in which women wrote, Walker describes several archetypes that proliferated in women's poetry of the period: the "sanctuary" poem, in which the speaker retreats to a bower of refuge to escape a violent assault upon her body or mind and experiences a feeling of freedom and creativity; the "power fantasy" poem, in which images of flight and sexual aggression precede a sense of fulfillment; the "free bird" poem, in which the speaker identifies with a confined bird and longs to be free; and the "sensibility" poem, in which the speaker defines herself in terms of an immoderate and agonized hypersensitivity.[13] Emily Stipes Watts in *The Poetry of American Women from 1632 to 1945* also surveys the tradition of women's poetry and stakes out its major authors and literary motifs.[14] In her study of nineteenth-century American women's poetry, Watts contends that although women's poetry was not impious, political, or particularly assertive, women adopted a set of tropes, many based on classical mythology, that countered the prevalent Adamic myth in American culture. Similarly, examining the "social, religious and intellectual currents of her time,"[15] Paula Bennett places Dickinson in the context of other nineteenth-century women poets and argues that Dickinson's domesticity and womanhood were crucial to her development as a poet: "Her submergence into the women's sphere and her presentation of herself as 'poetess' (a *woman* poet) was, therefore, a good deal more than simply a role she played in order to keep from playing others" (13). For Bennett, Dickinson rejects masculine authority and uses nature to transcend the masculinist tradition: "Unable to reconcile herself to the concept of a transcendent God, Dickinson presents nature as a woman-centered and materially-based alternative to established religion" (20).

If nineteenth-century women attempted in their poems to free themselves from the oppressive weight of male dominance, however, they did so by conforming to the generic characteristics and typical themes and to the image of women proposed by the publishing world. It is tempting to read a twentieth-century feminist bias into nineteenth-century genteel culture, since our tendency as critics is to assume that women were strategic in promoting their own talent, though they never actually claimed they were more talented than male writers. Rather, much as female writers pretended to accept a self-effacing demeanor in print, their resistance to established poetic norms of expression amounts not to a strategy consciously directed against an oppressive culture, as some critics have argued, but to a discomfort with topics that were not equal to the actual experiences of their lives.[16]

On 7 July 1860, an anonymous article appeared in *The Springfield Republican*, perhaps written by Dickinson's friend and editor-in-chief, Samuel Bowles, on "When Should We Write":

There is another kind of writing only too common, appealing to the sympathies of the reader without recommending itself to his judgment. It may be called the literature of misery. Its writers are chiefly women, gifted women may be, full of thought and feeling and fancy, but poor, lonely and unhappy. Alas that suffering is so seldom healthful. It may be a valuable discipline in the end, but for the time being it too often clouds, withers, distorts. It is so difficult to see objects distinctly through a mist of tears. The sketch or poem is usually the writer's photograph in miniature. It reveals a countenance we would gladly brighten, but not by exposing it to the gaze of a worthless world.[17]

It is striking how much the writer, who conflates women's writing with their lives and emotions, correspondingly denigrates the so-called "literature of misery" as sentimental, contending that such emotion "clouds, withers, distorts" and so prevents the poet from accurately representing life. His quasi-scientific desire for the poet "to see objects distinctly," not "through a mist of tears," elevates rationality over feeling. Perhaps Dickinson echoed such sentiments herself when she wrote in 1861 to Higginson about her verse, "The Mind is so near itself—it cannot see, distinctly—and I have none to ask—" (*Letters* 2,

403). Furthermore, a woman's poem is thought to mimic her nature and to serve as a "photograph in miniature," clearly a violation of the privacy cherished by the men and women of the age. As Eberwein notes, the poet's brother, Austin, consistently refused to allow photographs of himself to be published in Amherst town histories and often repeated to his daughter a dictum he had learned as a child: "Fools' names and fools' faces / Only appear in public places" (6). Bowles's statement that he would only reluctantly expose a woman's "countenance" to the "worthless gaze of the world" captures the spirit that would discourage women from publishing: if a genteel woman would not show her face all over, then shouldn't the female writer also refrain from submitting her innermost feelings to public scrutiny?

Feminist critics have ranked the "literature of misery" as an expression of female power. According to Walker, the "literature of misery" defined a poet's worth in terms of the capacity to convey grief, and women writers claimed special talent as a result of their suffering and self-sacrifice.[18] If we contend, as Walker does, that drawing on a "secret sorrow" allowed women "a sense of self-importance and an object for contemplation that they could claim as their own" (88), then we can find their poems assertive, since they frequently focus on domestic sorrows and personal trials. Placing at a high premium the ability to be moved by the dying, sentimentalists believed that the fact of sudden death was a reminder of the common bond of mortality and a means to convert the mourners. A popular New England poet, Hannah F. Gould, portrays "The Dying Child's Request" (1832) to act as a *memento mori* for others:

> "To brother—sister—playmates too,
>   Some gift I'd leave behind,
> To keep me, when I've passed from view,
>   Still present to their mind.

> "You'll thus to them my books divide,
>   My playthings give away;
> So they'll remember how I died,
>   When not so old as they."[19]

Portraying children, whose certainty of the afterlife and piety remained strong, these writers provide evidence for the nineteenth-century reader that faith persevered after death. Dickinson frequently asked the question more bluntly in letters to friends and relatives on the death of a loved one: "Did he go willingly?" Yet in the hands of the sentimentalists, stories of holy trials and patient deaths were part of a larger revolt against Calvinism, for they made the emotional "melting" of a contrite heart more central than resignation to death. The expression of boundless grief and the theme of spiritual renewal were generally thought to be elevated subjects that merited heartfelt "effusions," which could rescue the mourner from damnation if only he or she were appropriately moved. As Gould's poem demonstrates, women's elegies often idealized dying children as teachers and pious exemplars. At the same time, children's messianic calling reveals how domestic traits, such as piety and the desire to teach others, extended far beyond the home and into the culture at large. Certainly, the image of women performing their domestic duties with angelic charm and moral rectitude became part of the conservative ideology to which many women writers publicly conformed in the mid-nineteenth century. Yet they also betrayed considerable business sense and negotiated their careers with savvy. As Mary Kelley has noted, because their lives were separated into "private women" and "public stages," they seldom displayed to their editors and their reading public any self-consciousness over this disparity.[20]

These three critics—Walker, Watts, and Ostriker—demonstrate that a continuum exists in American women's poetry from its Puritan origins to the 1960s, yet they only gesture toward the importance of reading Dickinson against her female contemporaries and in their shared literary culture. They define the central images, such as the "secret sorrow" and the "free bird," that pervade women's poetry. They also demonstrate the link between women poets of the same tradition, radical and conservative, black and white, who reworked common themes concerning women's poetic creativity. Finally, each critic encourages us to read Dickinson against the spectrum of nineteenth-century women writers as either an "Individual Talent" in the midst of a women's "Tradition" (Walker), a master of the duplicitous style (Ostriker), or an exponent of a feminine poetic tradition (Watts).

Feminist critics have spawned the recovery of nineteenth-century American women's literature, an ongoing process that has profound implications for the reconstruction of the American literary canon. The doctrine of "separate spheres"—the idea that women's and men's lives were presumed to belong to the home and the larger world respectively—is a mainstay of arguments about nineteenth-century women's lives and literary careers and has itself undergone significant revision.[21] In their account of the rise of the bourgeois family in nineteenth-century America, Barbara Ehrenreich and Deidre English note that the collapse of the old-order agrarian life prompted the creation of new "public" and "private" spheres dividing the home and business world into women's and men's realms, and thus maintaining a hierarchical division of work and leisure, where women occupied a central role as purveyors of morals and primary educators of children.[22] Confined to *Kinder, Kirche, Küche*—children, church, and kitchen, in the popular prewar German formulation concerning women's lives—women of the middle classes were expected to raise children and run their households; in turn, men's roles as wage earners in the business world were confirmed. Writing in 1978, Nina Baym notes that the "domestic" is not a "fixed or neutral word in critical analysis," for it betokens to modern critics not only women's fiction set within the home but entrapment.[23] In contrast, nineteenth-century women writers did not see their lives as belonging to "separate spheres," but they saw the home as a place from which women could exert almost as much control in the world as men: "If worldly values could dominate the home, perhaps the direction of influence could be reversed so that home values dominated the world. Since they identified home with basic human values, they saw this as a reformation of America into a society at last responsive to truly human needs, a fulfillment of the original settlers' dreams" (48–49).

Among some feminist literary critics, reclaiming sentimentalism has provided a way to establish women's literature as a means of empowerment. As Shirley Samuels has argued in *The Culture of Sentiment* (1992), critics of sentimentality have often taken it to task for focusing on domestic and familial relations through which they addressed crucial national issues, such as slavery, despite their exclusion from political power.[24] Sentimentalists were at once chided for refraining from exercising power over issues of real political and social importance and, simultaneously, defined by a lack of ability to act outside the home. The doctrine of separate spheres thus embodies a "double logic of power and powerlessness": "a separation from the world of 'work' (and economic power) was compensated for by the affective power of the 'home'; in the use of sentimentality, separation from political action nonetheless meant presenting an affective alternative that not only gave political actions their emotional significance, but beyond that, intimately linked individual bodies to the national body" (4). Although Samuels does not claim that women assert themselves politically through sentimental literature, sentimentality, with its fusion of feminism and abolition, foregrounds women's concerns with the way power is managed in the culture at large.

Novels like Harriet Beecher Stowe's *Uncle Tom's Cabin* (1851–52) sowed the seeds of revolt in nineteenth-century American women's writing by advocating bonds between women. For Baym, the symbiosis between home and world is best exemplified by Stowe's novel. Stowe's Eva, for instance, is linked to a female power matrix: Mrs. Bird, Mrs. Shelby, Rachel Halliday, and Aunt Dinah manipulate men's behavior and rule from the kitchen. Eva is associated with the evangelical fervor of mothers. Desiring to convert the slaves through touch, she invokes the physical contact so common among evangelists. When she lays her hand on Topsy's shoulder, her father, the atheist St. Clare, is reminded of his mother's words: "we must be willing to do as Christ did,—call them to us, and *put our hands on them*."[25] By showing how St. Clare and other men associate Eva with the piety of their mothers, Stowe hopes to persuade the public to eliminate slavery through identification with Eva's tearful passing. For Stowe and other writers of her age, women could affect the course of history through their evangelical zeal and ability to arouse pathos.

If one considers the political and personal dimensions of women's lyrics, their self-portrayals are double-edged: they can be read either as affirming a belief in the ideology of submissive womanhood or as questioning women's roles. The satisfaction of woman's role as pious nurturer, for example, is described in Julia Ward Howe's "Woman":

> A vestal priestess, proudly pure,
>> But of a meek and quiet spirit;
> With soul all dauntless to endure,
>> And mood so calm that none can stir it,
> Save when a thought most deeply thrilling
> Her eyes with gentlest tears is filling,
> Which seem with her true words to start
> From the deep fountain at her heart.
>
> A mien that neither seeks nor shuns
>> The homage scattered in her way;
> A love that hath few favored ones,
>> And yet for all can work and pray;
> A smile wherein each mortal reads
> The very sympathy he needs;
> An eye like to a mystic book
>> Of lays that bard or prophet sings,
> Which keepeth for the holiest look
>> Of holiest love its deepest things
>
> . . . .
>
> A vestal priestess, maid, or wife—
>> Vestal, and vowed to offer up
> The innocence of a holy life
>> To Him who gives the mingled cup;
> With man its bitter sweets to share,
> To live and love, to do and dare;
> His prayer to breathe, his tears to shed,
> Breaking to him the heavenly bread
> Of hopes which, all too high for earth,
> Have yet in her a mortal birth.[26]

Howe portrays an embodiment of the womanly virtues of humility and silence. "Meek and quiet," she displays chastity as a "vestal priestess." Her association with the six priestesses who guarded the sacred flame in the temple of Vesta in ancient Rome is reinforced by Howe's characterization of her as "the fireside's dearest ornament" (l. 20) and also suggests that her role is essentially domestic. Quite as remarkable as the portrait of womanly virtue and household taskmaster, however, are its multiple contradictions: she is "proudly pure," but unprepossessing; "neither seeks nor shuns" praise; favors none, but serves all; and so on. Howe's portrait balances the qualities that a woman was ideally thought to possess, since she was not assumed to feel any actual desire, creating a two-sided portrait that preserves her ambiguity to the viewer, who can see in her placid expression "a smile wherein each mortal reads / The very sympathy he needs" (ll. 13–14). Simultaneously mirroring others and fulfilling their needs for sympathy, she is aptly summed up by the Romantic image of nature as a "mystic book" (l. 15). For Emerson and Wordsworth, the leaves of this mystic book hold the traces of God to an inspired mind. Lacking the intellectual capacity to interpret herself, woman is a symbol that must be interpreted by others, a vessel that contains all the desires projected onto her. Finally, she assumes a Christian role, sharing her husband's responsibilities and embodying the "hopes which, all too high on earth, / Have yet in her a mortal birth" (ll. 33–34). The speaker's concluding lines uncover the ambiguity:

> This is the woman I have dreamed,
> And to my childish thought she seemed
> The woman I myself should be:
> Alas! I would that I were she.
>
> (ll. 35–38)

Although these lines can be read as a straightforward acceptance of this image of femininity, they also might sardonically admit that such an ideal is undesirable: to her "childish thought" this image of woman seemed perfect, but in adulthood the speaker's wish to imitate this model is reduced to a sigh.

Elizabeth Oakes Smith's "The Wife" captures some of the same ambiguities:

> All day, like some sweet bird, content to sing
> In its small cage, she moveth to and fro—
> And ever and anon will upward spring
> To her sweet lips, fresh from the fount below,
> The murmured melody of pleasant thought,
> Unconscious uttered, gentle-toned and low.
> Light household duties, evermore inwrought
> With placid fancies of one trusting heart
> That lives but in her smile, and turns
> From life's cold seeming and the busy mart,
> With tenderness, that heavenward ever yearns
> To be refreshed where one pure altar burns.
> Shut out from hence, the mockery of life,
> Thus liveth she content, the meek, fond, trusting wife.[27]

This poem adopts birdsong as a central metaphor for a woman's poetic voice that depicts her supposedly "natural" and spontaneous being. Comparing a wife to "some sweet bird" in its "small cage," Oakes Smith suggests that women resemble birds in their naive expression of "pleasant thought," which rises "from the fount below . . . / Unconscious uttered" (ll. 4–6). Furthermore, home life stands in opposition to "life's cold seeming and the busy mart," suggesting that men can be redeemed by the values and virtues of the home. In serving as the earthly repository of the "one pure altar" of heaven, wife and home become more real than the world outside, where life's "cold seeming" and "mockery" of true existence reign. Indeed, although the description in the last eight lines is of the wife, it might as easily apply to a husband, who after a long day, turns with "one trusting heart / That lives but in her smile" to the inner sanctum of the home. Paradoxically, however, the home is also sustained by her (or his) "placid fancies," and her "content" (mentioned twice in the poem) relies on a denial of reality. At the poem's end, "fond" connotes naively credulous as well as caring and implies that the wife is foolish for not realizing that her husband's ascendency over her is sustained by her confined existence.

Rather than portray a woman as placidly content, neither desirous herself nor accepting the desires of others, even Dickinson's more conventional speakers often lament the fate of unappreciated women, as in the following lyric:

> Poor little Heart!
> Did they forget thee?
> Then dinna care! Then dinna care!
>
> Proud little Heart!
> Did they forsake thee?
> Be debonnaire! Be debonnaire!
>
> Frail little Heart!
> *I* would not break thee—
> Could'st credit *me*? Could'st credit me?
>
> Gay little Heart—
> Like Morning Glory!
> Wind and Sun—wilt thee array!
>
>   (J, 192)

Reminiscent of Burns's Scottish lays with its dialectic "dinna," the poem adopts the sentimental imagery and repetitive phrasing reminiscent of bird calls and typical of women's poetry. But Dickinson transforms the conventional sorrowing of a traduced women by casting the speaker as one who courageously bemoans the fate of the forgotten and ill-used "little Heart."

Rather than extol a woman's state in life as teacher and purveyor of values, Dickinson's speaker challenges the "little Heart" to be stoic in the face of abuse. If the heart is forgotten, the speaker urges forgetfulness; if forsaken, gaity; if broken, faith in a *woman* rather than a man. Dickinson overturns the romantic conventions upon which poetry is based, where a man's attention determines a woman's social role and her estimation of herself. Ultimately, the poem suggests that the "little Heart" will receive its final commendation and the fulfillment of its promises only in death. The comparison to "Morning Glory," which evokes the resurrection, suggests that the heart will find its final release in the ground, where it will be arrayed by "Wind and Sun" rather than the attributes of worldly love. Far from locating the source of women's power in an inner spiritual "fount," as do Smith and Howe, Dickinson centers women's freedom in nature and, more ambiguously, in death. Even in this early poem, she creates an allegory of romantic detachment that contradicts the hierarchies of activity and passivity upon which courtship is based.[28] More generally, her poems adapt the language of sentimentalism to question the essentializing view that women were an unthinking fount of emotions and to promote Dickinson's inclusion in a community of other women writers. As the following chapters show, Dickinson's poetry emanates from an artistic and intellectual sensibility born of her native New England and shared with other women, a recognition of whose own artistic achievement has been long overdue.

Chapter 2

"This—Was a Poet"
Emily Dickinson and Nineteenth-Century Publishing Standards

It is the woman above all—there never have been women, save pioneer Katies; not one in flower save some moonflower Poe may have seen, or an unripe child. Poets? Where? They are the test. But a true woman in flower, never. Emily Dickinson, starving of passion in her father's garden, is the very nearest we have ever been—starving.

—William Carlos Williams, *In the American Grain*[1]

There are women so intensely feminine that they would not write to publish if they could; too proud, because too wise to expose their feelings to a world made up of persons with whom they neither hold communion, nor have sympathy.

—Elizabeth Sheppard, *Rumors* (Leyda 2, 88)

I thought that being a Poem one's self precluded the writing Poems, but perceive the Mistake.

—Emily Dickinson (*Letters* 2, 525)

"The whole tendency of the age is Magazine-ward," wrote Edgar Allan Poe concerning the proliferation of magazines and periodicals in nineteenth-century America.[2] Perhaps referring humorously to the heavenward direction of much pious and uplifting sentimental poetry and fiction, so popular in his era, and written primarily by women, Poe brilliantly goes on to define a woman's relationship to her literary composition. Cannily aware of the way women's lives and poems were often confused, he claimed that "a woman will never be brought to admit a non-identity between herself and her book."[3] We may take his comment that a woman writer's art will never stand apart from her life also as a strategy consciously adopted by literary women. As he notes, they would never "admit" that their lives and works were not identical, because they saw the conflation of a woman's life and art as an opportunity to hide behind a shield of modest femininity. Deemed the embodiment of values, women's poems were read as extensions of the female sex, and allowing their books to represent themselves publicly entitled the poets to a greater degree of freedom in their personal lives than they might otherwise have been afforded.

Perhaps the most important fact of her literary biography is Dickinson's decision not to publish. In doing so, she distinguished herself as the only American Renaissance writer who valued her own conception so completely that she was willing to forego publication. Even Higginson, litterateur and friend, advanced her poems before the public in his 1890 "An Open Portfolio" only "with some misgiving, and almost with a sense of questionable publicity," yet he readily acknowledged the authenticity of her creative vision: "Wayward and unconventional in the last degree; defiant of form, measure, rhyme, and even grammar; she yet had an exacting standard of her own, and would wait many days for a word that satisfied."[4] In light of the history of the critical discourse surrounding women's poetry, the Dickinson-Higginson relationship might be recast in terms that highlight the dismissiveness that is a normative response of a critic to a woman writer. Like the character from Elizabeth Sheppard's novel, *Rumors*, Dickinson profited by the attitude toward the lives and careers of many female authors, deemed too "feminine" to seek notoriety in print and too "wise" to circulate their verse widely among unappreciative readers.[5] Instead, she forsook publication once she realized her artistic conception would be violated and adapted the standard of moral propriety that encouraged women to shy away from the light of public exposure. She countered the prevailing opinion that women should refrain from discussing any but pious and domestic topics and sought an alternative to publication as a means of circulating her verses.

Many critics have discussed Dickinson's fascicles—the forty stab-bound and hand-sewn packets into which she copied her verse that were discovered in her bureau after her death by her sister, Lavinia—either as a form of self-publication or as an ordering device that gives method and meaning to her poetry.[6] As Martha Nell Smith has argued in *Rowing in Eden: Rereading Emily Dickinson*, these textual exchanges between the poet and her correspondents, especially her beloved sister-in-law, Susan Gilbert, and important male friends, comprise themselves a type of "publication" and amount to a method of "workshop" composition that counters the prevailing myth about her supposed isolation as a writer.[7] Dickinson "published" her poems by circulating them in her letters; she may have circulated manuscript books to Helen Hunt Jackson. Far from mere "fair copies," the fascicles are an invaluable source for discerning the poet's intentions and her compositional techniques, as the script itself becomes a form of iconic design. These holographic performances, in which lines gain or lose intelligibility with their calligraphy, are largely defeated through conventional print reproductions of her poems.

Dickinson's circulation of manuscripts, various handwriting styles, and visual puns all suggest that she found more autonomy and room for free play in the unrestricted page, and the vein of criticism that sees her as a scribal publisher raises provocative issues about her absorption of periodicals, newspapers, and giftbooks, all of which trumpeted the standards of women's verse. Dickinson's choice not to publish was influenced by the publishing constraints to which women were subjected. As Karen Dandurand has argued, Dickinson was fully aware that her poems were "going round" the newspapers, a nineteenth-century euphemism for reprinting and circulating verses, often without permission from the original source.[8] If so, then one might assume that it was perhaps not the idea of publication that so disturbed her as the loss of control over her poems once they were in the hands of editors. As she remarks to Higginson in an early letter, "I marked a line in One Verse—because I met it after I made it—and never consciously touch a paint, mixed by another person—" (*Letters* 2, 415). Rather than submit to the legitimating strategies and dictates of editors and publishers, she chose to refrain from publishing altogether.

Why did Dickinson reject the opportunity to print her verses and make the boldest quest for poetic originality among her contemporaries? How (and to what degree) did other women serve as examples? How far were these poets able to modify, redefine, and explode the prevalent definition and presentation of women's verse in nineteenth-century America? Characterized by most nineteenth-century critics as pious, natural, and unpremeditated, women's poems and their lives were often conflated. In fact, so often were women's books and lives compared that their poems came to be referred to as "embodiments," "waifs," and "children," which needed to be "fathered" under the auspices of a male critic or editor before appearing before the public. Dickinson deemed publication "the Auction / Of the Mind of Man" (J, 709), and therefore refused to allow the bulk of her poems to be printed, lest publication reduce her "Human Spirit / To Disgrace of Price—" (J, 709).

The publishing milieu contributed greatly to the formation of a nineteenth-century reader's taste. Recently, critics have focused on reconstructing the literary milieu or print culture to ask questions about how and why authors wrote. In *Beneath the American Renaissance*, David S. Reynolds draws on and demonstrates the influences of a variety of "high" and "low" discourses in American print culture, including temperance literature, evangelical tracts, and abolition newspapers on major authors, like Dickinson, Melville, and Whitman. He underscores Dickinson's allegiance with the sensibility and political sympathies of her age, even as she transforms its materials: "If the women authors of the literature of misery sought to establish an artistic middle ground between the effetely Conventional and the openly feminist, so Emily Dickinson explicitly rejected both the 'Dimity Convictions' of traditionalists and the public methods of women's rights activists, while she made the era's boldest quest for specifically artistic exhibitions of woman's power."[9] By focusing on Dickinson's specifically "artistic exhibitions of woman's power," Reynolds privileges the aesthetic over the sociological, making it difficult for him to speak of the value of much women's poetry of this era. Wishing to maintain a distinction between "high" and "low" literature, Reynolds contends that major authors rework, modify, and, ultimately, transform subliterary genres into works of art. This argument, though, masks the intrinsic artistic value of much women's writing and, conversely, the sentimentalism with which many of Dickinson's own lyrics are imbued. The hierarchical equations upon which his and other critics' arguments rest—canonical/noncanonical, radical/conservative—are put into question when we begin to consider that Dickinson adopted many of the same fictions and myths as other women writers, cultural materials that were shaped by editors' and critics' perceived role for women.

By the 1840s, magazine publishing had become a major source of revenue for established writers, and new female writers profited by the widespread distribution of their work as well. Genteel magazines, such as *Scribner's Monthly*, *Graham's Magazine*, *Harper's*, and *The Atlantic Monthly*, set the standards of literary taste and encouraged the development of a national audience for women's domestic fiction and verse. Producing Gothic tales, Western travelogs, sentimental poetry, short stories, and novels, such writers as Harriet Prescott Spofford, Caroline Kirkland, Harriet Beecher Stowe, and Alice and Phoebe Cary reaped profits. Encouraged by the ever-widening market for sensation fiction, sentimental romance, travel pieces, and periodical literature of all types, women gained notoriety, which in turn served their financial interests. Publishers branched out to the southern and western states. From about 1790 to 1830, magazine publishing had become increasingly centralized in New York and Philadelphia, where most well-known male authors, such as Whittier, Prescott, Longfellow, Lowell, and Hawthorne, had their works distributed. As British reprints of successful authors began to diminish the American bookselling trade, however, famous writers, as well as those women who were trying to break into the market, increasingly turned to magazines to publish their works. As Charvat notes, the burgeoning of magazines created a demand for poetry by which popular poets, including Longfellow and Whittier, were to profit; others, including Julia Ward Howe, Louisa May Alcott, Celia Thaxter, and Helen Hunt Jackson, eventually did as well.[10]

While the standardizing of men's and women's literary works in magazines made publishing successful as a business venture, it also promoted a unified norm of taste and required drastic artistic compromises. Even noteworthy authors had to bow their intentions to the demands of editors at powerful publishing houses. Hawthorne, for instance, came close to ruining his career by catering to his publisher, Ticknor & Fields, when they insisted that he keep turning out new works for his audience.[11] Poe, too, railed against the magazines and newspapers that he believed lessened literature's worth by demanding light and easily digestible reading: "Whatever the talent may be brought to bear upon our daily journals, (and in many cases this talent is very great,) still the imperative necessity of catching, *currente calamo*, each topic as it flits before the eye of the public, must of course materially narrow the limits of their power."[12] Like their male counterparts, women were commercially viable and successful in being published insofar as they adapted to the expectations of the publishing world.

A woman who epitomizes success through submission to publishing constraints is Susannah Rowson. Her *Charlotte Temple* (1791), a seduction novel printed in England before her departure for America, was the most popular novel in America before Scott's historical romances. Rowson's book not only demonstrates her willingness to conform to publishers' expectations but also models the way women's literature would be published later in the nineteenth century. While her *Reuben and Rachel* (1796), a novel set in the era of Columbus on American soil, failed miserably, it is significant that she ventured outside the conventions of the strictly European seduction novel precisely to satisfy the American reading public's newfound taste for historical romance. As Charvat tells us in *The Profession of Authorship in America*, "This readiness to consult the market and adapt to it her literary stock-in-trade, which was didacticism, gives Mrs. Rowson standing as an early American writer of true professional temperament."[13] Although Charvat's comment evinces the dismissal among many critics of women's literature, he correctly surmises that, from the 1790s onward, to be a successful writer, either male or female, meant tailoring literary works to the expectations of the publishing world.

In *Doing Literary Business: American Women Writers in the Nineteenth Century*, Susan Coultrap-McQuin argues that nineteenth-century women writers were among the most widely recognized in America and the most undervalued. By 1830, fully a third of published authors were women; by 1850, female writers accounted for nearly one half of the most popular writers in the nation.[14] Despite their success, women were denied both recognition and authority for their work. Indeed, Coultrap-McQuin takes as her central question their persistence in the face of tremendous obstacles: "How can we explain women's persistence and success as writers in the face of attitudes and behaviors that could render them invisible?" (3). She explains this success in part as a result of their courtly dealings with their "Gentleman Publishers," more resembling a marriage than a professional relationship with their editors. The paternalistic attitude an editor took toward his authors was mutually beneficial and symbiotic: he provided gentlemanly services, including paying bills, performing personal favors, advancing money, and advising on investments, while the author, more often than not, responded with loyalty and trust that ensured a continued commitment to his publishing house. Gentleman Publishers "sought to develop trusting, paternalistic, personal relationships with their authors; they claimed to have personal goals beyond commercial ones to advance culture and/or to provide a public service; and they assumed the role of moral guardian for their society" (34). Undoubtedly, part of the implied rationale for an editor's fatherly behavior toward women was that he acted as a buffer between the hard financial realities of the publishing world and their delicate sensibilities, but his prevalence in all aspects of the author's life did not lessen (and perhaps even affirmed) his decision-making power and role as arbiter of taste. Female writers found their cordial and supportive relationship with editors willing to publish their work both a boon and a burden: they gained a wide audience and could earn their living as writers but only by submitting their poetry to editors' dictates and conforming to a docile and agreeable public image.

Known primarily as Poe's vindictive literary executor, Rufus Griswold set the terms by which women's verse was described in the 1848 preface to his well-known anthology, *The Female Poets of America*. When we consider that Griswold's volume was widely distributed and very influential, his preface reveals several dominant ideas about women's writing in this era. He denigrates the intellectual value of women's poetry by contending that it relies heavily on an expression of the emotions. Because he believes that feeling is all-important in women's poetry, he correspondingly gives less credence to their intellect: "It is less easy to be assured of the genuineness of literary ability in women than in men."[15] Alluding to the unspent feelings that he believes underlie women's poetry, he further claims that the "finest and richest development" of the moral rectitude that was considered most developed in women might reflect "some of the qualities of genius" (7).

Griswold implies that women who are fully occupied with a loving family have no need to write poetry. He alludes to the unspent emotions of their poems, as if they exhibit a kind of debased Wordsworthianism: they betray "a soul rapt into sympathy with a purer beauty and a higher truth than earth and space exhibit," which is revealed to be only "the natural cravings of affections, undefined and wandering" (7). Thus their actual philosophical pondering can easily be confused with the nostalgia and sentiment of women's writing, which may be the product of women who have squandered their time and energies on poetry instead of keeping their homes: "We are in danger, therefore, of mistaking for the efflorescent energy of creative intelligence, that which is only the exuberance of personal 'feelings unemployed.' We may confound the vivid dreamings of an unsatisfied heart, with the aspirations of a mind impatient of the fetters of time, and matter, and mortality" (7).

Griswold claims that female writers, whose works center on the home and family, are purveyors of virtue and serve an important function in preserving culture in the midst of an ever more demanding male business world. Women of the middle class were expected to raise children and run their households; in turn, editors and critics confirmed the prevalent ideology concerning women's domestic lives, praising them as pious teachers and bastions of values. In keeping with this attitude, Griswold remarks that the influence of women's innately moral quality "never is exerted but for good" in the culture at large (8). Women's outpourings, which he claims are characterized by "the infusion of our domestic spirit," will temper the developing national "school of art" into a state of "civil refinement" (8). He writes:

It has been suggested by foreign critics, that our citizens are too much devoted to business and politics to feel interest in pursuits which adorn but do not profit, and which beautify existence but do not consolidate power: feminine genius is perhaps destined to retrieve our public character in this respect, and our shores may yet be far resplendent with a temple of art which, while it is a glory of our land, may be a monument to the honor of the sex. (8)

In contending that women's literary activities compensate for the business ideology of men, Griswold also proposes the conservative ideals that enshrine woman as a moral exemplar and household ornament. In addition, the subtly sexualized language—the "temple of art" on "our shores" may invoke the *mons veneris*—pervades the description of women's poetry by editors. Finally, Griswold's desire to commend a woman's art for the "honor of the sex" only keeps her absent from any real power—on an idealized pedestal, in the home, and firmly in her place.

If Griswold expresses a view typical among male editors of this period, Caroline May is an example of a woman who expresses the same condescending, patriarchal attitudes toward women's poems. In her 1848 preface to *The American Female Poets*, she comments on the profusion of women's poems in newspapers and bound volumes, contending that "poetry, which is the language of affections, has been freely employed among us to express the emotions of a woman's heart."[16] She remarks that women's poetry has been underrated because of its popularity, leading many Americans to value the works of women in other countries over native female authors. "As the rare exotic," she notes,

costly because of the distance from which it is brought, will often suffer in comparison of beauty and fragrance with the abundant wild flowers of our meadows and woodland slopes, so the reader of our present volume, if ruled by an honest taste, will discover in the effusions of our gifted country-women as much grace of form, and powerful sweetness of thought and feeling, as in the blossoms of woman's genius culled from other lands. (vi)

As the comparison between American women's poems and "the abundant wild flowers of our meadows and woodland slopes" suggests, women's lyrics were often figured as flowers in a "fertile garden of literature" (vi), which emphasizes both the decorative and the spontaneous nature of their poetry. Furthermore, May's characterization of women's poems as "effusions" suggests an outpouring of emotions or spirit, a commonly accepted notion, given women's supposedly more intensely emotional natures, and it recalls the attar or perfume to which their poetry was often compared. Critics contended that women's feelings needed to be pressed out, often through personal trials and suffering, before they were incorporated in poetry; Griswold concludes about Lydia Sigourney, a popular infant elegist and author of books of etiquette and advice for women: "it is only because the flower has not been crushed that we have not a richer perfume" (93).

The very number of women's poems was also used to denigrate their achievements. In 1874, an anonymous reviewer of Stoddard's new edition of Griswold's anthology writes that seventeenth- and eighteenth-century female poets are less experimental and less prolific than women in the nineteenth century. The reviewer, who is probably a man, bases this assumption on the fewer poems extant by women poets from the two previous centuries. According to the reviewer, the smaller output of poets like Bradstreet and Wheatley proves that the female sex was at that time more "sure of its place" and more true to its duties, implying that women who published forsook their proper roles as wives and mothers.[17] Although he admits that the increase in nineteenth-century American women's writing might stem from "the increase of general intelligence" or "the genius of women," he concludes that their prolificacy probably also signals a "special restlessness . . . their part of modern discontent that wreaks itself in numbers" (120), an allusion perhaps to the first protests for women's suffrage. Clearly, this reviewer seeks not only to belittle women's literary achievement, but also to turn their productivity against them.

According to the same reviewer, the (usually male) editor's task is to weed out good from bad poems by women:

To no one else is vouchsafed the fearful vision of pyramids of portfolios asking monthly inspection, and reams of waste paper attesting the censor's wrath and justice. By the side of this garland of the accepted and approved, an anthology of the rejected— may no one be indiscreet enough to cull it!—would complete a curious commentary on the position and wants of women in our republic of letters. (120)

Like a righteous Calvinist God, the editor exercises justice over the wicked: he dominates with "wrath and justice" over "pyramids of portfolios" in order to separate the chaff of bad poetry from the few pure grains. Indeed, "indiscreet" hints that women's failures were tantamount to mishaps too embarrassing, or perhaps too revealing, to be made public. Although "republic of letters" emphasizes the supposed democracy of the literary marketplace, this reviewer would perhaps prefer an aristocracy of letters and positions himself at the top of the literary pyramid. Editors clearly felt the weight of the more cultured, older, British literary tradition bearing down on their fledgling authors and so claimed that nature had a special role in encouraging great literature. Since women were so often reduced to their bodily nature, they were thought to have a peculiar alliance with the feminized earth. In his preface to *The Female Poets of America* (1848), for example, Griswold comments on the numerous submissions of American women to magazines, which he claims develop from a majestically endowed landscape rather than a rich culture or individual talent: "In the absence from us of those great visible and formal institutions by which Europe has been educated, it seems as if Nature had designed that resources of her own providing should guide us onward to the maturity of civil refinement" (8). In ascribing to women the power to guide others toward the "maturity of civil refinement," he bolsters the idea that female verse was spontaneous and natural, and he makes the individual woman writer responsible for her entire sex's advancement.

In his 1836 review of Sigourney's *Zinzendorff, and Other Poems*, Poe joins a chorus of male editors and critics in condemning a productive woman poet. Lydia Huntley Sigourney has a reputation as a great writer solely because she is popular with the reading public, "their names *being equally in the mouths of the people*."[18] The sheer number of her published poems creates a reputation for her where none should rightfully exist:

We know it to be possible that another writer of very moderate powers may build up for himself, little by little, a reputation equally great—and, this too, merely by keeping continually in the eye, or by appealing continually with little things, to the ear, of that great, overgrown, and majestical gander, the critical and biographical rabble. (123)

Popular writers like Sigourney were considered seductresses, since they made themselves visible to the male "majestical gander." In contrast to those who have "written a great work" and "by this single effort . . . attained a certain quantum of reputation" (123), a moderately talented writer can earn an equally large reputation by submitting a large number of poems "little by little" to periodicals. Indeed, their power is enhanced according to Poe by their being "continually in the eye" of the public, much like a prostitute who exposes herself to the glance of an inquiring client or whispers invitations. Not only do these less talented writers keep "continually in the eye," but they also appeal "continually with little things, to the ear," as if they secured the attention of the public with a catchy phrase. By describing Sigourney as if she were both cheating the public and prostituting herself, he reduces women's poetry to their duplicitous nature or body.

Editors demanded the pious and morally uplifting content of women's poetry to be mirrored in a smooth and untroubled meter. In 1852, an anonymous reviewer of Alice Cary's *Lyra and Other Poems* praised her verses for their metrical correctness and their sensitivity. In claiming that women poets expressed their emotions naturally and spontaneously, critics considered their best poems to be those in which the meter is correct and which appear to issue without forethought; conversely, they disparaged metrical innovations in women's verse, claiming that they gave the impression of laborious effort. Hence, the reviewer of Cary's book objects to its title poem because it "is too curiously wrought for the subject; it seems more like an experiment in poetry, than the sincere outpouring of grief."[19]

Between 1820 and 1885, editors often characterized women's verse as more affective, "natural," and unpremeditated than men's, and their portrait of women as unconscious wellsprings of emotion is amply represented by reviews of women's poetry.[20] In an anonymous 1871 review of Helen Hunt Jackson's *Verses* (1870) in *The Nation*, for example, a critic wonders if the poetry's harshness might come from Jackson's "seeming more intellectual" than she is and sums up the effect of her compact and realistic verse with an analogy that makes the critic a voyeur: "the feeling is clothed in a somewhat enigmatic form, and one finds it almost laborious to unclothe it and discover it."[21] The reviewer complains about the poetry's complexity as if he would prefer the whore to wear less. We can see that some nineteenth-century editors took the association between a woman's book and body to its extreme in equating publishing her poems with giving them a physical existence and implying that her thoughts needed to be clothed in proper language.

Nineteenth-century editors used childbearing metaphors to describe their control over the appearance of both anonymous verse and women's poems. This language of paternity or "legitimation," as I have termed it, has a double meaning: it signifies both that the critic promotes a poem as if he were conferring a secure identity on an illegitimate child and that he gives the poem his approval or authorization. In contrast, women claimed no corresponding maternity for their works. Although their seventeenth-century ancestress, Anne Bradstreet, wittily imaged her book in her dedicatory sonnet as a bastard child about to enter the world, nineteenth-century women poets figured their verses predominantly as "effusions," bodiless spirits that were the product of a momentary fancy or passing emotion for which they asked ample patience from the reader. To some degree, women perpetuated the stereotypical language of mindless, disembodied thought in their prefaces. Yet male editors continued to claim paternity (or, in Poe's case, assumed paternity) for women's literary works as a means of gaining the upper hand in print.

In his 1845 review of *The Waif*, a collection of poetry by unnamed authors edited by Longfellow, Poe aptly figures the poet who has plagiarized as a betrayed husband who has been duped into believing that his wife's child is his own. Even the title of Longfellow's collection (from which Poe is omitted) summons up the common convention that anonymous poems were like orphaned children, sent out into the world without benefit of name or parentage. Borrowed thoughts resemble a child who, once exposed to public scrutiny, is revealed to be another man's, much to the astonishment of its nominal father:

But, in either view, he thoroughly feels [his thought] as *his own*—and this feeling is counteracted only by the sensible presence of its true, palpable origin in the volume from which he has derived it—an origin which, in the long lapse of years it is almost impossible *not* to forget—for in the mean time the thought itself is forgotten. But the frailest association will regenerate it—it springs up with all the vigor of a new birth— its absolute originality is not even a matter of suspicion—and when the poet has written it and printed it, and on its account is charged with plagiarism, there will be no one in the world more astounded than himself.[22]

Much as a duped father may be the last to realize that his wife's child is not his own, a poet who has unwittingly absorbed and repeated the words of another author in his own work may find himself suddenly under siege, so that "there will be no one in the world more astounded than himself" at the charges of literary thievery. Concluding his remarks with a defensive strategy, he claims that artistic originality is always in question, adding defensively that "all literary history demonstrates that, for the most frequent and palpable plagiarisms, we must search the works of the most eminent poets" (759). In Poe's convoluted logic, he not only places himself above other authors, but he portrays himself as the victim at the hands of an unruly woman.

Editor John Keese, in his 1843 preface to Elizabeth Oakes Smith's *The Sinless Child*, reinforces the image that women's poetic efforts are unskilled, extemporaneous, and require an editor's approval. The title of Smith's popular long poem describes the child heroine, Eva, whose father has died and who lives out her short life in her mother's care. In presenting Smith's book as if he were taking on an almost generative role, Keese seeks to combine his duties as a publisher—a figure he believes others perceive as a mere businessman, pandering to the demands of the marketplace—with the more respected "editorial labours" of the "literary fraternity."[23] Clearly, even the phrase "literary fraternity" shows that male critics dominated the literary establishment. Keese criticizes the belief that the publisher has a purely "mechanical" role in printing and distributing verse, much as man might be said to have a purely "automatic" function in reproduction. "And why, indeed," he wonders, it may be observed in passing, should not a bookseller aim at being something more than the mechanical salesman of printed paper! Are *his* pursuits, of all others, the most hostile to literary culture? Is he presumed to exercise neither judgment nor taste in furthering the ends of trade; presumed to buy and sell only according to the existing demands of the literary market; while even the enterprise of the haberdasher is denied him, in anticipating the call for an article and introducing it to "the season." (viii)

Unlike a "mechanical salesman of printed paper," an editor must be a person with "judgment" and "taste" who uses his merchandising to form the taste of his readership. In contrast to a mere supplier of goods, the bookseller will decide which literature will be distributed, creating a demand for the product he supplies to the market, much as a "haberdasher" who anticipates "the call for an article" indirectly determines what will be sold that season. By arguing that booksellers should exert the power of taste and set the "fashion" in women's writing, Keese invokes the image of women readers and writers as fashion plates while underscoring the real effect that publishers and merchants had in creating a national demand for sentimental women's writing.

Keese wishes not only to exercise his taste, but also to appropriate the creative role of author. He defends his dual role as harbinger of taste and editor of the text:

Surely, in this country, at least, no pursuit is thus conducted [which allows the bookseller to exercise taste in publishing and distribution]; for which on the one side, the producer is constantly obliged to act as his own factor; on the other, whether it be the staple of cotton, or the fabrication of pin-heads, every intelligent dealer makes himself more or less familiar with the processes of nature or of art, in the production of the article. In fact, whether the "operation," be in wheat or tobacco, in books or burlaps, it is this exercise of his own intelligence, which alone gives soul to enterprise, and distinguishes the energy of the operator from that of a mill-horse or steam-engine. (viii–ix)

Like the editor, the bookseller should both distribute goods and know how they are produced. On the one hand, Keese contends that the "producer" must be his own "factor"—literally, a commission-merchant, one who buys and sells for another person. On the other hand, he distinguishes his role as an agent for the author's literary productions from his involvement in the methods of production. Not only is "every intelligent dealer" the source of his own publicity and distribution of his goods, but he also "makes himself, more or less familiar with the processes of nature or of art, in the production of the article," exercising his "intelligence" in order to give "soul" to his enterprise.

For Keese, the publisher animates the literary enterprise, thus mimicking the role of a physician or midwife who delivers a baby. He uses two more sets of oppositions. In the first, he contrasts organic life with manufactured goods—"whether [the production] be the staple of cotton, or the fabrication of pin-heads . . . whether the 'operation,' be in wheat or tobacco, in books or burlaps"—claiming that production of either natural or man-made goods requires the dealer's intervention. In the second, he prefers "intelligence, which alone gives soul to enterprise," to the raw "energy" of an unthinking animal or machine. "Intelligent" recalls the distinction editors frequently made between a male author's or critic's reputedly superior intellect and a female author's spontaneous, affective creativity. In aligning his role with that of a soul-giver, he claims that he can animate the processes of production. In making himself into an intelligent creator who can embody women's writing in print, he reenforces the terms by which women's verse was judged throughout the nineteenth century.

In concluding, Keese endorses *The Sinless Child* by publishing it under his auspices. He distances himself from any part in the poem's first appearance, for he does not wish to trespass on the work of another editor:

The writer of this, cannot claim to have been among the first to welcome the advent of a fresh and original poem, whose inspiration seems drawn from the purest well-springs of thought and fancy; nay, as already hinted, he admits that it was only the frequent demand for the work at his publishing office, under the presumption that it had already assumed the form of a book, which induced him, in the first instance, to procure a copy, and make a personal examination of its beauties. He *does* claim, however, that in the many months which have passed away since that first perusal, no effort has been spared, upon his part, to have it brought before the public in a fitting shape. (xi–xii)

In contrast to his earlier remarks that a bookseller might exert his own taste rather than respond only to the wishes of his customers, Keese states that the already "frequent demand for the work at his publishing office" first drew his attention to it, adding carefully that "it had already assumed the form of a book" when he first "procure[d] a copy, and ma[de] a personal examination of its beauties." He treats with much more care the feelings of the other editor than of the author herself, even though he states at the beginning of the essay that the reason for "'defining his position'" as editor is to explain his almost familial role in "the existing literary fashion of one friend editing the works of another, who still lives to write" (vii).

In Keese's presentation of Smith's book, we see the extreme lengths to which an editor would go in legitimating women's poetry. Giving a "fitting shape" to a book of poems not only alters the poet's work to conform to current literary standards, but it also authorizes them before they undergo public scrutiny. Following Keese's logic, one might say his attention to the "fitting shape" of women's poetry once again places emphasis on its divergence from the expected aspects of their writing—on form rather than content, analysis rather than synthesis, idea rather than feeling. He tries to keep a rigorous standard for his own work, as he does for the women writers whose works he edits:

The hesitation and diffidence of the party chiefly interested in such a step, will be appreciated and understood by those who, living by their daily literary toil, and often giving their name to the public, with some hasty effusion, designed to meet the immediate call upon their pen, still preserve a high intellectual standard within their own minds, and distrust their best productions when put forth as the consummate effort of their literary powers. (xii)

Unlike women writers, who supposedly dash off spontaneous lyrics, Keese and other editors are at risk of producing "some hasty effusion," since they live by their more workaday "literary toil" and cater to the needs of the marketplace. Dickinson's observation with regard to publishing—"Poverty—be justifying / For so foul a thing"—applies to editors as well as writers (J, 709). Editors and publishers feared ruining their own reputations if they published an immature poem and allowed their "intellectual standard" to be lowered. Keese concludes that "it is with honest and heartfelt gratification therefore, that the writer of these remarks has availed himself of the high privilege of superintending the present volume . . . under *his own name*" (xii; emphasis original) as editor. Almost as if he were conferring a secure identity on "The Sinless Child" herself, Keese puts a stamp of approval on Smith's verse for all "those who love pure poetry and respect womanly feeling" (xii).

Nineteenth-century American women poets turned the image advanced by the publishing world to their advantages. For most, publishing verse based on the everyday experience of domestic life afforded moderate to considerable fame and monetary success. Their poems centered on holy lives, patient trials, and Christian consolation in family life. In her introduction to *The American Female Poets* (1848), May affirms that the work of women writers was considered most fitting when it paid tribute to the home and its pious values: "home, with its quiet joys, its deep pure sympathies, and its secret sorrows, with which a stranger must not intermeddle, is a sphere by no means limited for woman, whose inspiration lies more in her heart than her head. Deep emotions make good foundation for lofty and beautiful thoughts" (vi). As Walker notes, there is an erotic component hinted at in May's "with which a stranger must not intermeddle."[24] Certainly, children's deaths, domestic discord, and abolition acquired erotic overtones in women's poetry and prose. But May's comment also points to the way women's exclusivity concerning private matters stakes out a domestic territory that they wished to make only theirs. Women clung to anonymity and pseudonymity as a way to guarantee privacy. For that reason, many women give little or no actual biographical information about themselves to collections: "To say where they were born seems quite enough while they are alive. Thus, several of our correspondents declared their fancies to be their only facts; others that they had done nothing all their lives; and some,—with a modesty most extreme—that they had not lived at all" (viii).

May's description of women writers' responses to questions about their lives could be a summary of Dickinson's own modest speakers, whose self-effacing poses she undermines, as in the following lyric:

> I'm Nobody! Who are you?
> Are you—Nobody—too?
> Then there's a pair of us!
> Don't tell! they'd banish us—you know!
>
> How dreary—to be—Somebody!
> How public—like a Frog—
> To tell your name—the livelong June—
> To an admiring Bog!
>
> (J, 288)

4. banish us] *advertise*   7. your] *one's*

Far from belittling herself, the speaker of this lyric heightens her importance by calling attention to herself and conspiring with the reader as an accomplice. As Alicia Suskin Ostriker has noted, this lyric reveals Dickinson's "duplicitous" stance: the poem "means both what it says and its opposite . . . contrary meanings coexist with equal force, because they have equal force within the poet."[25] Far from simply mocking the desire to be "Somebody," the speaker deliberately differentiates and thereby calls attention to herself as a "Nobody." Furthermore, she subtly resists the meek image of nineteenth-century American women. "Nobody" accepts anonymity, yet literally lacks a physical self—no body—the opposite of the critics' contention that women were closely aligned with the body. The variant reading to "advertise" sounds dreadful to a speaker who resists publication and perhaps fears being overrun with admirers, yet "They'd banish us" suggests the alternative is even more dire (especially when one considers the possible echo of Hal's promise to "banish" Falstaff in Shakespeare's *Henry IV*, I [II.iv.456]). Nobody more boldly compares being "Somebody" to repeating one's name ad infinitum, "like a Frog," to a crowd of dull-witted flatterers, "an admiring Bog." This lyric makes anonymity a prize, shared with another, thus solidifying the speaker's relationship to the reader and rejecting the notoriety that publication could bring. The speaker embodies the duplicitous nature of women, especially writers, who demurely hid behind the shelter of initials or anonymity but widely distributed their work.

Given the critical climate in which women poets wrote, it is not surprising that they often took a publicly self-effacing attitude toward their own careers. Since the era of Bradstreet, the widespread belief that women's intellect was inferior to men's had engendered a tradition of male authentication and legitimation in the presentation of American women's verse. Thus, Bradstreet's book of poems is preceded by letters and tributes by prominent male friends, attesting to her literary talent. Black women writers endured an even more extreme authentication, as their very identity as human beings, much less as poets, was in question. Published in 1783, more than a century after Bradstreet's book, Phillis Wheatley's *Poems On Various Subjects, Religious and Moral* contains a letter by her former master attesting to her education, which made her writing credible to the public. By the nineteenth century, such legitimizing gestures had become thoroughly embedded in the editorial discourse surrounding women's poetry. Women writers in this period continued to ask the public to be tolerant in reading their poems, expressing shock and embarrassment that their verse was subject to public scrutiny, and often foregrounding the unpremeditated nature of their writing. "They have sprung up like wild flowers in the dells, or among the clefts of the rock; wherever the path of life has chanced to lead," writes Sigourney in the preface to her 1834 *Poems*.[26] She blames the short and fragmentary nature of her lyrics on pressing domestic cares:

Some of the poems contained in the present collection were written at an early age. Others interspersed themselves, at later periods, amid domestic occupations or maternal cares. The greater part were suggested by passing occasions, and partake of the nature of extemporaneous productions. All reveal, by their brevity, the narrow intervals of time which were devoted to their composition. (v)

Sigourney's claim that most of her poems are "extemporaneous productions" and her contention that their "brevity" reveals "the narrow intervals of time" in which they were written suggest to the reader that her poems are designed to commemorate the passing moment, that they are the work of an amateur rather than a professional poet. Perhaps Sigourney's tendency was to compose quickly, yet the large and ornate study she had built for herself from the profits of her poems' publication suggests an attention at least to the outward signs of her position as an established writer. Her self-effacing attitude in print contrasts strongly with the actual circumstances of her professional life and suggests that such a mode of self-presentation had become largely a posture for women writers of the day.

Women writers frequently attest to the private nature of their verses, even when they publish them. Helen Hunt Jackson compares her poetry to flowers thoughtlessly strewn about by children in the dedicatory sonnet to her 1875 *Verses*:

> When children in the summer weather play,
> Flitting like birds through sun and wind and rain,
> From road to field, from field to road again,
> Pathetic reckoning of each mile they stray

They leave in flowers forgotten by the way;
Forgotten, dying, but not all in vain,
Since, finding them, with tender smiles, half pain,
Half joy, we sigh, "Some child passed here to-day."
Dear one,—whose name I name not lest some tongue
Pronounce it roughly,—like a little child
Tired out at noon, I left my flowers among
The wayside things. I know how thou hast smiled,
And that the thought of them will always be
One more sweet secret thing 'twixt thee and me.[27]

In likening the composition of her poems to the "pathetic reckoning" of the flowers that children have carelessly strewn about, she reflects the common myth that women's versifying was thoughtless and unpremeditated. These discarded flowers, which we confront "with tender smiles, half pain, / Half joy," evoke our sense of pity and regret at the loss of childhood. Jackson then compares the appearance of her poems to this same half-careless, half-pitiful scattering, implying that she created her verses in a similarly unreflective way: she has "left [her] flowers among / The wayside things." Jackson's analogy between the children's wavering path and her own circuitous method of writing reinforces the common view that women's poems were accidents of the moment. Moreover, her disparaging remarks typify women's habit of apologizing for the fragmentary and unplanned nature of their poems. Because the code of privacy prevented women from naming others in public, Jackson refuses to identify the person to whom she dedicates her book, "whose name I name not lest some tongue / Pronounce it roughly." In fact, leaving her "flowers among / The wayside things" might refer elliptically to a sexual relationship. Not only does this person share an intimacy with the author, for she hints that he or she "hast smiled" and that this remembrance will be "one more sweet secret thing" between them, but only she and her lover share knowledge of what prompted the writing of her poems—a knowledge that affirms their secret bond. Jackson's poem describes her verses as private transmissions between a woman and her lover in keeping with the popular ethic of privacy.

As we have seen, Dickinson came of age as a poet in an era that relegated women's literary endeavors to the private and personal, even when they found their way into published form. The frequent anonymity and pseudonymity of female poets, as well as their commonly perceived status as dilettantes and amateur artists, drove them to exploit another popular venue: the literary portfolio. Like an artist's sketches, which could be worked up and revised as finished products, literary "sketches," fragments, vignettes, and other pieces not meant for publication were contained in these portfolios. In an 1840 review-essay, "New Poetry," Ralph Waldo Emerson recognized its essentially private and unfinished nature:

Is there not room then for a new department in poetry, namely, *Verses of the Portfolio*? We have fancied that we drew greater pleasure from some manuscript verses than from printed ones of equal talent. For there was herein the charm of character; they were confessions; and the faults, the imperfect parts, the fragmentary verses, the halting rhymes, had a worth beyond that of high finish; for they testified that the writer was more man than artist, more earnest than vain; that the thought was too sweet and sacred to him, than that he should suffer his ears to hear or his eyes to see a superficial defect in the expression.[28]

Emerson's essay concludes his discussion of this "new department" with William Ellery Channing's "Boat Song," yet his comments pertain to women's poetry as well. Although initiated by Washington Irving's *The Sketch Book* in 1820, the portfolio tradition takes on a distinctly feminine cast by mid-century with best sellers such as Sarah Parton's *Fern Leaves from Fanny's Portfolio* (1853). Emerson praises the "charm" and "sweet" nature of these "confessions," adopting a sentimental and feminized rhetoric and evoking the common portrait of women's writing as artless and private. For Emerson, the privacy and unfinished nature of writing stems from his belief that publication is a violation of the soul, an ethic held by many of the transcendentalists, including Dickinson, Thoreau, and other forgotten authors, like Charles Lane. The elevation of fragments over finished work, a popular trend among the Romantics, advocates the modest strains of amateur poets, like Channing, who rise above the desire to publish and so stay true to their original conception, over the "high finish" of the consummate literary professional. Although he claims the fragmentary nature of these lyrics testifies that "the writer was more man than artist," he jokingly contends that these writers believe themselves to be minor divinities, too rarefied to broadcast in print an imperfect expression of their exemplary relation to God.

Both their dilettante status and their presumed relation to the divine made the portfolio an apt genre for women writers. The idea that verse should remain private, a convention that kept genteel women from publishing in the newspapers and journals, paradoxically freed women to make themselves known through circulating their manuscripts. Perhaps it is this ethic of privacy among the transcendentalists that encouraged Emerson to praise the portfolio tradition when he writes that "we should be loath to see the wholesome conventions, to which we have alluded, broken down by a general incontinence of publication, and every man's and woman's diary flying into the bookstores, yet it is to be considered, on the other hand, that men of genius are often more incapable than others of that elaborate execution which criticism exacts" (*E&L*, 1170–71). Indeed, Emerson remarks in his preface that *Parnassus* had its origin as a type of journal or blank book for his favorite readings: "This volume took its origin from an old habit of copying any poem or lines that interested me into a blank book."[29] Even at the time Emerson was writing, in mid-nineteenth-century

America, "incontinence" connoted a lack of self-restraint, particularly in sexual relations. Although he makes no distinction between the sexes when he remarks that "every man's and woman's diary" goes "flying into the bookstores," he reserves for "men of genius" the right to produce works that may not meet the critical standards of the day. On the other hand, women were encouraged to be publicly silent and blamed for publishing, almost as if they had broken sexual mores.

Moreover, the portfolio tradition spawned numerous collections of anonymous verse, which reinforced the prominent genteel convention that authorship should not be acknowledged to the general public. Guessing the names of well known authors was a common parlor game. The popularity of these literary endeavors attests to the public's enjoyment in subverting the decorum of the publishing world by guessing the identities of the authors. Helen Hunt Jackson encouraged her friend and correspondent Dickinson in 1878 to submit the poem beginning "Success is counted sweetest" to *A Masque of Poets*, one of the popular "No-Name Series" of anonymous literary productions, to which Jackson was herself a contributor. Significantly, more than one reviewer of the collection mistakenly attributed Dickinson's poem to Emerson, an error that the series editor, Thomas Niles, observes in a letter to the poet: "You were entitled to a copy of 'A Masque of Poets' without thanks, for your valuable contribution which for want of a known sponsor Mr Emerson has generally had to father" (*Letters* 2, 626). Not only did Emerson exert a profound influence on the thought and form of Dickinson's work, as Niles's remark suggests, but the literary world also sought to ascribe a "paternity" to women's poems. In his other interchanges with Dickinson, Niles obviously values his reputation as a "Gentleman Publisher" over commercial success. In answering her query about Cross's biography of George Eliot, Niles notes that "'H.H.' once old me that she wished you could be induced to publish a volume of poems"; politely refusing to insist, however, he demurely adds, "I should not want to say how highly she praised them, but to such an extent that I wish also that you could" (*Letters* 2, 726). In 1883, after again inquiring about Cross's biography of Eliot, Dickinson received a letter from Niles admitting that there were rumors Cross was still at work, and shortly afterwards, a copy of Mathilde Blind's *Life of George Eliot*, just recently published by Roberts Brothers, arrived. In response, the poet sent him her copy of the Brontë sisters' poems, possibly to suggest that they would prove worthy of biography as well. Nevertheless, Niles returned the "precious volume," apparently without understanding its implication, and added: "I will take instead a M.S. collection of your poems, that is, if you want to give them to the world through the medium of a publisher" (*Letters* 3, 769).

In the preface to Dickinson's posthumously published *Poems* (1902), Thomas Wentworth Higginson places her squarely in this tradition of dilettante writers when he claims that her poems "belong emphatically to what Emerson long since called 'the Poetry of the Portfolio,'—something produced absolutely without the thought of publication, and solely by way of expression of the writer's own mind."[30] Although Higginson recognizes her originality, he put her unconventional poems into print apologetically, as if their unfinished surface reflected on him:

> Such verse must inevitably forfeit whatever advantage lies in the discipline of public criticism and the enforced conformity to accepted ways. On the other hand, it may often gain something through the habit of freedom and the unconventional utterance of daring thoughts. In the case of the present author, there was absolutely no choice in the matter; she must write thus, or not at all. (iii)

Not subject to "the discipline of public criticism" and its "enforced conformity," Dickinson rejected poetic conventions in a way that seems to us motivated by an inner vision akin to Emerson's poet-scholar's obstinacy. Even though Higginson acknowledges the benefit one could derive by standing above more mediocre expression, such irregularities cast doubt for him on her ability as a poet. In his memories of the poet, he recalls her almost as a mythical being, beyond the realm of human comprehension: "I saw her but twice face to face, and brought away the impression of something as unique and remote as Undine or Mignon or Thekla" (v). He alludes to the seemingly rough and unfinished nature of her poems and to their metrical irregularity when he observes that they have "flashes of wholly original and profound insight into nature and life; words and phrases exhibiting an extraordinary vividness of descriptive and imaginative power, yet often set in a seemingly whimsical or even rugged frame" (v). Recalling Emerson's remark in "Self-Reliance" that "I would write on the lintels of the door-post, *Whim*," rather than "spend the day in explanation" (*E&L*, 262), "whimsical" belies the deliberate, artful, and self-possessed nature of her poetry. Rather than attribute her poems to "self-reliance," Higginson adopts the discourse surrounding women's poetry and likens them to flowers: "In many cases these verses will seem to the reader like poetry torn up by the roots, with rain and dew still clinging to them, giving a freshness and a fragrance not otherwise to be conveyed" (v–vi). Staunchly accepting the criteria by which women's verse was judged in this era, Higginson was predisposed to rate Dickinson's poems as too delicate and perhaps even abnormal to endorse their publication wholeheartedly.

To be sure, Higginson recalls criticizing her verse from a perspective common among nineteenth-century American editors, and his remarks about the poet reveal that he viewed her initially very much in the tradition of other women poets when he tried to make her conform to publishing standards. In his essay, "Emily Dickinson" (1901), he writes that she differed from the normative standards of punctuation by using "chiefly dashes," noting that "it has been thought better, in printing these letters, as with her poems, to give them the benefit in this respect of the ordinary usages."[31] Contemporary critical reflections on Dickinson's verse that attend to the placement of words on the page, punctuation, and the like have suggested how fully she relied on handwriting with its calligraphic flourishes and excesses as a means to convey her poetic intentions. As Susan Howe reminds us, "Poetry is never a personal possession. The text was a vision and gesture before it became sign and coded exchange in a political economy of value."[32] Higginson characterizes Dickinson's handwriting as "not in the slightest degree illiterate, but cultivated, quaint, and wholly unique" (250); he notes that her letter "was in a handwriting so peculiar that it seemed as if the writer might have taken her first lessons by studying the famous fossil birdtracks in the museum of that college town" (250). Thus he imagines that she mirrors the print of dead birds in her own idiosyncratic cursive. When we recall that women's poetic speech was frequently thought to resemble birdsong, his remark seems characteristic of the popular conception of women's unpremeditated versifying. Moreover, he describes the irregularity of "her habit as to capitalization, as the printers call it, in which she followed the Old English and present German method of thus distinguishing every noun substantive" (250). Apparently, he did not appreciate that she may have capitalized not only nouns, but also pronouns, adjectives, and prepositions to highlight the elements of her personal mythology. In supervising the 1890 *Poems*, which he edited with Mabel Loomis Todd, Higginson regularized Dickinson's verse by repunctuating it and eliminating capitals except at the beginnings of lines, for he claims that she manifested a "defiance of form" and valued her intent over formal correctness: "she was intent upon her thought, and it would not have satisfied her to make the change" (256). To his credit, he eventually gave up his effort at normalizing her work, even though he did so only because he deemed her to be unrepentant and lost: "she interested me more in her—so to speak—unregenerate condition" (262). Ultimately, as St. Armand has noted, Higginson's "naturalist's eye" predominated over his judgment as editor, almost as if she were one of the stuffed specimens in Amherst College's laboratory.[33] Higginson turned from hunter to observer: "I could only sit still and watch, as one does in the woods; I must name my bird without a gun, as recommended by Emerson" (276).

Dickinson sought to distinguish herself from assertive and perhaps demanding advances made by other women writers. Contemporary accounts of exchanges between women and their editors, as we will see in the following chapters, convey why she was reluctant to associate herself with their tactics. Dickinson was familiar with Henry Wadsworth Longfellow's novel, *Kavanagh* (1849). In writing to his wife shortly after his first visit with Dickinson, Higginson comments: "One day her brother brought home Kavanagh hid it under the piano cover & made signs to her & they read it: her father at last found it & was displeased" (*Letters* 2, 475). A dark, comic novel, *Kavanagh* is a tale of New England village life that portrays an exchange between a "poetess" and her editor that parallels aspects of the Dickinson-Higginson friendship. The character Mr. Churchill, a schoolmaster, represents the writing life and reveals the depth to which each character misinterprets his own calling or the reality of life around him. Like John Marcher, the unenlightened protagonist of Henry James's "The Beast in the Jungle" (1903), whose tragic fate is never to realize his destiny, Churchill yearns to write a romance but is frustrated due to his dreamy, romantic nature and to the demands of personal and professional acquaintances on his time. Intending to compile "a series of papers on Obscure Martyrs,—a kind of tragic history of the unrecorded and lifelong sufferings of women, which hitherto had found no historian, save now and then a novelist," he fatally lacks a sense of perspective and overlooks, of course, the native saint of his village, Alice Archer.[34] Having never revealed her love for the minister Kavanagh (the title character) or betrayed her confidence to her bosom friend, Celia, after discovering Celia's love for him, Alice stands as a mute tribute to stoical New England womanhood: "Mr. Churchill never knew, that, while he was exploring the past for records of obscure and unknown martyrs, in his own village, one of that silent sisterhood had passed away into oblivion, unnoticed and unknown" (113–14). Churchill as hagiographer betrays the potent—and often misguided—interest men showed in writing the lives of women who were expected implicitly to exemplify the ideals of motherhood and femininity, as Longfellow dryly notes in the title to one of his character's proposed lyceum lectures: "'What Lady Macbeth Might Have Been, Had Her Energies Been Properly Directed'" (115). The joke is well taken, yet has an ounce of seriousness: had Lady Macbeth or Alice Archer been fulfilling her correct domestic duties, she would have been more successful in her role as woman or wife.

Mr. Churchill's encounter with an amateur versifier, Miss Cartwright, however, suggests the lengths to which women poets might go to see their works in print, in contrast to genteel and demure ladies whose respect for the dictates of "True Womanhood" were paramount. A "damsel sitting in his armchair" when he arrives in his study one afternoon asks for his help in publishing her verses:

"I have come to ask a great favor of you, Mr. Churchill, which I hope you will not deny me. By the advice of some friends, I have collected my poems together,"—and here she drew forth from a paper a large, thin manuscript, bound in crimson velvet,— "and think of publishing them in a volume. Now, would you not do me the favor to look them over, and give me your candid opinion, whether they are worth publishing? I should value your advice so highly!"

This simultaneous appeal to his vanity and gallantry from a fair young girl, standing

on the verge of that broad, dangerous ocean, in which so many have perished, and look-ing wistfully over its flashing waters to the shores of the green Isle of Palms,—such an appeal, from such a person, it was impossible for Mr. Churchill to resist. He made, however, a faint show of resistance,—a feeble grasping after some excuse for refusal,—and then yielded. He received from Clarissa's delicate, trembling hand the precious vol-ume, and from her eyes a still more precious look of thanks, and then said,—
    "What name do you propose to give the volume?"
    "Symphonies of the Soul, and other Poems," said the young lady; "and, if you like them, and it would not be asking too much, I should be delighted to have you write a Preface, to introduce the work to the public. The publisher says it would increase the sale very considerably." (100–1)

Not only does this encounter satirize the demands male literati, like Longfel-low, must have felt female authors made on their time, but it also records for us an image of the poetess who both assertively pushes her interests among liter-ary professionals and relies on meek femininity to secure her way. Furthermore, the description of her manuscript and its title—*Symphonies of the Soul, and Other Poems*—points to the way women's works were received in nineteenth-century America and the bodiless, spiritual quality thought to be central to their conception.

    Unlike the fictional Miss Cartwright, Dickinson betrayed neither the requi-site business acuity nor the self-promotion necessary for commercial success. Yet the scene in some respects parallels Dickinson's own strategic approach to Higginson about her verses. Like Miss Cartwright, who flatters her mentor's vanity and seeks his "candid opinion, whether they are worth publishing" (100), Dickinson asks Higginson similarly to tell her what is "true" (*Letters* 2, 403). Undoubtedly, the "simultaneous appeal to his vanity and his gallantry from a fair young girl" mixes the desire to act uprightly and the wish to please the opposite sex, a combination of attitudes at work also in the concluding line to Dickinson's first letter to Higginson, her "Preceptor": "That you will not be-tray me—it is needless to ask—since Honor is it's own pawn—" (*Letters* 2, 403). Not only does she rely on the moral rectitude of what Coultrap-McQuin refers to as a "Christian Gentleman," the moral and intellectual counterpart to the "True Woman" according to the doctrine of the separate spheres, but she also assumes that as a gentleman he would sacrifice himself for a lady's bene-fit, like a pawn in a chess game. Although she was not above deferring to Hig-ginson's advice and deploying genteel feminine behavior in her efforts to se-cure his attention, she distances herself from the commercialism of her age and demonstrates her understanding of the limits and advantages of their relation-ship. Higginson writes that he received four poems with her first letter ["Safe in their Alabaster Chambers—" (J, 216), "I'll tell you how the Sun rose—" (J, 318), "The nearest Dream recedes—unrealized—" (J, 319), and "We play at Paste—" (J, 320)]; although his comments reveal that he thought some of her best poetry tritely sentimental, he later learned to appreciate her originality. He classes the poem beginning "The nearest Dream recedes—unrealized" (J, 319), for example, "among the most exquisite of her productions, with a singular felicity of phrase and an aerial lift that bears the ear upward with the bee it traces" (251):

> The nearest Dream recedes—unrealized—
> The Heaven we chase,
> Like the June Bee—before the School Boy,
> Invites the Race—
> Stoops—to an easy Clover—
> Dips—evades—teases—deploys—
> Then—to the Royal Clouds
> Lifts his light Pinnace—
> Heedless of the Boy—
> Staring—bewildered—at the mocking sky—
>
> Homesick for steadfast Honey—
> Ah, the Bee flies not
> That brews that rare variety!
>
> (J, 319)

The lyric points to the uncertainty of attaining a predestined place in the ever-receding mansion of "Heaven." Like the "June Bee," which heralds the beginning of summer and the end of the school year's confinement, salvation beckons but constantly eludes us, much as the bee rises to "the Royal Clouds" and leaves the boy "Staring—bewildered—at the mocking sky." Whether or not Dickinson intended to show her awareness that Higginson might not understand her poetry, he admits his confusion at her cryptic metaphors and shrewdly recognizes that he might easily substitute for the boy in the poem, who vainly tries to capture a "June bee": "The bee himself did not evade the schoolboy more than she evaded me; and even at this day I still stand somewhat bewildered, like the boy" (252).

If, in her first tentative exchanges with Higginson, Dickinson outwardly adopts a self-effacing demeanor, she also reveals her discomfort with his criticisms of her poetry by evoking the same rhetoric of embodiment and dress that pervades the editorial discourse of the period.[35] Assuming a pose that resembles the posture other women writers took toward their editors, she only tentatively acknowledges authorship of her work in her correspondence with him. He notes that "the most curious thing about the [first] letter [that he received from her] was the total absence of a signature" (250). Instead, she includes her first and last names, written in pencil, on a separate card in its own envelope and not on the poems she included. Indeed, Dickinson may well have wanted to separate herself as far as possible from her father's and grandfather's New England renown and to establish her own fame. True to his era, however, Higginson sees only the most genteel aspects of a woman's modesty, rather than the strategy of a professional author at work: "The shy writer wished to recede as far as possible from view" (251).

Dickinson viewed Higginson's criticisms almost as if they incised her body, and her response to his request for more poems further suggests her cautious rejection of his criticism. In her first letter to Higginson, she asks him to tell her if her verse is "alive"; "Should you think it breathed—and had you the leisure to tell me, I should feel quick gratitude—" (*Letters* 2, 403). Punning on the word "quick," she implies that if the poem is alive in his estimation, she will be, too. He recalls in his essay that "I remember to have ventured on some criticism which she afterwards called 'surgery,' and on some questions, part of which she evaded, as will be seen, with a naïve skill such as the most experienced and worldly coquette might envy" (253). His metaphor of coquetry invokes the language of prostitution that has underwritten editorial discourse about women's poetry. Such language also demonstrates that he understood that she kept back as much as she told him about her poems, that she taunted him by seeming to defer to his advice while she mocked it.

Moreover, her use of the metaphor of "clothing" in her next letter to Higginson suggests how closely editors and critics associated a woman's body with her poetry. Although she responded to his tentative reproaches by sending more poems, she excuses herself in the letter that accompanied them for not being able to gratify his wish for ones that were more "orderly": "While my thought is undressed—I can make the distinction, but when I put them in the Gown—they look alike, and numb" (*Letters* 2, 404). Dickinson probably refers to dressing her poems for public view, as well as to the regulating effect that the "Gown" of form has on her thought. The importance of that regularizing "Gown" is clear in her next letter to Higginson, to whom she turns for guidance in containing the potentially explosive power of imagination: "I had no Monarch in my life, and cannot rule myself, and when I try to organize— my little Force explodes—and leaves me bare and charred—" (*Letters* 2, 414). Adopting the rhetoric of dress that proliferated in the editorial discourse surrounding women's verse of this period, she rejects the more normative sensibility that Higginson unsuccessfully tried to instill in her. Her remark also might serve as a preconceived response to a critic whose contemporaries, as we have seen, imagined that women's poetry was embodied in print and "clothed" in a regular, smooth-sounding meter.

Her next few letters to Higginson continue to stress the necessity of her poetic form, even as she maintains a conventionally submissive attitude toward him. He might have suggested, as St. Armand postulates, that she instead attempt prose fiction, like the popular sensation writer Harriet Prescott

Spofford,[36] whom Dickinson admired, since in her third letter the poet thanks Higginson for his honest criticisms and replies with a courteous but definitive refusal: "Your first—gave no dishonor, because the True—are not ashamed—I thanked you for your justice—but could not drop the Bells whose jingling cooled my Tramp—" (*Letters* 2, 408). Whether she actually anticipated his suggestion that she "delay 'to publish'" or made up her mind shortly after his discouragement, she thenceforward forsook publication as a means to disseminate her work: "I smile when you suggest that I delay 'to publish'—that being foreign to my thought, as Firmament to Fin—If fame belonged to me, I could not escape her—if she did not, the longest day would pass me on the chase—and the approbation of my Dog, would forsake me—then—My Barefoot-Rank is better—" (*Letters* 2, 408). Higginson must also have suggested that her poems lacked metrical regularity, for she punningly noted that she would continue to display her metrical "foot" despite his advice. "Barefoot" carries a range of connotations for Dickinson's speakers: a sanctified soul, a dead body, an innocent child, and, most significantly in terms of "rank," a poor person. Later, she again rejected in mock-fear his criticisms that her meter is irregular, while nevertheless maintaining a mildly self-effacing demeanor: "You think my gait 'spasmodic'—I am in danger—Sir—You think me 'uncontrolled'—I have no Tribunal" (*Letters* 2, 409). Dickinson might well have been derisively classed by Higginson as one of the neoromantic poets of the so-called "Spasmodic School," including Elizabeth Barrett Browning, who yearned toward cosmic themes while they exploited intensity and formlessness. Yet she still asks him for the occasional favor of reading her poetry to see "if I told it clear" and says "'twould be control, to me—" (*Letters* 2, 409). She resisted Higginson's suggestions to revise the form of her poems, while continuing to seek his advice.

In light of Higginson's respectful dismissal of her writing and the popular characterization of women's poetry as private, untutored, and affective, Dickinson's choice not to publish is hardly surprising. Much as the journal gave transcendentalists like Thoreau and Emerson a private forum for ideas and fragmentary sketches, the lyric provided Dickinson an unpublished daybook, an almanac of moods and feelings, that she forever transformed in the exercise of her craft. When she remarks in a letter to Higginson that "My Business is Circumference," she pointedly distances herself from the desire for commercial success and allies herself instead with Emerson, for whom "Circumference" signifies the extensiveness of divinity in his essay, "Circles": "St. Augustine described the nature of God as a circle whose centre was everywhere, and its circumference nowhere" (*E&L*, 403). Reluctant to submit to what she believed were the profiteering motives of publishers, she remarks to Higginson in 1862 that "two Editors of Journals came to my Father's House, this winter—and asked me for my Mind—and when I asked them 'Why,' they said I was penurious—and they, would use it for the World—" (*Letters* 2, 404–5). The editors in question, who may have been Samuel Bowles and Dr. Josiah Gilbert Holland, are characterized as self-righteous, designing men who wanted to profit from the publication of her "Mind." They accuse her of "penury" for not printing her poems for the good of others; she, however, indicts them for greedily wishing her to publish under the guise of charity. To Louise Norcross in 1872, she writes derisively of a woman, probably Elizabeth Stuart Phelps, who requested a similar submission under the banner of feminine "duty": "Of Miss P—I know but this, dear. She wrote me in October, requesting me to aid the world by my chirrup more. Perhaps she stated it as my duty, I don't distinctly remember, and always burn such letters, so I cannot obtain it now. I replied declining. She did not write to me again—she might have been offended, or perhaps is extricating humanity from some hopeless ditch" (*Letters* 2, 500). Unlike many of her counterparts, Dickinson refused to submit to the rigors of the publishing world, and she rejected both the constraints women especially faced and the profiteering of most successful authors, even under the guise of charity.

Although she detached herself from the careerist ambitions of many versifiers, the standard image of the meek and retiring poetess allowed Dickinson to maintain a lifelong friendship from which she could question her "preceptor's" own deeply held beliefs. Higginson might easily have classed her with other nineteenth-century women writers, whose "secret sorrows" were commonly thought to provide the basis for poems on the loss of love and the deferral of a romantic union in life. Dickinson transformed the rhetoric of "secret sorrows" and the common depiction of women's poems as delicate blooms in her poems on female creativity. Hearkening back to the common description of women's verse as flowers and its meaning as a heady perfume, for example, Dickinson transforms "Attar" to describe the way the distillation of everyday experience in poetry, its "Essential Oils," may not be the province of men alone:

> Essential Oils—are wrung—
> The Attar from the Rose
> Be not expressed by Suns—alone—
> It is the gift of Screws—
>
> The General Rose—decay—
> But this—in Lady's Drawer
> Make Summer—When the Lady lie
> In Ceaseless Rosemary—
>
> (J, 675)

In *Emily Dickinson: A Poet's Grammar*, Cristanne Miller contends that Dickinson anticipates metaphors of female creativity in the twentieth century and, through her use of paradoxes and syntactical ambiguity, produces a "multiplicity of meaning and an indeterminate reference, two characteristics that open questions of meaning but frustrate the referential or informative communication most language provides."[37] If we also contend, as does Miller, that "Dickinson plays off the century's widespread conception of woman as the ministering angel in the house and of poet as sensitive, suffering soul" (31), then we can see how Dickinson's linguistic play allows her to question the role of poet as defined by the nineteenth-century publishing establishment. Symbolic of women's beauty and passion, the rose defends a claim to her right to be both woman and poet: the linguistic overtones of "expressed" and the pun on male "Suns" suggest that women as well as men can tap the hidden resources of human suffering. The double method of extracting "Attar" from a rose—through drying under the sun and crushing its petals—amounts to passive and active forms of violence, "the gift of Screws." Given the emphasis early in the poem on the agency of the "Suns" in extracting meaning, "Attar" further redefines the role of the female poet as potent. "General Rose" serves as a type of death and femininity, since it is closely associated with woman's beauty and its transience. Although this "General Rose" decays, the "Attar" subsists and can exude the aura of summer, even after the author's body lies interred in "Ceaseless Rosemary." Indeed, the similarity between the flowers laid away in a drawer and the lady's corpse confined to its coffin conflates the poetry and its author, and these parallel images suggest that lyrics can resurrect and come to substitute for the actual poet, much as Dickinson's own lyrics were rescued from oblivion in her bureau drawer by her sister, Lavinia. Adopting images popular among nineteenth-century critics and writers alike, who were thought to have sprung up like flowers so copiously throughout New England, Dickinson suggests her lyrics can refresh and renew their reader.

Aware of the definition of women's verse pervading the literary marketplace, Dickinson elsewhere defines the role of the poet in a way that distinguishes her from other poets:

> This was a Poet—It is That
> Distills amazing sense
> From ordinary Meanings—
> And Attar so immense
>
> From the familiar species
> That perished by the Door—
> We wonder it was not Ourselves
> Arrested it—before—
>
> Of Pictures, the Discloser—

The Poet—it is He—
Entitles Us—by Contrast—
To ceaseless Poverty—

Of Portion—so unconscious—
The Robbing—could not harm—
Himself—to Him—a Fortune—
Exterior—to Time—

(J, 448)

The impersonal phrasing of the first line ("This" and "It is That") and the characterization of the poet as male deliberately set Dickinson at arm's length from the popular nineteenth-century definition of the poet. The poet distills "amazing sense" and "Attar" from "the familiar species / That perished by the Door," rather than the courtly rose or other effete plant. Like Roger Chillingworth in Nathaniel Hawthorne's *The Scarlet Letter* (1850), who states, "my old studies in alchemy . . . and my sojourn, for above a year past, among a people well versed in the kindly properties of simples, have made a better physician of me than many that claim the medical degree," the speaker could claim specialized knowledge of herbs and plants others ignore.[38] Not only Indians, of course, were familiar with the medicinal properties of wildflowers and other plants, but women also acquired knowledge about plants through folklore and other women. The poet's talent lies in "arresting" the meaning of such trivial and everyday pursuits, and the result paradoxically "entitles" us to "ceaseless Poverty," as if the poet reminded us consistently of our own deprivation. The syntactical ambiguity and inversions of the last two stanzas raise the possibility that the poet's talent is inner-directed, a sentiment shared by other transcendentalists. If we take "to Him" to modify "Portion," then the poet's talent seems central to the stanza, but if "to Him" modifies "Himself," then the poet becomes himself a "Fortune" who is "Exterior—to Time—." The radical lack of self-awareness imbedded in this final possibility supports the supposed "unconscious" nature of much women's poetry. Rather than merely subscribe to the belief that women's poetry issued freely and spontaneously, however, Dickinson contends that the poet's talent exists outside the cult of personality so popular in the nineteenth century, outside of history, and even outside of time itself.

Given the emphasis on women's appearances in nineteenth-century America, Dickinson also undoubtedly recognized the powerful symbolism of the white gown she habitually wore for the last twenty years of her life. Dress signified such basic facts as social rank and occupation; it also indicated whether the family had recently experienced a death and signified the mourner's relation to the deceased. Her most significant poem concerning publication describes the color white:

Publication—is the Auction
Of the Mind of Man—
Poverty—be justifying
For so foul a thing

Possibly—but We—would rather
From Our Garret go
White—Unto the White Creator—
Than invest—Our Snow—

Thought belong to Him who gave it—
Then—to Him Who bear
Its Corporeal illustration—Sell
The Royal Air—

In the Parcel—Be the Merchant
Of the Heavenly Grace—
But reduce no Human Spirit
To Disgrace of Price
                                   —(J, 709)

Remarking on the meaning of white in nineteenth-century literature, Gilbert and Gubar note that its noncolor signifies female vulnerability and madness in Dickens's Miss Havisham; mortality in Tennyson's Lady of Shalott, and the power of imagination that destroys itself in Wordsworth's Lucy Gray.[39] White is the color of spiritual election, physical virginity, and metaphysical ambiguity; and when placed in the context of publication, this color refers more obviously to a blank page. Invoking perhaps, as Galway Kinnell has noted, the slave auction, the poem plays on the registers of blackness and whiteness, as they refer not only to the abolition movement but also to the liberation of the mind from the fetters of print.[40] The only group who escapes the speaker's condemnation are those who need an income—perhaps the very women writers who often sustained themselves and their families through printing their works. Yet she dismisses such depredation of the spirit for herself, preferring to remain unsullied by the tawdry motivations of the literary marketplace. In fact, if we place her remarks in the context of the editor's wish to become a substitute creator, then she displaces the role of editor with God—she wishes to go "White—Unto the White Creator." Much as Dickinson wore white in order to show that she could not be easily interpreted by the era's standards for feminine appearance, her poetry resisted the standards of interpretation adopted by the literary world.

For Dickinson, the critical discourse about nineteenth-century American women's poetry and the persistent desire on the part of editors to legitimize women's verse determined not only the social terms of her relationship with

Higginson, but also the vocabulary in which their first tentative exchanges about her poetry were to be carried out. Even while she questioned the criteria by which Higginson judged her verse, her conventional relationship with him suggests the absence of perceived alternatives for a woman who sought to be published in the nineteenth century. It is against the backdrop of the prevalent definition of women's verse by editors and critics that we can best gauge Dickinson's own use and revision of these conventions. Rather than ignore the constraints that the publishing world would have placed on her poetry, we should consider how its striking originality, so forward-looking in its sensibility, responds to cultural pressures that shaped women's lives and works in the period—pressures that throw into even bolder relief the genius of Dickinson's art.

"A MORN BY MEN UNSEEN"

Chapter 3

"Feet So Precious Charged"

Dickinson, Sigourney, and the Child Elegy

As his mental powers unfolded, his perceptions were not strikingly acute, but his habits of fixed attention prominent, and remarkable. They gave almost a solemnity to his infant countenance, so earnestly would he regard with a full, grave eye, every speaker who addressed him. Long ere the completion of his first year, in the silent watches of the night, his mother would find, on accidentally waking, that bright eye scanning her face with strange intensity . . . Often, as with magnetic influence, that searching, prolonged gaze of the babe that knew no sound of speech, seemed to draw her soul into his own, till she almost felt awe mingling with the love that had no limit.

—Lydia H. Sigourney, *The Faded Hope*[1]

The widow . . . leaves Eva to learn the wants and tendencies of the soul, by observing the harmony and beauty of the external world. Even from infancy she seems to have penetrated the spiritual through the material; to have beheld the heavenly, not through a glass darkly, but face to face, by means of that singleness and truth, that look within the veil. To the pure in heart alone is the promise, "They shall see God."

—Elizabeth Oakes Smith, *The Sinless Child*[2]

> Pass to thy Rendevous of Light,
> Pangless except for us—
> Who slowly ford the Mystery
> Which thou hast leaped across!
> —Emily Dickinson (J, 1564)

Emily Dickinson's assurance of God's love was deeply troubled by the deaths of children. Ravaged by tuberculosis and childhood diseases, most children born in the nineteenth century died before reaching adolescence; of those, more than half died before they reached the age of five. Neither the severe Calvinist God of Jonathan Edwards nor the merciful "Everlasting All" of Isaac Watts's hymns could rationalize adequately the death of an innocent child. "Ah! dainty—dainty Death! Ah! democratic Death!" writes Dickinson to the Hollands in fall 1876. "Grasping the proudest zinnia from my purple garden,—then deep to his bosom calling the serf's child" (*Letters* 2, 341). While she betrays the Whig politics of the elite class, who feared the loss of personal property in the leveling of social classes, as Betsy Erkkila has argued, she must acknowledge death's ultimate Jacksonian democracy: it claims both high and low, the zinnia from her "purple garden" and "the serf's child."[3]

Widely hailed as "The Sweet Singer of Hartford" and as the première infant elegist of nineteenth-century America, Lydia Sigourney was part of a widespread cult of death in nineteenth-century America. In *The Faded Hope* (1853), she memorializes her son, Andrew, whose extraordinarily idealized portrait is consonant with the terms by which dying children were depicted in this period. Like Eva, the pious and otherworldly heroine of Elizabeth Oakes Smith's popular long poem, *The Sinless Child* (1843), Andrew has a special relationship to nature, deciphering its phenomena as if they were part of a language that revealed a spiritual truth. We are told that "Among his earliest developments of character, were a strong will and great truthfulness . . . His own faults were narrated with entire simplicity."[4] Showing early a spiritual vision and nearly supernatural prescience, he uses language as a transparent medium, slowly gaining the use of words, as if too great a facility would signal the beginnings of adult sophistry: "He was not rapid in his acquisition of language, but gave close attention to the import of the words that he learned, and applied them steadfastly, and without circumlocution, to their respective images" (11). Indeed, that he depends on his older sister's speech during her daily Scripture lessons to gain his first knowledge of the Bible suggests that he is close to an unspoiled truth that is traditionally distorted by the written word.

Eva, too, interprets nature as if it were a language that manifests God's will. In one of the short prose introductions to each section of her poem, Smith writes that Eva seems unnaturally close to her mother and grows up solely in her care, since her father died before she was born. "Given to the world in the widowhood of one parent, and the angelic existence of the other . . . ," she

is gifted with the power of interpreting the beautiful mysteries of our earth . . . More than this, she beholds a divine agency in all things, carrying on the great purposes of love and wisdom by the aid of innumerable happy spirits, each delighting in the part assigned it. She sees the world, not merely with mortal eyes, but looks within to the pure internal life, of which the outward is but a type.[5]

Eva's perfect insight into the spiritual side of life allows her to see beneath the veil of existence. Perceiving the "outward" world merely as a "type" of the inner, she becomes the agent of God's supervening will. She is surrounded by the sight of ministering angels, and finds solace in the spirit world, despite her mother's blindness to their beauty. Like Andrew, Eva perceives the glimmerings of the spiritual world and communicates her vision to those around her.

Like many of Dickinson's child speakers, Andrew picks up a "crumb" of knowledge here and there to sustain himself, and ultimately builds himself into a self-proclaimed religious authority. His attention and "docility" during his sister's lessons allowed him, Sigourney writes, "to gather here and there a crumb. . . . Still, in his silent gathering of fragments, the little basket of the mind became better stored than was anticipated. Especially were moral and religious precepts accumulated, and treasured" (14–15). While still practically an infant, he revealed his spiritual precocity by transforming the animals on his father's farm into his disciples, who, as Sigourney drolly notes, "were as unique as their preceptor,—being no other than a large flock of poultry" (15). Although he related to all the animals and plants around him as if they were pupils awaiting his pious instruction, he evinced a particular fondness for the flowers in his father's garden. For the most part he gently confided in them, displaying his general "friendship for the humblest creatures" (17), yet he also "established a code of justice, not unmarked by penal statutes" (18). Exercising his sway arbitrarily over his "realm," he punished any "too aspiring plants, that overshadowed and domineered over the humbler ones," by levelling them. Even the "imagined exultation" of one plant, which stood taller than a newly felled one, brought the "usual judgment" (18).

Sigourney's description of Andrew as both a benevolent "preceptor" and a Draconian enforcer of God's will confirms for us the precarious and double-sided position the dying child had for Dickinson and her contemporaries. In writing to her sister-in-law, Susan, on the death of Susan's eight-year-old son, Gilbert, Dickinson suggests that the knowledge the child gains by dying allows him to assume the role of spiritual teacher. Privy to the mystery of death, a dead baby assumes an authority over adults, who would willingly receive his instruction. Once her nephew's "Playmate," the poet seeks a lesson in heavenly faith from a new "Preceptor": "Gilbert rejoiced in Secrets—His Life was panting with them—With what menace of Light he cried 'Don't tell, Aunt Emily!' Now my ascended Playmate must instruct *me*. Show us, prattling Preceptor, but the way to thee!" (*Letters* 3, 799). Like Gilbert's, Andrew's early death casts an aura of holiness and spiritual precocity over his life. In punishing the surrounding flowers in a way that imitates God's exercise of justice, Sigourney's Andrew fully represents a divine authority. Like Jesus in the temple, he can exhibit both righteous anger and benevolent goodness. Yet his act of arbitrary destruction also resembles the angry frustration of a child, who would tyrannically exercise control over an environment in which he is himself powerless.[6] The portrayal of him as an angry feller of flowers, moreover, echoes the frequent characterization of children as flowers, an image that captures their fragility and delicacy; like blooms, children may be felled before they have reached their full maturity. Both Dickinson and Sigourney portray a child's tragic death as well as its vengeful acts in life, suggesting that children rebelled against their fates in a world where they were never meant to survive for very long.

In the child elegy, Dickinson expresses her dissatisfaction with the contemporary consolatory myth that the child enjoys a blissful existence after death. Like Sigourney's tribute volume, her poems frequently empower the child, who revenges himself for his early death on those who are left behind. Rather than offering the grieving family reasons to let the child go, she reverses the standard consolation format by depicting a dead child who himself mourns for his family. She thus undercuts the consolation offered to the mourner by openly portraying the pain and anxiety that the child undergoes in life and death. Even in poems that do not specifically commemorate the death of an actual child, she suggests that the promise of an untroubled reunion between parents and child in heaven is ultimately delusive. In this chapter, I will selectively sketch the use of the child elegy by American women writers in the nineteenth century, looking at a number of nineteenth-century poems lamenting an infant's death, particularly by Sigourney, in order to show how Dickinson's poems adopt and revise the conventions of the child elegy. Rather than offer condolence to the bereaved parents as the typical nineteenth-century version does, her poems suggest that a reunion beyond the grave is only a fiction in the minds of the mourning family.

Although their poems set out several standard features of child elegies, American women poets of the nineteenth century tend to focus even more than their predecessors on the pious and exemplary character of the dying child.[7] Like the elegies that commemorate an infant's death in the seventeenth and eighteenth centuries, the poems of nineteenth-century female poets regularly compare the infant to withering or severed flowers, alluding to the child's truncated life, to its delicate health, and to its smeared beauty.[8] Moreover, they console parents by encouraging them to compare their child's perhaps eventually painful state on earth with its blissful existence in heaven, and they look forward to a comforting reunion between parents and child after death. Yet American women poets of the nineteenth century focus to a greater extent than before on the exemplary and pious character of the dying child. In these poems, the dying child teaches a lesson in holy living to its parents.[9] The child often departs willingly, a testament to his faith in God's promise to prepare a place for him in heaven. Often speaking at the point of death, the children in these poems confidently assure those who are left behind that they will achieve a painless and contented existence in heaven. Furthermore, they willingly give their possessions away as keepsakes, cherished objects which will preserve the memory of their holy lives and encourage loved ones to emulate their pious be-havior. Possessed of a sure salvation, the children of these poems faithfully an-ticipate a reunion with their families in heaven.

In "The Dying Child's Request" (1832), Hannah F. Gould, a popular New England poet, depicts a child who displays an exemplary Christian attitude to-ward death. Assuring his mother that those he leaves behind will be more pre-cious to him in heaven because they are absent, he foretells his own death and consoles her with the promise that they will reunite in heaven:

> "There's something tells me I must go
> Where Christ prepares a home,
> To which you all, left now below,
> In little while shall come."[10]

Although he displays an unimpeachable faith in salvation, his promise that his family and friends will join him shortly after he dies eerily hints at the mortal end of those who mourn for him. Moreover, he wants his mother to distribute his possessions as keepsakes in order to incite his family and friends to live moral lives and imitate his actions so that they might join him in heaven. He asks her first to divide his belongings among his siblings and friends, then to give the money from his small savings to a missionary:

> "Then from my money-box you'll take
> The little coins within,
> To use as means, for Jesus' sake,
> In turning souls from sin."
>
> (ll. 21–24)

Evangelism, like an unshakable faith in an afterlife, was a hallmark of the spiritually prescient child, who spent most of his or her short life encouraging others to follow Christ's teachings. His dying moments, with which the poem concludes, demonstrate his unwavering belief in the promise of a life after death. He remarks on the spirits he sees hovering around him, eventually los-ing his ability to see, yet the radiance of his soul disperses the gloom of his dying moments:

> The morning sun shone in, to light
> The chamber where he lay;
> The soul that made that form so bright,
> To Heaven had passed away.
>
> (ll. 37–40)

Although the child's vision darkens, the poem suggests that, just as the sun brightens the room, his soul will remain a beacon to all who look to him for moral inspiration.

Although many female poets consoled parents on a child's death with the promise of everlasting life, others found little consolation in popular myths of the afterlife. Helen Hunt Jackson's "The Prince Is Dead," for example, depicts two families, one royal and one common, who suffer equally at the death of their sons:

> A room in the palace is shut. The king
>   And the queen are sitting in black.
>   All day weeping servants will run and bring,
> But the heart of the queen will lack
> All things; and the eyes of the king will swim
> With tears which must not be shed,
> But will make all the air float dark and dim,
> As he looks at each gold and silver toy,
> And thinks how it gladdened the royal boy,
> And dumbly writhes while the courtiers read
> How all the nations his sorrows heed.
>   The Prince is dead.
>
> The hut has a door, but the hinge is weak,
> And to-day the wind blows it back;
> There are two sitting here who do not speak;
> They have begged a few rags of black.
> They are hard at work, though their eyes are wet
> With tears which must not be shed;
> They dare not look where the cradle is set;
> They hate the sunbeam which plays on the floor,
> But will make the baby laugh out no more;
> They feel as if they were turning to stone,
> They wish the neighbors would leave them alone.
>   The Prince is dead.[11]

Like many of her poems, this lyric contrasts two settings in order to accentuate the deaths that have taken place. Wealthy and poor suffer alike, and only the habits of mourning vary: whereas the king and queen can shut the door of the chamber where the child lies, the poor couple must continue to work and live in the same room. Remarkable for how subtly she portrays the mourners, the poem implicitly contrasts the need to contain one's grief—"With tears which must not be shed" (l. 6; l. 18)—with the bluntness of emotion and the directness of expression of the poor and with the king as he "dumbly writhes" at the courtiers' announcements. Jackson's evocation of wealth and its inability to console grieving parents ultimately questions the satisfaction of consolatory fictions.

Dickinson undercuts the delusory way of thinking about death offered in child elegies such as Gould's. The excessive and prolonged grieving that the sentimental tradition relished kept the child perpetually present, a consoling reminder of reunion after death to the family who was left behind. Such practices, moreover, found their embodiment in the popular artifacts of the Victorian cult of death. Figurines, miniature portraits, locks of hair, and other keepsakes served to keep the child's image almost physically preserved. Popular female elegists consoled parents by affording them a tangible image of spiritual perfection to cherish, one nearly as real as the porcelain likeness of a crying infant placed under a glass dome in the parlor, or as the portraits of children, depicted in a familiar environment with a vase of flowers or their favorite toys in the foreground.[12] Indeed, many poets who returned again and again to the child elegy gained materially by this theme; their very lives as authors depended heavily on their writing poems on the deaths of infants. Dickinson criticizes the Victorian mourner who, overly preoccupied with the loss of the dead, may seem himself to be more dead than alive. She overturns the roles of mourner and mourned, implicitly posing the question, "Who's dead, and who's alive?" Commenting more generally on the pain that both adults and children suffer in life, she questions the underlying assumptions in the elegies of the day that promise an undisturbed heavenly reunion. For Dickinson, a child's death leads only to a very circumscribed grave:

> There was a little figure plump
> For every little knoll—
> Busy needles, and spools of thread—
> And trudging feet from school—
>
> Playmates, and holidays, and nuts—
> And visions vast and small—
> Strange that the feet so precious charged
> Should reach so small a goal!
>
> (J, 146)

The "little knolls" are mounds above children's graves. A paratactic sequence joined by "and"—including "Playmates," "holidays," "nuts," and other objects and events—conveys the breadth of each child's experience. It also hints at the "littleness" of their activities and concerns, which are cut short by their deaths. These trivial concerns are indeed "vast," especially when compared to the smallness of the graves, for they point to lives yet to be lived. Louisa May Alcott's "Our Little Ghost" (1866) sentimentally describes a child's daydreams:

> Fancies innocent and lovely
>   Shine before those baby-eyes,—
> Endless fields of dandelions,
>   Brooks, and birds, and butterflies.[13]

As the title suggests, Alcott's poem invokes the specter of child mortality but defends against its threat by portraying the living child as a playful "spirit" who haunts the family home. Like Dickinson, Alcott lists the items of the child's reverie in a paratactic sequence—"Brooks, and birds, and butterflies"—yet she renders the elements of its vision sentimentally, in contrast to Dickinson's more workaday "Busy needles," "spools of thread," and "trudging feet." Dickinson's poem, moreover, does not offer a protective guarantee against the child's death, as does Alcott's. Instead, the paratactic sequence of the final stanza describing the child's vision gives way in the last two lines to a periodic sentence, in which the speaker refrains from further enumerating the objects of the child's world. "Strange" bitterly understates the child's death, as if it betokened a God with very skewed values. Rather than claim that the dead infant has gained a satisfying heavenly reward, the speaker implies that the "small" goal of the grave does not match the child's vast value. Indeed, if we read the penultimate line as containing a pun on metrical "feet," we can better characterize Dickinson's response to the child elegies of other nineteenth-century women poets: while the infant elegies of the sentimentalists predict a blissful salvation in heaven for a dead child, the feet so precious charged of Dickinson's poem lead only to an actual grave, suggesting that the child should be valued in life, rather than sentimentalized in death.

Because of their youth, children were supposed to be linked closely to nature and supernaturally aware of the immortality they had just left behind by being born, of, as Wordsworth says, "splendour in the grass, of glory in the flower."[14] The size and appearance of children in this era's funerary portraits indicate cultural attitudes toward death. Painted in 1805 by the folk artist John Brewster, Jr., *Francis O. Watts With Bird* is one example of a popular genre of posthumous art that flourished in nineteenth-century America (Fig. 1). Many portraits and book illustrations depict a gigantic dead child who dwarfs the landscape. In Brewster's painting, a two-year-old boy holding a bird on his finger towers over an idealized background of hills and trees. As A. Bruce MacLeish notes: "The boy's good nature and delicacy are emphasized by his lacy clothes, the bird in his hand, and the light that makes him stand out from the somber background" (592). Artists often sought to capture the personality, occupation, or habits of those they portrayed in telling details, but the boy's clear and serene expression, his diaphanous nightgown and glowing figure point away from earthly pursuits toward his celestial state. Moreover, he holds the bird by a string: tethered to fate, he seems the plaything of an arbitrary God. Finally, the disproportion of the huge boy to the miniature background suggests not only the vast importance of the dead child to his family but also the fear of death among the living.

Variations in size, such as one sees in *Francis O. Watts With Bird*, occurred frequently in paintings around the turn of the nineteenth century. Another

Fig. 1. *Francis O. Watts with Bird*, by John Brewster, Jr., 1805. Oil on wood panel, $35\frac{1}{2} \times 26\frac{1}{2}$ inches. Courtesy of the New York State Historical Association, Cooperstown.

Fig. 2. *Emma Van Name*, by Joshua Johnson, c. 1805. Oil on canvas, 29 × 23 inches. Courtesy of The Alexander Gallery, New York.

painting, *Emma Van Name*, by Joshua Johnson, the first professional black portrait painter in America, reflects the artist's talent for painting large family portraits, including full-length standing figures of children. Of the eighty portraits currently attributed to Johnson, forty-six include children—outnumbering those of any other painter working in Baltimore in these years.[15] Dating from around 1805, *Emma Van Name* depicts a child whose smallness is almost surreal when compared to the huge goblet of strawberries by her side. Sacred to the Virgin Mary, strawberries may suggest innocence and ripeness for death (Fig. 2).[16] Replicated in her pink dress and shoes with coral jewelry, the color red also links her to adult female sexuality. Indeed, the phallic whistle that she carries around her neck, designed to ward off old women's curses, hints that her protectors would guard her virginity and shield her from the subsequent loss of power that motherhood and marriage entailed.

By mid-nineteenth century, paintings of oversized infants were replaced by scenes that emphasized family love and mourning customs. A posthumous portrait of 1844, *Edward W. Gorham*, by Joseph Whiting Stock, depicts a boy who mischievously sits with hammer, tacks, and string before a chair (Fig. 3). The playfulness, naturalness, and spontaneity of the scene indicate that families wished to remember children as they appeared in life. In *Sidney Grey Ford*, another posthumous portrait dating from around 1843, an unknown artist depicts the child dressed in the short frock and trousers commonly worn by both boys and girls in the first half of the nineteenth century. Posed with a favorite toy before a garden wall, the boy looks directly at the viewer, while a cemetery gate topped by funerary urns visible in the background points to the boy's early death. A tuft of morning glories ("quick to bloom and quick to fade"),[17] confirms that he is divided from the world of the living and becomes a reminder of the precariousness of life for adults as well as children.

Nineteenth-century artists and poets adopted a common cultural trope for the dying child: a withered or severed bloom. Some popular sentimental elegies give an ironic twist to this standard trope by pairing a growing child with a flower, only to portray the dead child taking revenge on the bloom by crushing it. In "Two Sundays" (1870), Helen Hunt Jackson depicts a child who tears apart the flowers around her, playfully snapping their stems, until she is herself cut down. Not only is the baby pictorially framed by the "lowly" doorway, which is made even "lower" by the flowers, but her liminal position also hints that she has barely entered the world when she dies:

I.

A baby, alone, in a lowly door,
Which climbing woodbine made still lower,
Sat playing with lilies in the sun.

The loud church-bells had just begun;
The kitten pounced in the sparkling grass
At stealthy spiders that tried to pass;
The big watch-dog kept a threatening eye
On me, as I lingered, walking by.

The lilies grew high, and she reached up
On tiny tiptoes to each gold cup;
And laughed aloud, and talked, and clapped
Her small, brown hands, as the tough stems snapped,
And flowers fell till the broad hearthstone
Was covered, and only the topmost one
Of the lilies left. In sobered glee
She said to herself, "That's older than me!"

II.

Two strong men through the lowly door,
With uneven steps, the baby bore;
They had set the bier on the lily bed;
The lily she left was crushed and dead.
The slow, sad bells had just begun,
The kitten crouched, afraid, in the sun;
And the poor watch-dog, in bewildered pain,
Took no notice of me as I joined the train.[18]

The opening two sections of Jackson's poem place the child in a natural and apparently normal environment, only to foreshadow her death. Her tanned "small, brown hands" hint she is healthy. The use of iambic tetrameter with anapestic substitutions also imitates the normal rush of events, but the couplets encourage us to see each activity as discrete and unconnected to a larger, divine plan: a baby, "alone," plays in a doorway, thus vulnerable to the intrusion of outside forces. While church bells ring, suggestive of the church's domain, a kitten "pounced" on "stealthy" spiders, and a watch-dog gazes warningly at the speaker. Both kitten and dog threaten creatures around them, as if they foretold the evil and arbitrary act of the child's destruction. Moreover, the poem's eerie solemnity is enhanced by the symbols scattered throughout that associate her with Christ's passion and death: the lilies the child plays with symbolize resurrection, the "gold cup" of the flowers recalls the chalice, and her awareness of time, her "sobered glee," brings a distinct change in mood.

The infant proves fragile as the plants around her. The second stanza begins with a trochee or spondee, whose strong, slow beats reflect the solemn mood. These beats fall on the words "Two strong men," underscoring the slowed pace of the funeral cortège, which contrasts with the more buoyant feeling of the

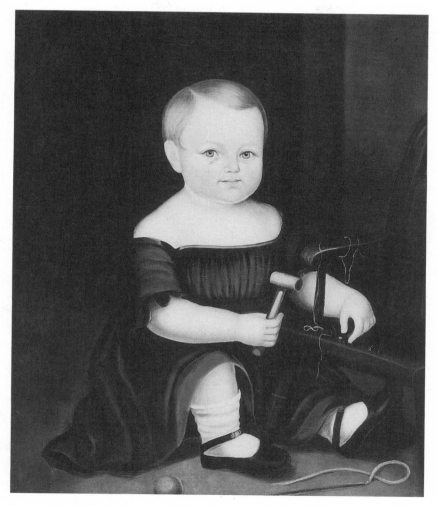

Fig. 3. *Edward W. Gorham*, by Joseph Whiting Stock, 1844. Oil on canvas, $30\frac{1}{8}\times 25$ inches. Courtesy of the New York State Historical Association, Cooperstown.

first two stanzas. Furthermore, their "uneven steps" mimic a toddler's tentative steps, recalling the dead infant they are carrying to the grave. In a moment in which the baby seems to enact vengeance after its death, its coffin crushes the lily that was previously out of her reach; set on the "lily bed" where she used to play, the casket smashes the last flower. Profoundly ironic, the recurrent trope of the broken flower implies that the child has been crushed in death, yet her act of control in breaking the stems is acted out again by her coffin.

Although events from the first stanza recur in the second half of the poem, they seem discrete and unconnected to the baby's demise, an irony all the more emphatic when we note that both sets of events occur on the same day of the week. Every aspect of the scene that previously registered the child's vitality now reflects its death: the "loud church-bells" become "slow, sad bells"; the once pouncing kitten now "crouched, afraid, in the sun"; and the threatening dog is "in bewildered pain." The title also underscores the irony of the child's death: God's day for sanctification, Sunday holds no blessings. Death has intruded into the baby's life, leaving the isolated speaker, who was originally treated as an intruder by the watch-dog, to join the train of mourners. God becomes the ultimate, arbitrary hunter, who devours little children even on the Sabbath and introduces an awareness of mortality into the child's world. Although the child in Jackson's poem mischievously destroys the flowers around her, her aggressive behavior naively presages the poem's more central act of destruction—her death. Yet the child's aggression and her unwitting act of revenge on the lily prove that the fear and anxiety surrounding death was not wholly redressed by nineteenth-century consolatory fictions and pious dictums in nineteenth-century America.

Many child elegies portray a dead infant's ascent to heaven as a growth in stature. An example of the disparity between a dead infant's gigantic stature and a dwarfish landscape is Emma Alice Browne's "Measuring the Baby" (1883). A child is measured periodically until its death, when it is transformed by another kind of growth:

> We measured the riotous baby
>   Against the cottage wall;
> A lily grew at the threshold,
>   And the boy was just so tall!
> A royal tiger lily,
>   With spots of purple and gold,
> And a heart like a jeweled chalice,
>   The fragrant dews to hold.
>
> His eyes were wide as blue-bells,
>   His mouth like a flower unblown,
> Two little bare feet, like funny white mice,
>   Peep'd out from his snowy gown;
> And we thought, with a thrill of rapture,
>   That yet had a touch of pain,
> When June rolls around with her roses
>   We'll measure the boy again!
>
> Ah, me! In a darkened chamber,

With the sunshine shut away,
Thro' tears that fell like a bitter rain,
We measured the boy to-day!
And the little bare feet, that were dimpled
And sweet as a budding rose,
Lay side by side together,
In the hush of a long repose!

Up from the dainty pillow,
White as the rising dawn,
The fair little face lay smiling,
With the light of Heaven thereon!
And the dear little hands, like rose-leaves
Dropt from a rose, lay still—
Never to snatch at the sunbeams
That crept to the shrouded sill!

We measured the sleeping baby
With ribbons white as snow,
For the shining rose-wood casket
That waited him below;
And out of the darkened chamber
We went with a childless moan:—
To the height of the sinless Angels
Our little one has grown![19]

Like other elegies on the deaths of children in this period, this poem takes measuring the baby as its central metaphor. As in "Two Sundays," the child's height is measured against a lily that "grew at the threshold" of a cottage or other "lowly" dwelling. Popular in poetry of this type, this liminal image suggests that the baby has barely ventured out into the world when it is struck down, while framing the image of the child in memento-like fashion. Illustrations to such poems often depict these children bounded in a doorway, as here (Fig. 4). The baby's highly realistic features, in contrast to the sketched-in floral garland, gateway, and lily, suggest that the illustrator combined a photograph with an ornamental frame, a common technique of mid-nineteenth-century mortuary tributes, in which the advances of photography supplemented the handiwork of an earlier era. In comparison with his elflike surroundings, the infant's huge size emphasizes the overwhelming effect of his death on his family and the tragedy that an infant's death meant to the larger culture. Yet the towering infant also seems threatening, since he resembles a doll, an image of terror and the grotesque. Indeed, the turn in Browne's poem occurs when the boy is measured for a coffin; "we measured the baby" continues as a refrain describing the boy's preparation for burial until the end, when his death

Fig. 4. Illustration of Emma Alice Browne's "Measuring the Baby," in *What Can a Woman Do?; or, Her Position in the Business and Literary World* (Detroit, Mich.; St. Louis, Mo., Cincinnati, Ohio: F. B. Dickerson & Co., 1885), n.p.

is described as a kind of growth: "To the height of the sinless Angels / Our little one has grown!" Although the elegy promises that the child has been assumed into heaven with the "sinless Angels," his physical size gives him an ascendency over death by letting him tower over both flowers and adults alike. Like the baby in Jackson's "Two Sundays," whose overweening ego admits that another being exists, Browne's poem displays through the toddler's enormity the family's love. His enormity hints that the fear of death was not contained by nineteenth-century consolatory fictions, and the unreality of his stature, especially when compared with the illustration, hints that even for a nineteenth-century readership the child's ascension was similarly fictional.

Browne's poem resonates with Dickinson's poems about "Amplitude" or "Awe." Dickinson's lyrics invoke the invitation and envoi of gravestone inscriptions in order to undercut the Victorian myth that we can expect a blissful reunion with the dead in heaven. In one elegy, the child-speaker relates her thoughts while being carried to her grave; she imagines self-pityingly how her family might have responded to her absence during their holiday celebrations:

> And would it blur the Christmas glee
> My Stocking hang too high
> For any Santa Claus to reach
> The Altitude of me—
>
> (J, 445)

Having assumed in death the proportions of a giant or having simply moved to a higher place, the speaker has separated herself from her family's celebrations and earthly pleasures. Like the heavenly growth of the baby in Browne's poem, the child's height poignantly reminds us of its distance from earth. But unlike Browne's poem, which retells the baby's death from the perspective of her family, this elegy depicts an insider's view of the grave, one which ultimately rejects the memories of home life in favor of a reunion after death with those who are still alive. Since her first thoughts only "grieved" her, the speaker has decided to think "the other way" and to imagine her family's eventual reunion with her in heaven:

> But this sort, grieved myself,
> And so, I thought the other way,
> How just this time, some perfect year—
> Themself, should come to me—

Readers in Dickinson's era must have been familiar with references to the long-awaited reunion that was promised to mourning relatives. Rather than offer the normative consolation of other child elegies, however, the conclusion to this poem portrays the dead child's point of view instead of the grieving family's. The perspective of the mourner is shifted from living parents to dead child, partly to point out the arbitrary nature of such consolation, and partly to accord the child the power of revenge over those who are still alive. Like an epitaph that warns that the reader of the tombstone would come to the same end as the dead soul who ostensibly speaks its words, this poem implies that the entombed child beckons its parents to come. Speaking as disembodied voices from the grave, epitaphs frequently call for the onlooker to halt and contemplate the grave of a fellow mortal, only to remind the reader that— sooner or later—he will return to the same spot.[20] Just as surely as we mourn the dead here on earth, they mourn for us and expect us to join them in heaven.

Lydia Sigourney modified the belief that the entire family would be reunited by portraying a reunion after death between a mother and her son. In doing so, she helped solidify the idealization of mothers which was current at the time, depicting a relation between mother and son that excluded the father and accorded women a special role as instructors and protectors of their children.[21] Dickinson invoked many of these standard consolatory myths, but only in order to contradict the easy translation of earthly doubts into heavenly hopes by writers like Sigourney, to whom I will now turn. In her elegies, Lydia Sigourney portrays a pious and idealized bond between a mother and her infant son. She built on a consolatory fiction, which was already standard in nineteenth-century America, that forecast the gathering together of the entire family beyond the grave. Yet she consoled grieving mothers in particular with the promise that they will rejoin their dead children in heaven. No doubt Sigourney was responding in her child elegies to the deaths of three of her own infants, as well as of her son, Andrew, whose care superseded every other relationship in her life. In publishing her tribute volume, *The Faded Hope*, Sigourney memorialized her son's death, and she wrote countless poems on the deaths of male infants, although she never wrote one on the death of her husband.[22] Her poems reflect the culmination of the sentimental cult of motherhood, where women's moral purity and innocence allowed them a privileged position as the primary nurturers and teachers of their children. While Sigourney accorded mothers and their sons a privileged role in her elegies, she remained well within the conventions of the period that predicted a reunion of grieving parents and children in heaven.

One can consider Sigourney's life as an example of the contradictory lives led by women writers, whom Mary Kelley has called "literary domestics."[23] As for many other nineteenth-century American women writers, no contradiction existed for Sigourney between pursuing writing professionally and leading a conventional life as a daughter, a wife, and a mother. Her commitment to her parents led her early in life to renounce the thought of marriage in order to support them through teaching and publishing,[24] yet her literary work became more professional and less altruistic as she became increasingly successful. Once she experienced the monetary success that a sizeable readership could bring, she began to turn out a prodigious number of contributions to gift volumes, periodicals, and annuals of all types. As her biographer, Gordon S. Haight, notes, with the bias typical for critics of his generation who discuss women's writing, Sigourney displayed in private a business sense that was considered uncommon at the time for women: "It is uncertain whether she practiced sweet patience consistently at home; but with her publishers she displayed a persistent sharpness of business dealing that was scarcely to be expected from a poetess."[25] She nevertheless kept up a smooth facade in public, embodying a conciliatory attitude in her relations with her editors and exhibiting a correctly feminine demeanor to her readership.[26] In fact, Sigourney was so far from finding her professional and private lives contradictory that, even after she had attained considerable success, she continued to view writing as a domestic activity, drawing up on ledger sheets the number of visits given and received, books read, pieces of clothing sewn or knit, and the number of pages of prose or lines of poetry written over the course of a year.[27] That she apparently viewed writing as a task on a par with household ones suggests how closely "private" woman and "public" duty were intermingled.

Perhaps Sigourney's conservative viewpoint offers one reason why she could overlook any contradiction, either in her life or her poetry. She implicitly encouraged the view, which was common at the time, that the lives of women and children were inherently similar and intimately connected. Editors and authors frequently referred to an innately moral quality that they believed made women naturally fit to safeguard the moral values of society and to assume the responsibility of converting others, especially men. Prominent writers, like Sigourney, reinforced this portrayal of women as pious and holy apostles. Sigourney wrote numerous advice manuals for women and their children, including such confidential and instructive volumes as *Letters to Young Ladies* (1833), *Letters to Mothers* (1838), and *Whisper to a Bride* (1850). These books depict mothers, as well as their children, as spontaneous teachers, whose untutored intellects were conduits for moral truth and virtue. Moreover, the ideal Victorian matron was generally conceived to be sexless and desireless, much as children were presumed to be free of erotic tendencies. In one poem, Dickinson claims that these gentlewomen are "Soft—Cherubic Creatures—," whose genteel "Dimity Convictions" make them so resemble childlike angels that Christ is embarrassed to redeem them (J, 401). Frequently compared throughout this period to flowers, women and children embody a cultural ideal of decorative beauty and highly prized fragility. In portraying the continuity between the lives of mothers and their dying children, Sigourney could write fully in the knowledge that her description of mothers as faithful and childlike adhered to the conservative limits which circumscribed the era's depiction of women.

Unlike Sigourney's son, who remains a perpetual child in his mother's eyes, the saintly child heroines of novels and poems attain moral perfection only in adulthood. Having escaped the influence of civilized society, novelist Sylvester Judd's Margaret absorbs moral truth from the natural life around her at the Pond where she lives in isolation with her family. Like Pearl in *The Scarlet Letter* (1850), Margaret seems an elf-child; when she is asked doctrinal questions by parishioners after attending her first religious service, she responds quizzically, evoking cries of dismay from those around her. But Margaret's story continues into adulthood, when she meets her suitor and eventual husband, Mr. Evelyn, who provides her with a more normative religious sensibility and with whom she sets out to convert the unregenerate of the small town of Livingston.[28] Her role in saving the town's souls suggests that the prescient girl continues her saintly mission on earth into adulthood.

Even after a spotless young woman dies, she imitates the role ascribed to mothers in guarding over the spiritual fates of those who are still alive. Once grown to womanhood, Smith's Eva meets Albert Linne, "a gay youth, whose errors are those of an ardent and inexperienced nature, rather than of an assenting will . . ." (115). Destined never to consummate an earthly relationship, Eva assumes the responsibility of caring for the state of her lover's soul, a duty for which women were believed to be naturally suited in life. Indeed, Eva's mother and neighbors are baffled by her deep comprehension of life, yet they contend that she "is unlike her sex only in greater truth and elevation" (41). Her chaste passion for Albert finds its culmination in heaven, from which, having progressed from "The Sinless Child" to "The Spirit Bride" (138), she acts as his guiding-spirit and constant protector. The child heroines in these works grow up to assume the responsibility accorded adult women in saving those around them, while their male counterparts, like Andrew in Sigourney's tribute volume, *The Faded Hope* (1853), can only extend a moral influence after death through an alliance with their mother's piety.

Sigourney's portrayal of Andrew, whose resistance to organized religion especially proved an obstacle for Sigourney, reveals the extent to which she tried to control his life.[29] Unlike his sister, Andrew had not had a conversion experience, an event which Sigourney and others of her generation considered necessary for proof of salvation. Unconcerned with the state of his soul as a teenager, Andrew talked of going west and settling a tract of land he had inherited from his father, claiming there he would be judged on the merits of his character. Sigourney responded with prayers, asking her friends to join her in supplication that he might be converted after all.[30] He gradually came to accept more of his mother's dictates, as he physically weakened. When he refused to discuss his sickness, Sigourney commended his stoic resilience but reproved his behavior, especially as he resisted her attention to his needs: "There was a strange pride about him, as if yielding to sickness, or accepting nursing care, savored of effeminacy or of giving unnecessary trouble" (211). Finding that he relies on her for companionship in his illness, she exults in their hours of conversation, imagining that at these times "every veil was rent, every mist removed" from between them (212); "If from eccentricity, or waywardness, or failure in reciprocity, she had at any time doubted the depth or force of his love, that doubt was put to rest forever" (213). Although he died at nineteen, he became in sickness "an increasingly tender, trustful and child-like spirit"

(222). With a childlike dependence and despite a lifelong aversion to accepting gifts of money, he was reduced in his weakened state to accepting them thankfully, and Sigourney takes satisfaction in finally gaining her triumph: "The pride of life had passed away. His soul was humbled. Scarcely, without grateful tears could his mother perceive, that everything from her hand, was accepted with the docility of a little child" (224–25).

Andrew appears both effeminate and childlike in Sigourney's description, and his death resembles those of other nineteenth-century child prophets. Like fully one half of the adolescents who died in this period, he was plagued with a disease that by the late nineteenth century was associated with young women through its representation in drama, opera, and novels—tuberculosis.[31] Like the young English poet John Keats, he appears in sickness to have acquired a feminine delicacy which only added to his already pale, delicate features: "The burning rose on the cheek, contrasting with the pure forehead, gave to the violet eye, flashing through its long fringes, unearthly brightness and expression" (215). Moreover, Andrew's habits resemble more those a woman than of a young man: he is thankful for "neatness, and tasteful arrangement" in the presentation of his last meals, and he strictly refuses to take a daily dose of cod-liver oil mixed in a glass of brandy and water due to an "early temperance-pledge" (228). Finally, even his resigned and beatific expression at the moment of death points to his mother's continued presence. Having predicted the exact hour and minute of his death, he resembles a child angel: "As the clock struck the hour of high noon, and the hand of his own watch touched the point of twelve,—he fell asleep, like an infant on the breast of its mother" (236). Andrew's holy example is memorialized by his mother, who hears the injunction "'Write!'" from a heavenly voice after his death and whose response suggests that her writing serves to sublimate her grief: "Glorious words! floating out upon the summer air, from consecrated lips, with holy healing" (237–38).

Like the dying child in nineteenth-century literature, who often consigns cherished objects to others in order to console them through his pious example, Andrew attentively gives away keepsakes, which form an integral part of the deathbed ritual in Victorian America. Much as Eva in Harriet Beecher Stowe's *Uncle Tom's Cabin* (1851–2), who provides comfort to her father's slaves on her death by cutting off her "long, beautiful curls" as gifts,[32] Andrew gives "a colored servant woman . . . to whom in boyhood, he had so perseveringly endeavored to teach the sciences" a keepsake designed to preserve her memory of him (231). Stowe's Eva, too, fervently wishes to make the slaves literate, remarking to her shocked mother that, if she had her jewels to use as she wished, she would "'sell them, and buy a place in the free states, and take all our people there, and hire teachers, to teach them to read and write'" (263). Both he and Eva try to teach those who are less advantaged than they are: education as well as evangelism formed a part of the nineteenth-century child exemplar's standard equipment in converting souls to the good.

Sigourney's poems on the deaths of male infants promise a grieving mother that she will be reunited with her dead son in heaven. In doing so, Sigourney suggests that the bond between a boy and his mother surpasses every other family tie.[33] Indeed, I would argue that she redefines the standard consolatory format in a way that was consistent with its conservative aims but which clearly set the mother and son's bond above all other family relationships. Her 1834 *Poems* usually identify these children either as male infants or make no reference to their gender; although Sigourney periodically memorialized the deaths of young women and girls in her verse, the vast majority of the poems in this volume deal with the deaths of both infant sons and their mothers.

In her elegies, a dead mother often encourages her son to join her beyond the grave, portraying a heavenly existence as more pleasant and natural than life on earth. Or, in another variation, a speaker who looks on from outside the family circle consoles the grieving mother with the prospect of a reunion with her infant son in heaven, an idealized version of the mother and child's relationship on earth. Taken together, Sigourney's poems imply that the relation between a mother and her son was so intense that a continuity existed between their lives even after death. The more material Victorian conception that the family circle would be reconstituted in heaven allowed mothers to keep a firm hold on their dead children's lives and to continue to possess them almost as if they were cherished mementos.[34] Rather than portraying a female speaker who receives comfort only from the promise of Christian salvation, Sigourney assures mothers of a material reunion with their infants in heaven.

To gain a fuller sense of the intent of her poems, one can consider the range of speakers in Sigourney's elegies. A brief catalog of her most frequently used speakers reveals that a mother and child's bond underlies every infant elegy: a mother enjoins her dead or dying child to die in order to avoid the pain and temptation of earth; a dead mother wishes her living child a happy and moral life; a generalized speaker describes a woman's joyful reunion with her dead infant in heaven; an observer of a child's funeral discourses to the bystanders about the mother's and father's sorrow; and, most commonly, a speaker who witnesses a scene of public mourning over a mother's death predicts that her child will continue to follow her holy example. Of the dozen or so child elegies in Sigourney's 1834 *Poems*, more than half focus on the mother's bond with a male infant.[35] In general, these poems begin with a mother's or child's death and then gradually reveal the logic by which the survivors can learn to accept their loss. Occasionally, they open by presenting a mother's death and offering a consoling message to her son, only to redress that loss by suggesting that she has already gained her long-awaited reward by joining her dead infant in heaven. Finally, her poems inevitably end with an upward glance, as an infant ascends to his dead mother's embrace or a mother is enjoined to "Look up!" for the compensation she lacks on earth.

Sigourney's "To a Dying Infant," a typical poem of this genre, portrays a speaker who encourages her child to ascend to heaven so that he can avoid the pain and temptation of earth. This poem somewhat resembles elegies of the seventeenth and eighteenth centuries, which console bereaved parents and relatives with the thought that the child has achieved salvation in heaven. She draws on the consoling myth that a child will be better off in heaven by depicting death as an escape from life's pain and uncertainty. Unlike earlier elegists, however, she adopts the popular nineteenth-century consolatory fiction that death is only a form of sleep. Rather than console herself on her infant's death with the thought of salvation, the mother in this poem sends her child to its heavenly sleep so that he will not sin:

> Go to thy rest, my child!
>   Go to thy dreamless bed,
> Gentle and undefiled,
>   With blessings on thy head;
> Fresh roses in thy hand,
>   Buds on thy pillow laid,
> Haste from this fearful land,
>   Where flowers so quickly fade.
>
> Before thy heart might learn
>   In waywardness to stray,
> Before thy feet could turn
>   The dark and downward way;
> Ere sin might wound the breast,
>   Or sorrow wake the tear,
> Rise to thy home of rest,
>   In yon celestial sphere.
>
> Because thy smile was fair,
>   Thy lip and eye so bright,
> Because thy cradle-care,
>   Was such a fond delight,
> Shall Love with weak embrace
>   Thy heavenward flight detain?
> No! Angel, seek thy place
>   Amid yon cherub-train.[36]

In claiming that the infant will maintain its purity by ascending to heaven, the speaker seeks to keep her hold over it. Although this poem begins as if it were going to be a lullaby, details slowly emerge to reveal that the child is dying (as the title, of course, has already told us). The mother charges her child, who is still "undefiled," to go to its "rest" in a "dreamless bed" in the hopes that its innocence will be preserved in heaven. The image of withering blooms in the last part of the stanza evokes a familiar trope of innocence, the "sweet moral blossom," which lasts only a short while before the temptations and pitfalls of the world mar its beauty. Contending in the second stanza that the infant should ascend to its "home of rest" in order to prevent its purity from being lost, the speaker attempts to extend her influence over her child even after its death. For Sigourney, heaven was not unlike the domestic sphere, where women and children remained above the world's moral and sexual corruption. From this "celestial sphere" of chaste innocence, dead mothers continued to exert a powerful influence as their children's first and most significant teachers of moral values. Although this speaker will apparently survive her baby, her wish that it die before treading "the dark and downward way" of sin allows her to imagine that it is still hers, since it will never enter the contaminated world. In the final stanza, she relinquishes the loving "cradle-care" of her infant as if she still had control over its fate. Her fantasy that she might actually be able to prolong the infant's life even momentarily in the "weak embrace" of love indicates her wish to cling to her dying child.

If Sigourney's mothers often seek to arrest their infants' heavenward flight, other poems frame almost visually a scene of mother or child's death in an effort to present a comforting keepsake to the reader. In "Baptism of an Infant, At Its Mother's Funeral," for example, a speaker wonders at the scene of death before her, which juxtaposes a mother's funeral with an infant's christening:

> Whence is that trembling of a father's hand,
> Who to the man of God doth bring his babe,
> Asking the seal of Christ?—Why doth the voice
> That uttereth o'er its brow the Triune Name
> Falter with sympathy?—And most of all,
> Why is yon coffin-lid a pedestal
> For the baptismal font?
>
> (ll. 1–7)

The tableau of father, priest, and baby is described in stark blank verse, which focuses attention on the image of the still figures who stand around the mother's casket. The speaker describes the scene as if drawing aside a veil from a tableau, only to append an instructive or consolatory moral. Like their opening scenes, the titles of Sigourney's poems provide a verbal snapshot of the central event, as the poem gradually reveals what the title already revealed. The titles often refer to scenes of nature worship, religious drama, or human tragedy, as the following ponderous ones suggest: "Solitude," "A Cottage Scene," "The Last Supper," and the immensely popular "Death of an Infant."

In "Death of an Infant," the child assumes center stage, almost as if he were a painting or piece of statuary that attracted the observer's notice:

> Death found strange beauty on that polished brow
> And dashed it out.—
>   There was a tint of rose
> On cheek and lip.—He touched the veins with ice,
> And the rose faded.—
>   Forth from those blue eyes
> There spake a wishful tenderness, a doubt
> Whether to grieve or sleep, which innocence
> Alone may wear.—With ruthless haste he bound
> The silken fringes of those curtaining lids
> Forever.—
>   There had been a murmuring sound,
> With which the babe would claim its mother's ear,
> Charming her even to tears.—The Spoiler set
> His seal of silence.—
>   But there beamed a smile
> So fixed, so holy, from that cherub brow,
> Death gazed—and left it there.—
>   *He dared not steal*
> *The signet-ring of Heaven.*

Joanne Dobson has argued that the use of conventional images, conversational tone, and grammatical regularity in this poem encourage us to accept the consolation offered at the end in the final, manifest metaphor: "In this lone metaphor, Heaven's promise of eventual reconciliation bridges the sentimental breach implicit in the deathbed scene. The 'wishful tenderness' of affectional desire will be rewarded with reunion in the afterlife."[37] Only the beginning of the third stanza, where the transposed syntax, archaic diction, and moderately complex sentence structure signal "the child's subjectivity, its 'wishful' desire to live" (271), impedes the easy transition from image to feeling. In addition, Sigourney's theatrical description and the images drawn from the vocabulary of sculpture and painting—the baby's "polished brow" and cheeks and lips with a "tint of rose"—add to the characterization of the dead infant as an object for public display. Like a merciless stage manager, death rings down the child's "curtaining lids" forever, yet the curtain rises triumphantly again in the poem's conclusion to enshrine the child's image permanently. Although the "Spoiler" has set "His seal of silence" (ll. 12–13) on the baby, his holy smile so awes the onlooker that "even Death gazed—and left it there.—" (l. 14). Stamped with the *"signet-ring of Heaven"* (l. 15), the baby's beatific look stops death from stealing the only cherishable memory left to the grieving parents.

A speaker who looks on a death from outside the family circle often exposes the innermost feelings of the mourners, especially important when a mother is no longer present to formulate an instructive moral for a child who survives her. Maternal mortality continued at a high rate throughout the nineteenth century, and pregnancy frequently heralded the death of the mother due to miscarriages and stillbirths, difficult or premature labor, the high incidence of puerperal fever, and medical procedures such as the cesarean section, which were almost always fatal.[38] Stepping into scenes of deathbed agony or funeral mourning, the observer in these poems laments a death that, because it occurs at home, might otherwise be overlooked. In "Baptism of an Infant, At Its Mother's Funeral," the speaker seeks in a series of questions to understand why the mother's death has occurred, only to be answered by the tears of the mourners as the mother's coffin is unveiled. She then foretells the baby's sorrowful life, almost as if she were herself speaking for its absent mother:

> ——Tears were thy baptism, thou unconscious one,
> And Sorrow took thee at the gate of life,
> Into her cradle. Thou may'st never know
> The welcome of a nursing mother's kiss,
> When in her wandering ecstasy, she marks
> A thrilling growth of new affections spread
> Fresh greenness o'er the soul.
> Thou may'st not share
> Her hallowed teaching, nor suffuse her eye
> With joy, as the first germs of infant thought
> Unfold, in lisping sound.
>
> (ll. 16–26)

Although his mother has died, the child lives out his mother's pious life on earth in her place, a claim borne out by the emotional and intellectual influence she continues to have on her infant. Marking the child's entry into life, the tears of the young mother's mourners baptize him: "—Tears were thy baptism, thou unconscious one, / And Sorrow took thee at the gate of life, / Into her cradle" (ll. 16–18). "Sorrow" is itself personified as a mother who will take the child into "her cradle," as if substituting for the real mother who died. As this image suggests, the grief the child suffers as a result of his mother's death serves to counsel him through life. Although deprived of her care on earth, he will grow up more aware of God's power, and hence will emulate his mother's piety:

> Yet may'st thou walk
> Even as she walked, breathing on all around
> The warmth of high affections, purified,
> And sublimated, by that Spirit's power

Which makes the soul fit temple for its God.
——So shalt thou in a brighter world, behold
That countenance which the cold grave did veil
Thus early from thy sight, and the first tone
That bears a mother's greeting to thine ear
Be wafted from the minstrelsy of Heaven.

(ll. 27–36)

Living in an environment imbued with "The warmth of high affections," which
have been "purified, / And sublimated" by his mother's death, the infant nevertheless will imitate her pious actions and achieve a union with her in spirit
until he rejoins her in heaven.

Sigourney contends that a mother influences her child as its teacher, a doctrine which she discusses at some length in her *Letters to Young Ladies* (1838):

It is in the domestick sphere, in her own native province, that woman is inevitably a
teacher. There she modifies by her example, her dependants, her companions, every
dweller under her own roof. Is not the infant in its cradle, her pupil? Does not her smile
give the earliest lesson to its soul? Is not her prayer the first messenger for it in the court
of Heaven? Does she not enshrine her own image in the sanctuary of the young child's
mind, so firmly that no revulsion can displace, no idolatry supplant it? Does she not
guide the daughter, until placing her hand in that of her husband, she reaches that
pedestal, from whence, in her turn, she imparts to others, the stamp and colouring which
she has herself received? Might she not, even upon her sons, engrave what they shall
take unchanged through all the temptations of time, to the bar of the last judgment? Does
not the influence of woman rest upon every member of her household, like the dew upon
the tender herb, or the sunbeam silently educating the young flower? or as the shower,
and the sleepless stream, cheer and invigorate the proudest tree of the forest?[39]

This passage reveals that nineteenth-century mothers fulfilled a crucial role
in educating their young children in ways acceptable to society. As her infant's
first teacher, a mother makes an impact on it that lasts all its life and maintains
her earthly control over it even after her death. She notably erects in its mind
her own "image" rather than God's as an example of holy love, the infant having completely internalized her influence, as if she were its "idol." From there,
she instructs it in behavior proper for an adult, encouraging her daughter to
marry and her son to adhere to the values of a moral life. Moreover, she insures
that these roles be endlessly perpetuated by setting her daughter on an idealized
"pedestal" from which she will instill the same values in her own children, "im-
part[ing] to others, the stamp and colouring which she has herself received."
Significantly, she considers a mother's earthly influence to be stronger over her
daughter than over her son, as her remark that she might exert her sway "even
upon her sons" suggests. Sigourney's faith in a girl's extreme malleability

points to her belief that women actively replicate the era's prevailing ideals of
femininity. Although she depicts the "influence of woman" as a nurturing force,
the way she emphasizes its pervasiveness and its persistence in the images
taken from nature of the "sunbeam silently educating the young flower" and
"the sleepless stream" flowing endlessly through the forest suggest just how effective she imagined this influence could be.[40]

In "Death of a Beautiful Boy," Sigourney alludes early on to the pain the
child suffers as a result of his mother's early death, only to suggest that he lives
out his short life in her shadow. Although his mother is absent, she is present in
his life in myriad ways:

> I saw thee in thine hour of sport, beside thy father's bower,
> Amid his broad and bright parterre, thyself the fairest flower;
> I heard thy tuneful voice ring out upon the summer air,
> As though some bird of Eden poured its joyous carol there,
> And lingered with delighted gaze on happy childhood's charms,
> Which once the blest Redeemer loved, and folded in his arms.
>
> I saw thee scan the classic page, with high and glad surprise,
> And saw the sun of science beam, as on an eaglet's eyes,
> And marked thy strong and brilliant mind arouse to bold pursuit,
> And from the tree of knowledge pluck its richest, rarest fruit,
> Yet still from such precocious power I shrank with secret fear,
> A shuddering presage that thy race must soon be ended here.
>
> (ll. 7–18)

Playing beside his "father's bower," the boy lives in a garden-world dominated by the presence of his masculine parent, yet the "fairest flower" points
to the continued influence of his mother. An allusion to Milton ("*Proserpin
gath'ring flow'rs / Herself a fairer Flow'r by gloomy Dis / Was gather'd . . .*"),[41]
this phrase uses the common trope of a culled flower to signify early death.
Sigourney alludes to Milton's Proserpine, who, like the feminized Andrew, is
fated to join the world of the dead while still young. Like the young women in
numerous other nineteenth-century poems, he sings in a "tuneful voice" reminiscent of a "bird of Eden."[42] The comparison to an animal, an "eaglet" whose
mind is aroused to the "bold pursuit" of knowledge, recalls the theories of the
post-Enlightenment Romantic philosophers, who contended that children are
primitive and unspoiled examples of human goodness, rather than depraved
sinners, as the Calvinists believed.[43] With the rise of evangelical religion in the
first half of the nineteenth century, the image of the spontaneous affection and
untutored intellect of children became a new model of holy behavior, one
which parents themselves needed to embrace in order to achieve salvation and
to which mothers were thought to contribute through their roles as nurturing
teachers. Sigourney adopts the motif of the Garden of Eden to develop this link

between the naive mind of an infant and his mother: the boy assumes Eve's role in searching after knowledge, plucking its "richest, rarest fruit." His attachment to his mother and his reunion with her in heaven is like an Oedipal scenario, yet the violence of this conflict turns inward as both mother and child die and the father remains absent and unscathed. Foretelling that the sensitive boy will live only a short time, the speaker predicts in the last line of the poem the boy's ascent to a domestic celestial sphere, where a "sainted mother's arms" will affectionately clasp him once again (l. 24). Like the act of stanza two's "Redeemer," who maternally "loved" the boy as soon as he saw him and "folded" him in his arms (l. 12), the promised embrace of his mother after death implies that they will continue their earthly relationship in heaven. In this final phrase, the mother herself takes the place of the "Redeemer" in Sigourney's view of a feminized heaven.

For Sigourney, a mother's influence over her son takes its cue at least partly from the popular image of a maiden weeping over a willow-shaded tomb that appears as a common motif in sentimental funerary iconography. Having internalized his mother's absence, the boy often increases in emotional sensitivity as he matures, a trait which is captured in the image of the growing willow tree. The weeping willow symbolized for nineteenth-century mourners the new, gradualist doctrine that promised heavenly salvation to those who suffered emotional pain and grief on earth. As Barton Levi St. Armand explains, this conventional image aptly conveyed the consoling mythology of spiritual regeneration: "The willow . . . was a traditional emblem of Christian mourning, since it shed its leaves like tears, seemed perpetually drooped in thoughtful reverie, and had the power to regenerate itself after being cut down (thereby foretelling the resurrection of the dead)."[44] The piteous shedding of tears and the merciful act of drying them often connect mother to son, as in the first stanza of "On the Death of a Mother Soon After Her Infant Son":

> There's a cry from that cradle-bed,
>   The voice of an infant's woe;
> Hark! hark! to the mother's rushing tread,
> In her bosom's fold she hath hid his head,
>   And his wild tears cease to flow.
>   Yet he must weep again,
>   And when his eye shall know
>   The burning brine of manhood's pain
>   Or youth's unuttered woe,
>   That mother fair
> With her full tide of sympathies, alas! may not be there.
>   On earth, the tree of weeping grows
>   Fast by man's side where'er he goes,
> And o'er his brightest joys, its bitterest essence flows.
>
>   (ll. 1–14)

As long as the mother lives, drying her child's tears is a show of care as well as an act of sympathetic bonding. Yet the boy may survive to experience other woes in life as an adult, which his mother will no longer be there to alleviate: although he may shed tears—"the burning brine of manhood's pain"—his mother's "full tide of sympathies" will not cleanse them. Indeed, the very shape of the stanza—with its narrow neck, wide body, and pedestal base- traces the outlines of a funerary urn, a further link to the iconography of mourning in nineteenth-century America. Rather than merely symbolize the tears shed for the dead, the "tree of weeping," like an ever-lengthening mea- suring stick, gauges the boy's developing spiritual maturity—the taller he grows, the more sensitive he will become to earthly woes. Even after his mother dies, the boy will adopt her sympathetic response to pain and continue to follow her example.

"On the Death of a Mother, Soon After Her Infant Son" further suggests that the close bond between mother and son prompts the mother's demise. Sigourney quickly shows in the succeeding stanzas that this faithful soul has already been rewarded with her child's company in heaven. Having completely given over her days to educating her son ("And from each rising sun / Till Night her balmy cup of silence poured, / For him the paths of knowledge she explored, / Feeding his eager mind with seraph's bread, / Till intellectual light o'er his fair features spread" [ll. 23–27]), she is subdued by his early death, and resigns herself to his fate. Her submissive posture echoes the traditional Christian attitude that encouraged adults to obey God's will as a child might a parent: "Yet she who bore him shrank not 'neath the rod, / Laying her chas- tened soul low at the feet of God" (ll. 32–33). In the last stanza, the speaker counsels all mothers to look forward to their children's company in heaven as compensation for their suffering on earth:

> Mothers! whose speechless care,
> Whose unrequited sigh,
> Weary arm and sleepless eye
> Change the fresh rose-bud on the cheek to paleness and despair,
> Look up! Look up to the bountiful sky,
> Earth may not pay your debt, your record is on high.
> Ye have gazed in doubt on the plants that drew
> From your gentle hand their nightly dew—
> Ye have given with trembling your morning kiss,
> Ye have sown in pain—ye shall reap in bliss;
> The mother's tear, the mother's prayer,
> In faith for her offspring given,
> Shall be counted as pearls at the judgment-bar,
> And win the gold of heaven.

(ll. 46–59)

Not only do mothers influence their children by acting as their earliest and most important teachers and protectors, but they can also join them in death by making the ultimate sacrifice as their sick nurse. The "speechless care" and "unrequited sigh" of these mothers are ignored, even as their bodies tire and their faces pale with anxiety and hopelessness. They constantly worry that their children might be taken away from them, gazing "in doubt" day by day on them and "trembling" with fear in the morning when they kiss them, lest they have died during the night. Sigourney promises in the conclusion to this poem that the mother who has mourned for a child on earth will be recompensed in heaven by just as much as she has suffered. Nevertheless, caring for a dying infant might promote a woman's heavenly reunion with her child in a very literal way, and the ailing health of the mother in this poem confirms for us once more that in Sigourney's elegies a mother's weary life is in many ways only an extension of her child's.

Dickinson was familiar with the Sigourney-style elegy that promised suffering mothers a reunion with their infants in heaven. Yet she adopts these conventions after her own fashion, and frequently writes elegiac meditations, which, while they do not lament the deaths of actual infants, draw on and transform the features of other child elegies. Barton Levi St. Armand remarks that Dickinson's "appropriation of the props of the Sentimental Love Religion and the popular gospel of consolation involve a process of personalization, internalization, exaggeration, and inversion."[45] Just as the death of Sigourney's son, Andrew, seems to underlie many of her infant elegies, the death of Dickinson's nephew, Gilbert, whom she called her "own Boy" (*Letters* 3, 853), occasioned some of her most lasting meditations on death, and prompted the elegaic tone of much of her later writing. In moments of genuine grief, she sublimated her pain to transform these accepted verse forms into her own statements concerning suffering, death, and the afterlife.

Like her contemporaries, Dickinson extols the dying child as a spiritual guardian, an infant prophet whose closeness to death makes him peculiarly able to preach to adults. But rather than dwell on an imagined prescience that forms part of its short but spiritually exemplary life, she claims that the child gains its knowledge of an afterlife only after it is dead. Her nephew, Gilbert, for instance, has discovered the answer to the mystery of death, which reaches beyond the ken of a living adult: "'Open the Door, open the Door, they are waiting for me,' was Gilbert's sweet command in delirium. *Who* were waiting for him, all we possess we would give to know—Anguish at last opened it, and he ran to the little Grave at his Grandparents' feet—All this and more, though *is* there more? More than Love and Death? Then tell me it's name!" (*Letters* 3, 803)[46] Despite her desire to find a "name" for existence after death, the secret of death still baffles Dickinson, and her attempt to understand it resembles a child's desire to learn to name an experience for the first time. In adopting the naive accents of a child, Dickinson affirmed the spiritual prescience of children.[47] Yet she parted company with sentimental elegists like Sigourney, who never afforded the dead child as much time as its parents to speak. Dickinson's appropriation of the myth of a postmortem reunion and of a child's prophetic knowledge allowed her aptly to convey her frustrations as a religious outsider, whose questions concerning death and the afterlife were destined to remain unanswered.

Dickinson believed that children had special access to the spiritual world and served as fitting examples of pious behavior for adults. Her letters to friends and relatives consoling them on the loss of children stress not only the "sweet velocity" (*Letters* 3, 799) of their lives, but also their faithful adherence to God's will: "'Come unto me.' Beloved Commandment. The Darling obeyed" (*Letters* 2, 636). No other death was more traumatic or grievous to Dickinson than that of her eight-year-old nephew, Gilbert, and her description of him in her letters is consonant with the terms in which dead children were described at the time. Writing in October 1883 to Susan Gilbert Dickinson, she notes his comet-like life in terms that echo funerary iconography: "No crescent was this Creature—He traveled from the Full—Such soar, but never set—" (*Letters* 3, 799). In this moving tribute, Dickinson acknowledges Gilbert's having passed beyond the ken of the living, like a sun/soul depicted winging its way toward heaven on gravestones. Furthermore, his encompassing knowledge of life and death makes him seem larger than life: "Wherefore would he wait, wronged only of Night, which he left for us—Without a speculation, our little Ajax spans the whole—" (*Letters* 3, 799). She compares Gilbert to Ajax, famed Greek hero of great stature and prowess, who fought against the Trojans, and she implies that he has transcended death in invoking the mythological warriors physical largeness. Yet the comparison is also a tender hyperbole, since Gilbert could measure up to Ajax's stature only in the eyes of those who loved him.

Dickinson deemed Gilbert's friend, Kendall Emerson, especially knowledgeable about her nephew's heavenly state, since he was with Gilbert when both were playing in a mudhole, and Gilbert contracted a fatal case of typhoid fever. The poet commemorated her eight-year-old nephew's death in three notes to Kendall. The timing of these letters, written at Christmas rather than on the anniversary of Gilbert's death, implies that his early demise reveals for her a tragic precocity. Like the Christ child, Gilbert was fated to suffer an untimely death. In her first note, in 1883, she asks for information about Gilbert's whereabouts after death with a childlike naiveté:

Dear Kendall—

Christmas in Bethlehem means most of all, this Year, but Santa Claus still asks the way to Gilbert's little friends—Is Heaven an unfamiliar Road?

Come sometime with your Sled and tell Gilbert's

Aunt Emily.

(*Letters* 3, 804–5)

In this, the most childlike of the three notes that Dickinson sent to Kendall, the poet pretends that Santa Claus seeks out "Gilbert's little friends" in order to bring them presents, then slyly asks if heaven is an "unfamiliar Road." She implies that the way to heavenly salvation is known only to those who, like Gilbert, have taken its path or who, like Kendall, have ventured close enough to death to make that road familiar.

Both of Dickinson's other letters stress the continued loss she feels at her nephew's death. In sending these notes every year as a tribute to Gilbert's memory, she implies that death might cut short Kendall's life as quickly as it did Gilbert's. In the second message, in 1884, she hints at the possibility that Kendall himself might have died during the intervening year:

Missing my own Boy, I knock at other Trundle-Beds, and trust the Curls are in—

Little Gilbert's Aunt—

(*Letters* 3, 853)

Ostensibly written to commemorate her nephew's death, the note also serves to make sure that Kendall has not died, that he is safe in his "Trundle-Bed," unlike her "own Boy," who is absent from home in his coffin. In her final note, in 1885, Dickinson once again warns Kendall that he might die as easily as Gilbert did:

Dear Kendall.

I send you a Blossom with my love—Spend it as you will—

The Woods are too deep for your little Feet to grope for Evergreen—

Your friend,

Emily—

(*Letters* 3, 894)

In enclosing a blossom with her note, she punningly alludes to the flower as a gift of money, yet symbolic of the transience of life, the flower also suggests Gilbert's early death and the possibility of Kendall's. She discourages Kendall from making a quest similar to the one he made with her nephew, lest his "little Feet" dangerously stray too far in the broad "Woods," which are "too deep." A symbol of perpetual life commonly used on gravestones, "Evergreen" suggests that Gilbert has become immortal as well as that his memory has remained fresh for the poet. Like the child in Browne's elegy, whose "little bare feet . . . were dimpled / And sweet as a budding rose" (ll. 21–22), Kendall has "little Feet" that symbolize the ease with which he, like Gilbert, might be assumed into heaven. Time has lessened her pain, allowing her some distance from her nephew's death; unlike the other two letters, which identify Dickinson as Gilbert's aunt, this one is signed simply, "Your friend."

Dickinson elsewhere assumes the guise of a naive child who is turned away from paradise in order to question God's seeming indifference to both adults and children who are denied His care:

> Why—do they shut Me out of Heaven?
> Did I sing—too loud?
> But—I can say a little "Minor"
> Timid as a Bird!
>
> Would'nt the Angels try me—
> Just—once—more—
> Just—see—if I troubled them—
> But dont—shut the door!
>
> Oh, if I—were the Gentleman
> In the "White Robe"—
> And they—were the little Hand—that knocked—
> Could—I—forbid?
>
> (J, 248)

Assuming the pose of a disobedient child who is shut out of the family circle, the speaker asks to be let into heaven, and this request resembles Gilbert's in his dying moments, when he asks to be allowed inside the gates of eternal life. The child hesitatingly asks the angels for another chance to prove his good intentions as a denizen of heaven, then posits a hypothetical case in his own defense: imagining himself in the last stanza as God or an archangel, the child implies that he feels doubly cheated in being shut out, as he reasons that, if he were in God's powerful place—if *he* were the doorkeeper of heaven—he certainly would not forbid a child's entry. The speaker thus refutes his unjust rebuff in heaven by testing the angels against the creed of "Do unto others as you would have them do unto you." Dickinson turns the table on Sigourney's familiar theme that children occupied a privileged place in heaven by portraying a child who is abandoned on heaven's doorstep, then inverts the child's lowly position with the archangel's at the poem's end to question his unjust exile on the boundary of paradise. The poet underscores the arbitrary power that God holds over the lives of infants and adults, who are denied the heavenly care and attention that the motto "Suffer the little children to come unto me" seems to promise.

Like others of her generation, Dickinson attests to a child's contentment after death. Sentimentalism provided a legitimate and therapeutic response to death, as in the following poem in which the speaker, who unwillingly travels to the grave, testifies to the dead child's happiness:

> Trudging to Eden, looking backward,
> I met Somebody's little Boy
> Asked him his name—He lisped me "Trotwood"—
> Lady, did He belong to thee?
>
> Would it comfort—to know I met him—
> And that He did'nt look afraid?
> I could'nt weep—for so many smiling
> New Aquaintance—this Baby made—
>
> (J, 1020)

Unlike the mothers in Sigourney's poems, who enjoin their children to die or hasten to follow them to heaven, the speaker is "trudging to Eden," as if she would prefer herself to remain here on earth. Following the characterization of dead children as once cherished, now lost, possessions, the speaker here asks if the mother previously owned this boy: "Lady, did He belong to thee?" But the dead child is no longer hers, and the speaker tentatively offers her knowledge of the boy's contentment as a consolation.

Furthermore, Dickinson alludes in "Trotwood" to the protagonist of Dickens's novel, *David Copperfield*, as a way of asserting that he continues in the family circle. The speaker puns that the child "would trot" to heaven and there meet an array of cheerful companions after death. Orphaned before birth by his father's death, David grows up solely in his mother's care. A wealthy, eccentric aunt, Betsy Trotwood, refuses to extend her riches to David at birth because, as a boy, he cannot take her first name. Indeed, his mother names him "Trotwood" in an attempt to satisfy his aunt, suggesting the extent to which women lay claim to his existence, even after they are no longer present in his life. Dickinson offers the thought of a happy comradeship among the dead as a much needed consolation on children's deaths. In a letter the poet wrote about two years after her nephew's death, she recalls Gilbert's dying vision of heaven as a kind of celestial playground: "October is a mighty Month, for in it Little Gilbert died. 'Open the Door' was his last Cry—'The Boys are waiting for me!'" (*Letters* 3, 891) Playfully reversing the hierarchy between adult and child, she responds that she opened the door, but she has seen him no more: "Quite used to his Commandment, his little Aunt obeyed, and still two years and many Days, and he does not return."

The motif of the dying child's escape from earth's tribulation, which appears frequently in Sigourney's poems, undergoes in Dickinson's verse a satiric reversal. Sigourney's "A Mother in Heaven to Her Dying Babe," for example, contends that the infant will attain salvation by dying in a pure state and avoiding the pains and temptations of adulthood:

> Long had he dwelt below,
>   Perchance his erring path,
> Had been through bitterness and woe,
>   On to his Maker's wrath
>
> (ll. 17–20)

Dickinson does not promise the same freedom from pain for the dying child. Instead, she invokes the very same pain and anxiety in order to assert that God leads innocent children through agony on earth:

> Far from Love the Heavenly Father
> Leads the Chosen Child,
> Oftener through Realm of Briar
> Than the Meadow mild.
>
> Oftener by the Claw of Dragon
> Than the Hand of Friend
> Guides the Little One predestined
> To the Native Land.
>
> (J, 1021)

Rather than focus on the child's anesthetized ascent to heaven, Dickinson counters the elegies of Sigourney and others by asserting that the infant suffers at God's bidding on earth. While the dying child in Sigourney's elegy escapes life's "erring path," which frequently leads "through bitterness and woe," the "Chosen Child"'s way in Dickinson's poem often goes through a "Realm of Briar." Before the child can commend its spirit into God's hands or submit to a mother's loving embrace after death, the guiding and protective "Hand of Friend," presumably God's, may convert to a "Claw of Dragon." "Predestined / To the Native Land" rather than the promised land of heaven, the child suffers on the ground with no sure promise of salvation.

Dickinson could think of nature as "the Gentlest Mother" (J, 790) who wills a peaceful "Silence" on her children, and in the following lyric she likens the release of both children and adults from life's pain to a benevolent mother's act of putting her children to sleep. She describes life as an unending thread, and prepares us with this image of homekeeping for the earth's role in gently alleviating life's suffering and pain through death:

> The Months have ends—the Years—a knot—
> No Power can untie

To stretch a little further
A Skein of Misery—

The Earth lays back these tired lives
In her mysterious Drawers—
Too tenderly, that any doubt
An ultimate Repose—

The manner of the Children—
Who weary of the Day—
Themself—the noisy Plaything
They cannot put away—

(J, 423)

The poem perhaps refers to the elderly, who "stretch a little further" the time al-
lotted them until death ends their "tired lives." Like pieces of yarn whose ends
are bound together, the months and years form a "Skein of Misery" that we cannot sever or unfasten. This image resembles the thread produced by the legendary Fates, the three sisters who were said to spin, measure, and cut the
length of each mortal life. Dickinson elsewhere characterizes the months as an
unending spool of yarn, which she would "wind" into "balls" until her lover arrives, putting them "each in separate Drawers, / For fear the numbers fuse—"
(J, 511). In the second stanza of this poem, however, "Earth" provides an escape to the pain and tribulation that people suffer in life by putting them to their
eternal sleep. Like a caring mother, she nestles their "tired lives" in her "mysterious Drawers" in the ground. This image of domestic care leads to the suggestion in the last stanza that we are like children who, exhausted by the day's
events, cannot put away "the noisy Plaything"—life.[48] Instead, these tired souls
must wait for a tender guardian to put them to their final rest. One might also
take "Themself" to modify "They," suggesting that the children are reduced to a
toy, the bauble in their own game. Such a variation recalls Sigourney's characterization of children as precious objects, who are reclaimed by a grieving
mother sending them to their heavenly sleep. By describing our mortal lives as if
they were overseen by a mother who relieves the pain and suffering of her children by laying them to their final rest, Dickinson draws on a trope familiar to
readers of Sigourney's elegies, yet she transforms the latter's act of domestic
pity into a universal benevolence, one conferred upon adults as well as children.
Although she implies that people of all ages can benefit from the earth's gentle
care, she suggests that we are as powerless as children to alter the course of our
lives.

In the following poem, which has been read as a move away from the "literature of misery" commonly associated with Sigourney and her followers, Dickinson undercuts the sentimentalized mourning over a child's death (Sewall 2,

329 n. 5). She portrays a dead child, who, just buried in the tomb yet in a state of semi-consciousness, has been reminded by a mourner's well-meaning pity that she is no longer alive:

> I cried at Pity—not at Pain—
> I heard a Woman say
> "Poor Child"—and something in her voice
> Convinced myself of me—
>
> So long I fainted, to myself
> It seemed the common way,
> And Health, and Laughter, Curious things—
> To look at, like a Toy—
>
> To sometimes hear "Rich people" buy
> And see the Parcel rolled—
> And carried, we suppose—to Heaven,
> For children, made of Gold—
>
> But not to touch, or wish for,
> Or think of, with a sigh—
> And so and so—had been to us,
> Had God willed differently.
>
> I wish I knew that Woman's name—
> So when she comes this way,
> To hold my life, and hold my ears
> For fear I hear her say
>
> She's "sorry I am dead["]—again—
> Just when the Grave and I—
> Have sobbed ourselves almost to sleep,
> Our only Lullaby—
>
> (J, 588)

4] Convicted me—of me— 15. us] me
11. we suppose] I supposed

The speaker's attachment to life and to possessions undercuts Sigourney's conception that dead children exist in an idealized state devoid of the cravings and desires of earth. The woman's remark, "'Poor Child,'" punningly hints that the child deserves pity because she has been dispossessed of material wealth as well as of her life. For the speaker, life's pleasures have grown to resemble unfamiliar objects, "Curious Things" or a "Toy," which she can never again possess. Moreover, she covets the gifts which she has heard "'Rich people'" buy for their children, naively thinking that presents might exist in heaven as well. In confusing the talk she has heard in life with the sight of a "Parcel" being "rolled—/ And carried" away, she mistakes the bundle, which probably contains another dead body, for toys. Even the idea that heaven's well-treated occupants are "Children, made of Gold" signals that she gauges their value according to a system of exchange.[49] Indeed, the phrase "Children, made of Gold," with its ambiguous reference both to the "Parcel" being carried to the grave and to the children who are already buried there, suggests not only that these children can receive gifts from their parents, but also that in some sense they have become mere toys or baubles themselves. In fact, the speaker enviously remarks that, "Had God willed differently," she might herself have been one of these privileged children. This economy of earthly possessions exposes one of the premises of Sigourney's elegies: that the mother owns and cherishes the dead child as if it were a precious object. Confined to her recollection of life and the worldly belongings of others, the speaker is reminded of what she has been denied in life by the woman's pity, and so arrives at an unwanted sense of self-consciousness.

Yet the child's dispossession points to an even more significant lack, for to accept the woman's pity would be to remind herself of the love she has been denied in life. In the first stanza, the speaker cries "at Pity—not at Pain—"; she is hurt by the pity of a nameless mourner, not by the pain of death. Unlike the infants of Sigourney's poems, who are promised a mother's loving embrace in heaven, this speaker cradles her own abstract "life," having been dispossessed of all but her hearing in the grave. When she again imagines the woman's hurtful pity, the speaker's remark is framed in free indirect discourse, which reflects her own psychic state: the woman's words are cast within quotation marks and the object of her pity takes a first-person rather than third-person singular pronoun ("'sorry I am dead'" instead of "'I'm sorry she's dead'"), so that the speaker sounds as if she were mourning her own death rather than ventriloquizing the voice of another. Like the growing sons who are deprived of maternal care in Sigourney's elegies, the speaker in this poem has internalized a tearful sympathy for her loss. Finally, the child laments especially the lack of a mother's care in the last stanza when she claims that she and the "Grave" have "sobbed ourselves almost to sleep, / Our only Lullaby—." This image suggests that the speaker longs for the forgetfulness of death, but rather than listen to a mother's voice singing her to sleep, she will lull herself into oblivion with the sound of her own sobs. Dickinson's sentimental portrayal of the dead child's thoughts here suggests how close she was in spirit to contemporary female elegists. Yet she is far from poets like Sigourney, who depict a mother's possessive influence over her dead child. Instead, Dickinson suggests that the child, alienated from its mother's care, suffers by the excessive pity that keeps it perpetually alive, when it would gratefully resign itself to the eternal sleep of the grave.

If Sigourney's elegies hint at a heavenly bond between women's lives and their sons', poems by other nineteenth-century women poets lamenting the deaths of children point to a more mundane link between death and a woman's sphere, to which a daughter is inevitably confined. In "The Little Maid" (1830), Anna Maria Wells, an American poet who was nearly as well known at the time as her half sister, Frances Sargent Osgood, depicts a young girl who grows up to live a restricted life of loneliness and poverty after her only brother has died:

> When I was a little maid
>   I waited on myself;
> I washed my mother's teacups,
>   And set them on the shelf.
>
> I had a little garden,
>   Most beautiful to see;
> I wished that I had somebody
>   To play in it with me.
>
> Nurse was in mamma's room;
>   I knew her by the cap;
> She held a lovely baby boy
>   Asleep upon her lap.
>
> As soon as he could learn to walk,
>   I led him by my side,—
> My brother and my playfellow,—
>   Until the day he died!
>
> Now I am an old maid,
>   I wait upon myself;
> I only wipe one teacup,
>   And set it on the shelf.[50]

Written as children's verse, this poem would have been read by most girls as a fantasy about their future lives, and it dramatizes the indelible impression that a son's death could make on a family's daughters, who were bound by convention to occupy the home without the promise of a son's eventual escape. The speaker begins life as a little maid, who performs her domestic duties for herself and her family while she hopes for companionship, until her brother's death consigns her to a life of lonely grieving. Distant from the girl's childhood and absent from her adult existence, her mother hovers only vaguely in the background. Her presence dimly appears in household cares and childbirth, as suggested by the "teacups" and by the baby's birth in the third stanza, pointing to these events as central ones in a woman's life. Although the birth of "a lovely baby boy" promises the girl companionship for a while, his death marks the end of both a socially normal childhood and adulthood. Having progressed from a "little maid" to an "old maid" by the poem's end, she continues to perform the same activity of keeping house she had played at as a girl and ends life in the same lonely way she begins. In fact, the girl apparently mourns her brother, as unmarried sisters often spent a lifetime fondly recalling a young brother who died. Once beyond marriageable age, a woman could substitute a lifelong dedication to her brother's memory for an actual marriage, especially during the Civil War era, when the deaths of young soldiers grew to staggering proportions and decreased the pool of eligible young men. This eroticized scenario of family devotion apparently allowed the grieving sister to find an outlet for the passion that was stifled for unmarried women in the proper Victorian household. Wells's poem depicts with startling clarity the circumscribed life of a woman who is bound by traditional mourning behavior to pay tribute to a dead brother's memory.

Before turning to a final poem by Dickinson that criticizes a girl's fate, we might ask a broader question concerning the infant elegy: why might poems on the deaths of children be a fruitful genre in which to look for commentaries on women's roles? Several of the cultural precepts that determined women's lives underlie the traditional elegy: a mother and child's bond was primary, and a woman's domestic role was at the center of her existence. Sentimental writers, like Sigourney, enshrined women on a "pedestal," which in turn kept them from attaining power outside the home. Since the infant elegy builds on women's primary role as domestic caretakers and moral exemplars, it allows them to console themselves on their loss by claiming an almost possessive hold over their dead children, who remained under their nurturing influence. Sigourney's lamentations on the deaths of sons not only bolster a woman's importance in the culture at large, but they also comfort bereaved parents and secure the elegist's place in the national consciousness. Rather than articulate their grief through original images, however, women poets mediated their lamentations through a number of sentimental tropes, such as "curtaining lids," "polished brow," and other expressions, and employed well-worn phrases in order to evoke a stock response from their readers. As Joanne Dobson notes about sentimental discourse, "A language close 'to the conversational norm' is a language that mediates its subject matter without either foregrounding itself or erecting linguistic barriers—such as learned diction, obscure tropes, or experimental uses of language—that impede comprehension. In other words, such a language operates as an apparently transparent medium for the conveyance of its subject matter and affect."[51] Deriving their metaphors from the language of nature and domestic life with which women were intimately associated, the poets sanitize grief in conventional language and convey emotion in terms that only circumscribe once again the familiar boundaries of a woman's experience—as housewife and mother.

If Sigourney's elegies hint at a heavenly bond between women and their children, Dickinson's poems question the link between motherhood and home duties that condemns women to a life of domestic cares. Another speaker questions a girl who dies as to why she sleeps, then claims she would have helped her die, if it had been possible:

> 'Tis Sunrise—Little Maid—Hast Thou
> No Station in the Day?
> 'Twas not thy wont, to hinder so—
> Retrieve thine industry—
>
> 'Tis Noon—My little Maid—
> Alas—and art thou sleeping yet?
> The Lily—waiting to be Wed—
> The Bee—Hast thou forgot?
>
> My little Maid—'Tis Night—Alas
> That Night should be to thee
> Instead of Morning—Had'st thou broached
> Thy little Plan to Die—
> Dissuade thee, if I c'd not, Sweet,
> I might have aided—thee—
>
> (J, 908)

The speaker attempts to rouse the "Little Maid" from her lethargy, only to conclude when the girl does not respond that she is better off dead than alive. Wondering why the girl does not rise and attend to her "Station in the Day," the speaker suggests that she should instead "Retrieve" her "industry." She goes on to define the girl's life as it found its common expression in contemporary literature: the girl's total existence forms a single "Day," which encompasses the traditional roles of girl, wife, and mother in the morning, noon, and evening of her life. By not fulfilling her "Station in the Day," the "Little Maid" has relinquished both her designated task in the family and her social duties as a future wife and mother; having given up the possibility of marriage and motherhood, she has abandoned "The Lily—waiting to be wed—" and "The Bee" as the day passes. The speaker then conventionally laments the child's death in the last stanza, regretting the endless sleep of mortality that prevents the girl's awakening to the "Morning" of her still youthful life. Indeed, we might take the speaker's final suggestion that if she could not have "Dissuade[d]" the girl from her "little Plan" to die she might have "aided" her as a dictum in line with Sigourney's belief that the innocent child is better off after death. Yet when we recall the speaker's previous attention to the child's social and familial duties, we find that the last two lines in fact question the role that the girl has been assigned all along. Imagining she could reason with the girl and "Dissuade" her from her "Plan," the speaker disingenuously claims that the child willfully chose to die, and decided to keep silent about it. By implying that the child has consciously decided to die, the speaker ascribes to her a willful determination not to exist. Furthermore, the speaker's use of "aided" is ambiguous: does she mean she might have eased the girl into death while she provided sympathetic comfort? Or that she might more actively have facilitated her decision to end her life? In summary, the speaker thinks that the "Little Maid"'s position in life is so constraining that she considers her earthly end preferable to a woman's life on earth, and she claims that she might have helped the girl once she had made her decision to die, much as if it had been a reasoned—and reasonable—choice.

Sigourney's poems console mothers with the belief that women's lives were continuous with their children's, a consolatory fiction which Dickinson rejects in her more radical interpretation of the child elegy. Sigourney partakes of the culturally sanctioned image of a woman as pious and domestic, but in her very idealization of the mother-son relationship, she suggests that women will be specially compensated for the pain they have suffered in life. While she expresses the sentimental consolation that was typical in poetry of this type, she diverges from the standard child elegy to accord women a more central place in the cultural mythology that predicted a gathering together of the entire family circle after death. Her example suggests that nineteenth-century American women writers were able to alter subtly the conventions of this form, even while they remained within its conservative limits. Although Dickinson adopts some of the same conventions in her elegies, she raises questions about the consolation offered by Sigourney and other nineteenth-century American female elegists. Rather than uphold Sigourney's theory of the mother's extended influence over her son, she rejects the possessive nature of the mother's bond and criticizes Sigourney's idealized conception of motherhood. In these and other poems, Dickinson casts doubt on the apparent comfort that a heavenly reunion offered to the grieving family and to mothers in particular. Finally, she suggests that the dead may willingly invite the living to join them, but that, once we do, the reunion we were promised proves to be only a fiction.

Chapter 4

"Alabaster Chambers"
Dickinson, Epitaphs, and the Culture of Mourning

> Have you ever been to Mount Auburn? If not you can form but slight conception—of the "City of the dead." It seems as if Nature had formed the spot with a distinct idea in view of its being a resting place for her children, where wearied & dissappointed they might stretch themselves beneath the spreading cypress & close their eyes "calmly as to a nights repose or flowers at set of sun."
>
> —Emily Dickinson (*Letters* 1, 36)

> It was, as we have intimated, a spot without beauty or bloom, like many others in New England; but in New England affections are green remembrances and enduring monuments; tears that mausoleums cannot always command were freely shed on this dry orchard-grass, and the purest purposes of life were kindled over these unadorned graves.
>
> —Sylvester Judd, *Margaret*[1]

> Oh may our follies like the falling trees
> Be stripped ev'ry leaf by autumn's wind
> May ev'ry branch of vice embrace the breeze
> And nothing leave but virtue's fruit behind
> Then when old age life's winter shall appear
> In conscious hope all future ills we'll brave
> With fortitud our disillusion bear
> And sink forgotten in the silent grave.
>
> —Anonymous Sampler Verse (1806)[2]

For many nineteenth-century American writers, heaven was a geographical, locatable entity, widely depicted in paintings, novels, and poetry. For Dickinson, finding its spiritual coordinates proved more difficult, as she was grounded in the awareness of early and arbitrary death rather than in a cheerful acceptance of religious platitudes. "Contentment's quiet Suburb," she writes in one lyric, is threatened by affliction, which ranges "In Acres—It's Location / Is Illocality—" (J, 963). The Victorian cemetery was not only the earthly repository for the dead, but in its rolling hills, ornate gates, and home-like tombs, it also prefigured a comforting vision of an afterlife as material as life. Dickinson's shift of focus from heavenly salvation to earthly life may be gauged by studying posthumous art, the "rural cemetery" movement, and her adaptation of the epitaph.

Funerary art and epitaphs provide insight into the inadequacy of nineteenth-century mourning fictions. She notes in a letter to Thomas Wentworth Higginson in July 1862 about her lack of a portrait: "It often alarms Father—He says Death might occur, and he has Molds of all the rest—but has no Mold of me, but I noticed the Quick wore off those things, in a few days, and forestall the dishonor—" (*Letters* 2, 411). When Dickinson mentions her lack of a "Mold," I assume she refers not only to photographs but also more broadly to a whole panoply of Victorian *objets d'art*, including plaster casts of hands, graveyard busts, embroidery, and funerary sculpture, that reified the dead and guaranteed an image to be lovingly cherished by those who survived them. The Victorian penchant for preserving a physical reminder of the dead led both to an elevation of high "feeling" in mortuary art and to a subsequent devaluation of such images as mass-produced kitsch. Dickinson's poetry offers a readjustment of vision, both from the vantage of the dead who beckon to us to join them and the living who are so accustomed to remembering the dead that they seem more dead than alive. Much as painters, sculptors, and writers set the image of the dead in canvas, stone, or verse, Dickinson displays the "State—Endowal—Focus—" (J, 489) that death confers by manipulating both epitaphic conventions and visual perspective in her lyrics.

Closer in style and thought to the sentiments expressed on Puritan gravestones than to the tearful consolation reflected in mid-nineteenth-century funerary art, Dickinson's elegiac meditations jolt the reader into an awareness of his or her own mortality through the use of a typical funerary device: the epitaph. Dickinson invokes the logic of epitaphic inscriptions in her poetry to suggest that the living and dead can reverse the roles assigned them by nineteenth-century mourning rituals. Rather than encourage mourners to look forward to a time when they will rejoin the beloved dead in heaven, as the nineteenth-century elegy so often does, her poems portray dead who unwittingly encourage their loved ones to die and come to them. By detaching the voice of the speaker from its normal conversational context, the epitaph underscores mortality and the absence that writing itself necessarily entails. I wish to examine the reversibility of the epitaph as well as how the representation of death in funerary art, mortuary paintings, and inscriptions reminds us perpetually of our own mortality. Dickinson's lyrics play on notions of presence and absence, on the possibilities of including the reader in a circuit of meaning that presumes one party is absent. Her subtle adaptation of many of the conventions of funerary art and inscriptions uses shifts in points of view to shorten our distance from the dead.

Epitaphs always carry reminders of mortality, since the voice of the dead (an obvious and patent fiction) foretells the death of the living. Given their special function as a message conveyed to the living by the dead, these inscriptions gain force as vatic proofs of an afterlife. In their study of the epitaph, Malcolm Nelson and Diana George note that in the traditional epitaph the "voice of the dead speaks to the ear of the living, reversing their roles: the deceased lives through the voice of the stone, defying death and yet reminding the living of their own mortality."[3] An epitaph from the Old Burying Ground (1769) in Brewster, Massachusetts, provides a typical invitation and envoi:

> Some hearty friend shall drop his Tear
> On my dry Bones and say
> "These once were strong as mine appear
> And mine must be as they."
>
> Thus shall our mouldering Members teach
> What now our senses learn:
> For Dust and Ashes loudest preach
> Man's infinite Concern.
>
> (637–39)

Close in thought and format to Dickinson's lyrics, this epitaph takes an abstract, tightly reasoned, and conceptual approach to death. What is significant is the ease by which the writer slips from a traditional epitaph (with its invitation to stop and ponder the remains, its connection to the reader's life, and its eventual send-off) to a more abstract lesson. As Nelson and George note, this epitaph is unlike others in its use of an observer's voice proclaiming the idea one normally finds expressed by the posthumous speaker (637). Typically, the dead person argues logically from the ground: death will overtake the mourner's life all too soon. But the second stanza's "Members" overturns even religious hierarchy and creates a communal voice for the dead and the living by punning on churchgoers and bodily limbs. Better than a minister's words, the remains of the dead "preach" the dissolution of the body and "Man's infinite Concern"—salvation. Thus, the epitaph chides the reader into an awareness of mortality, while simultaneously implying that living and dead are already members of the same, select society.

Dickinson would have been familiar with examples of New England epitaphs from seeing them in graveyards in Amherst, South Hadley, and the farmlands of western Massachusetts, but she was also exposed to epitaphs in a book owned by the Dickinsons, Helen Hunt Jackson's *Bits of Travel at Home* (1878). Although remembered today, if at all, as the author of *Ramona* (1881), a novel about an Indian man and his half-Mexican lover set in Old California, Jackson was a prolific travel writer who traveled throughout the United States and Europe. In her collection of travel essays set in New England, California, and Colorado, Jackson provides examples of epitaphs that summarize for us the mid-nineteenth-century American approach toward death. In "A Morning in a Vermont Graveyard," she describes the graves of early settlers, whose antique epitaphs resemble the terse reminders of mortality more typical of Puritan graveyards than the mid-nineteenth-century cemetery. In a passage worthy of Thoreau she describes a scene of natural splendor, archaic tombstones, and slowly encroaching industrialization:

It is the warmest spot I have found to-day; a high wall of soft pines and willow birches breaks the force of wind on two sides, and the noon sunlight lies with the glow of fire on the brown crisp grass. The blackberry vines, which this year have brighter colors than the maple-trees, flame out all over the yard in fantastic tangled wreaths of red, and the downy films of St. John's wort and thistle seeds are flying about in the air. Half an hour ago an express train went by, on the river bank, many feet below, and the noise seemed almost unpardonable so near the graves. Since then not a sound has broken the stillness, and the fleecy clouds have seemed to come down closer and closer until they look like thin veils around bending faces.[4]

The description of nature suggests that the scene evokes a visionary state in the speaker. Appropriately, the graveyard is bordered by pines and willow trees, especially indicative of mourning. Moreover, the "fantastic" overgrowth of vines and "downy films" of St. John's wort encourage the reader to contemplate the lives of the dead. Describing clouds that look like "thin veils around bending faces," she casts the graveyard in a visionary light, imaginatively identifying with Jemima Tute, whose gravestone sparks the essay ("how well she must still recollect the day" [201]).

Primarily recounting the life of Tute, pioneer and survivor of an Indian attack that killed her husband and young daughter, the essay details her capture and the deaths of other women in the fort. In the summer of 1755, Tute and the other women of Bridgman's Fort, having been left alone all day by their husbands who were tilling the fields, were attacked by Indians. Their husbands had themselves been attacked and some killed earlier. Jackson's discussion of Tute's life and epitaph at once pays homage to the dead and criticizes the desire to memorialize them in the prevailing fashion. She praises Tute as she recounts the attack on the fort and notes, quoting from a contemporary recollection of Tute written by an aide of George Washington: "She was still young and handsome, though she had daughters of marriageable age. Distress, which had taken somewhat from the original redundancy of bloom and added a softening paleness to her cheeks, rendered her appearance the more engaging" (203). Unlike her husband who died during the attack, Tute survived, was captured and ransomed, eventually remarried, and outlived her third and final husband. Like other eighteenth-century epitaphs, Tute's emphasizes the importance of reputation and social standing, especially important for women since they lacked other position in society: we are told she was "Successively relict of Messrs. WM. PHIPPS, CALEB HOWE AND AMOS TUTE"; that her eldest daughter married a Frenchman and that her youngest child died; that "By the aid of some benevolent Gentle'n, / And her own personal heroism, / She recovered the rest" of her children; and that, "Having passed thro' more vicissitudes, / And endured more hardships, than any of her cotemporaries," she had managed to keep her reputation intact ("No more can Savage Foes annoy, / Nor aught her wide-spread Fame destroy" [203]). Turning to the epitaph of Amos Tute, Jemima Tute's last husband, Jackson notes that the gravestone, although it is fifteen years older, looks modern and the inscription is clear: "It is strange that with the white marble ready to their hands on so many hillsides, the old Vermont settlers should have put so many of their records into keeping of the short-lived slate" (203–4).

Jackson concludes with a Thoreauvian description of the surrounding field and forest as a natural, pristine gravesite:

By a round-about road through pine and beech woods, dark with the undergrowth of shining laurel, we wind down from the hill into the town below. We shall pass another curious burial-ground on our left. It is not enclosed; has no tombstones; and, so far as anybody knows, there have been no interments in it for thousands of years. (207)

Characterizing a former swamp, filled in over the years, as a "curious burial-ground" and the teeth-marks of beavers as the "traces of builders," Jackson implies that nature itself constitutes a gravesite for all creatures. Although another author might make pious references at this point, Jackson makes the humorous observation that "the most distinguished, or, at any rate, the biggest person ever buried there, was an elephant" (207). She notes that "Two years ago, some Irish laborers dug part of him up. Even in a muck bed, among the Green Mountains, he was not any safer than he would have been in Trinity Church Yard in New York" (207). Despite the prevalent assertion that the dead were at rest in their natural "home," Jackson underscores their inability to be guaranteed an undisturbed rest. With clinical detail, she notes that what remains of the animal is "only forty inches of one tusk," and that tusk has been placed "on exhibition at the State Capitol, and has been mended with glue by the State Geologist" (207). Perhaps mocking the way the dead were adorned with prominent tombstones whose epitaphs displayed family ties and predicted their painless state in death, Jackson points to the futile attempts of human beings to repair their own mortality.

Jackson's essay exemplifies the way many nineteenth-century elegies and mortuary tributes attempted to preserve our memories of the dead. Unlike the inscriptions on tombs built during the eighteenth century, which emphasized reputation and social standing, nineteenth-century epitaphs stressed the emotional tie between the dead and the family. Epitaphs changed significantly from the Puritan to the Victorian eras, when the prolixity of the earlier epitaphs and their didactic refrains weakened to a "felt" silence. More frequently, nineteenth-century gravestones monumentalize the dead through elaborate imitation of natural structures, such as logs, stumps, trees, and stones, rather than through an epitaph. Foretelling the modern practice of recording only the names and dates of the deceased, the high Victorian cemetery often used inscriptions that simply identified the family relation and sometimes omitted the family name altogether: "Our Angel Boy," "Mother & Son," "My Wife & Daughter." Furthermore, the initial reverie of the dead in Jackson's essay commonly appears in nineteenth-century women's elegiac meditations; depicting female speakers who contemplate the dead and imaginatively commune with mothers, sisters, friends, or children, such essays and lyrics provide a pleasant contemplation and consoling recollection of the dead. Rather than assert that women's lives existed outside of any meaningful social or familial context, women's elegies draw a continuous line between their female forebears and their own lives.

In light of Jackson's description of an antique graveyard in Vermont, we might consider briefly another contemporary description of a Puritan graveyard in order to place Dickinson within the context of mid-nineteenth-century American mortuary tributes. Older graveyards were always located next to a church in the middle of a town or city, as if to enforce the unity of community and church life. Unlike the ornate Victorian cemetery, they acknowledged the harsh, unadorned truth that death is a part of life. Such an antique graveyard appears in Sylvester Judd's utopian novel, *Margaret* (1845). The eponymous heroine and her friend Isabel attend a funeral at the town's cemetery, which dates from the time of the first settlers:

This spot, chosen and consecrated by the original colonists, and used for its present purpose more than a century, lying on the South Street, was conspicuous both for its elevation and its sterility. A sandy soil nourished the yellow orchard grass that waved ghostlike from the mounds and filled all the intervals and the paths. No verdure, neither flower, shrub, or tree, contributed to the agreeableness of the grounds, nor was the bleak desolation disturbed by many marks of art. There were two marble shafts, a table of red sandstone, several very old headstones of similar material, and more modern ones of slate. But here lay the fathers, and here too must the children of the town ere long be gathered, and it was a place of solemn feeling to all.[5]

In stark contrast to the graveyard in Judd's novel, changes in cultural attitudes toward death in the nineteenth century encouraged the community to isolate and monumentalize for posterity the remains of the dead. Judd's graveyard lacks the meditative woods and decorative tombstones that allowed those who passed within the rural cemeteries' gates an opportunity for mournful but pleasantly consoling reverie. Unlike the three-dimensional memorial sculptures that became increasingly popular, the tablet and tombstones "of red sandstone, now gray with moss, bearing death's heads and cherub cheeks rudely carved, and quaint epitaphs, and the whole both sinking into the earth and fading under the effects of time" (1, 270), are decaying relics of an era that conceived of death as a two-dimensional event of heavenly salvation or hellish damnation.

Furthermore, new methods of interment and changes in taste regarding funerary sculpture in mid-nineteenth-century America underwrote this sentimentalization of death. The idea that the dead were as present as if they were still alive found its contemporary expression in the "rural cemetery" movement, which became prominent in the nineteenth century.[6] Responding to epidemics of yellow fever in 1819 and 1822 in Philadelphia and Boston and to another in New York City in 1822 that killed sixteen thousand around Trinity Church burial ground alone, the proponents of the new cemetery movement sought to protect the health of the general population by removing graves to the countryside. The movement away from the slate stones that were so popular among the Puritans toward funerary sculpture accompanied a more general desire to imagine salvation as a gradual process that depended on the capacity to suffer, on feelings rather than works. The founders of one of the earliest of the rural cemeteries, Mount Auburn, were so opposed to the form and conception of the church graveyard that they banned perpendicular slate slabs. Instead, larger monuments that were variations of neoclassical architectural elements—broken columns, sarcophagi, obelisks, and steles—referred to classical themes and were associated with the Romantic idealization of relics and unfinished structures. Imitations of natural forms, including chopped tree trunks or ivy-covered boulders, fashioned entirely of marble or granite, also appeared in burial grounds. More impressive as artifacts of high Victorian feeling than as testaments to holy living in the Puritan fashion, mid-century graveyard sculpture often omitted the last names of children, referring to them only by nickname, or by familial relation. Death could thus be naturalized, and earth serve as a tomb for all.

Eventually, the emphasis on a rural and natural home for the dead gave way to high Victorian tastes that preferred the ornamental garden to an arbor-shaded retreat for mourners. By the 1860s, Mount Auburn's trees were razed, hills and steep inclines leveled, swamps filled in, and ponds trimmed with granite to form more symmetrical shapes. The "rural cemetery" was propelled by a new impulse toward mid-century: it was designed not only to insure the health of the community, but also to memorialize the dead in a setting that was consoling and aesthetically pleasing to the nineteenth-century mourner. Ann Douglas characterizes the sense of placid contentment and nostalgic reverie that such a spectacle was meant to instill in the viewer: "The mid-nineteenth-century American went to the cemetery rather in the spirit in which his twentieth-century descendant goes to the movies: with the hopefulness attendant upon the prospect of borrowed emotions."[7]

For the middle class, memorializing the dead affirmed social position and promoted religious conformity. Like the typical elegy, which assured mourners that they would rejoin their loved ones in heaven, the new cemeteries conveyed a sense of permanence and prosperity. By the end of Judd's novel, Margaret and her husband, Mr. Evelyn, transform their small town of Livingston into an ideal religious community, Mons Christi, which is laid out on the order of the new "rural" cemeteries, complete with floral plantings, verdant hills, marble statuary, and an erected cross.[8] Despite the idealistic enthusiasm of its planners, the construction of this morally uplifting fictional landscape is contingent on a much-needed bequest of money, as was the new, actual venture at Mount Auburn. Having made a large financial investment, shareholders of the cemetery protected and adorned their portion of land, much as they might have a residence. Proprietors often placed wrought or cast iron fences around their lots, a habit that derived from the older cemeteries in which cattle were allowed to graze, and heavy granite curbings in the second half of the century further segmented the cemetery grounds. Part of the popular "Domestication of Death" throughout the period, as Douglas attests, this division of lots symbolized the owners' attachment to family and property status: "Nostalgia, here as elsewhere, functioned as a spiritualized form of acquisition."[9] Perhaps even more important than displaying wealth, however, parceling off the graves of family members with a border allowed the survivors to treat the dead as if they had homes of their own; the custom of erecting fences around graves softened the awareness of death for mourners, who could console themselves with the thought that they would rejoin loved ones in a domestic setting after death.

The graves in these new cemeteries stand as testaments to the loving attachment of families to their dead. In Judd's novel, Margaret watches her neighbors, the "drunken Tapleys from No. 4," who lead a life of dissolute revelry, as they solemnly "moved in a body to a corner of the lot, where four years before was laid their youngest child, a little daughter, marked by a simple swell of dry sod scarce a span long, and there at least they were sober" (1, 270). In contrast to the unadorned graves of the Puritan churchyard of Judd's novel, Victorian ornamental tombstones for children, usually only a quarter the size of an adult's, frequently bear the figure of a lamb or sleeping infant over a tablet, with an inscription that reads simply "Our Children" or "Our Angel Boy." Despite the vast difference in aesthetic taste that these stones of different eras represent, their common lack of names points to a practice dating from the seventeenth century, which could leave children unnamed over a year after their birth.[10] Parents thereby postponed the child's official entry into the family until he had passed through the period when he was most likely to contract a fatal disease. As anonymous testaments to the vast numbers of infants who died too young to be named (or too precious to have that name mentioned in public), tombstones reflect the family's deep emotional investment in the dead.

The fiction that the dead spoke and that they were fully naturalized in their setting also appears in William Wordsworth's "Essays upon Epitaphs" (1810). Like other Romantics who sought to naturalize death, Wordsworth extols nature as the ultimate tomb. In America, only eleven years later, Bryant wrote "Thanatopsis," a similarly strong defense of the way nature joins all people in death. Wordsworth expostulates upon the appropriateness of situating a cemetery in woods or fields: "I could ruminate upon the beauty which the Monuments, thus placed, must have borrowed from the surrounding images of Nature—from the trees, the wild flowers, from a stream running perhaps within sight or hearing, from the beaten road stretching its weary length hard by."[11] For Wordsworth, monuments had a picturesque quality when set against the natural landscape, and even the "beaten road stretching its weary length" conjures up images of a vast stream of humanity or even of a corpse, deepening the nineteenth-century viewer's sympathetic associations between the cemetery and the natural world.

Wordsworth attributes the erection of monuments to a twofold desire to guard the remains of the deceased and to preserve their memories: they provide "a record to preserve the memory of the dead, as a tribute due to his individual worth, for a satisfaction to the sorrowing hearts of the Survivors, and for the common benefit of the living" (96). According to Wordsworth, epitaphs are the foundation for many basic topoi of funerary icons—"Life as a Journey—Death as a Sleep overcoming the tired Wayfarer—of Misfortune as a storm that falls suddenly upon him—of Beauty as a Flower that passeth away" (96–97). Just as Wordsworth had advised the writer in the preface to *Lyrical Ballads* (1798) to write in a plain style, he notes that the tone of epitaphs should be solemn and express their grief in a "general language of humanity" (100). Not only is an impartial tone necessary to convey grief adequately, but "the common or universal feeling of humanity" must be appealed to for the epitaph to exalt the reader (101).

According to Wordsworth, the epitaph often suspends our powers of disbelief by portraying a posthumous speaker who assures the reader that the afterlife is pleasant:

The departed Mortal is introduced telling you himself that his pains are gone; that a state of rest is come; and he conjures you to weep for him no longer. He admonishes with the voice of one experienced in the vanity of those affections which are confined to earthly objects, and gives a verdict like a superior Being . . . By this tender fiction the Survivors bind themselves to a sedater sorrow, and employ the intervention of the imagination in order that the reason may speak her own language earlier than she would otherwise have been enabled to do. (104)

Consoling the reader with the idea that the speaker exists in a realm beyond pain, the writer of an epitaph supports the "tender fiction" that the dead are still alive. Yet this fantasy remains a "tender fiction," an open secret for the mourners, who console themselves partly by creating their own fictions about the deceased's continued existence.

Women elegists in this period sought to "bind themselves to a sedater sorrow," as Wordsworth notes, through the use of posthumous voice and the evocation of specifically female scenes of mourning.[12] Like male writers, many female writers invoked the visionary state that may take place in a dream to suggest the change in perspective accompanying the death of loved ones. Lydia Huntley Sigourney's "Dream of the Dead," for instance, depicts a speaker who during sleep imagines that the dead have rejoined her:

> Sleep brought the dead to me. Their brows were kind,
> And their tones tender, and, as erst they blent
> Their sympathies with each familiar scene.
> It was my earthliness that robed them still
> In their material vestments, for they seemed
> Not yet to have put their glorious garments on.
> Methought, 'twere better thus to dwell with them,
> Than with the living.
>
> (ll. 1–8)

The dead look much as they did in life, a fact the speaker attributes to her own earthly perspective. From her vantage point, she sees them "robed . . . / In their material vestments," still clothed in the flesh rather than in the "glorious garments" of the spirit. Her remark echoes the Christian doctrine that foretells the spiritual nature of the body after death: "It is sown in corruption; it is raised in incorruption: It is sown in dishonour; it is raised in glory: it is sown in weakness; it is raised in power: It is sown a natural body; it is raised a spiritual body" (1 Corinthians 15:42–44). For the speaker, the combination of the dead's inviting humanity and their enviable immortality softens the knowledge that she must join them herself. Far from being frightening and unapproachable, the speaker's view of a material heaven is so consoling that she is prompted to remark that the dead's life seems preferable to her own.

In Sigourney's "Dream of the Dead," the speaker encounters in her dream a variety of people, some of whom she was acquainted with in life and all of whom point to her desire to recapture her youth. The first is "a chosen friend, / Beloved in school-days' happiness, who came . . . / As she was wont"; then her dead mother, "Full of fresh life, and in that beauty clad / Which charmed my earliest love"; followed by "A stranger-matron," who, "sicklied o'er and pale," disappoints the speaker's injunction to hear her mother speak and inverts the mother's healthful image; and, finally, a dead infant, laughing and smiling as if it were still alive. All of them are "gentle forms / Of faithful friendship and maternal love" (ll. 40–41); all of them are female or too young to be gendered. Upon awakening from her dream, she finds that these spirits "Did flit away, and life, with all its cares, / Stood forth in strong reality" (ll. 42–43). In fact, once her dream has evaporated, the speaker is aware once again of the disappointment of her life, another feature women's poetic dream-sequences often share. Despite her knowledge of the true state of the dead ("Upon whose lips I knew the burial-clay / Lay deep, for I had heard its hollow sound, / In hoarse reverberation, *'dust to dust!'*" [ll. 32–34]), she finds this fleeting vision consoling:

> Sweet dream!
> And solemn, let me bear thee in my soul
> Throughout the live-long day, to subjugate
> My earth-born hope. I bow me at your names,
> Sinless and passionless and pallid train!
> The seal of truth is on your breasts, ye dead!
> Ye may not swerve, nor from your vows recede,
> Nor of your faith make shipwreck. Scarce a point
> Divides you from us, though we fondly look
> Through a long vista of imagined years,
> And in the dimness of far distance, seek
> *To hide that tomb, whose crumbling verge we tread*
>
> (ll. 44–55)

The speaker will cherish in her memory this vision of the dead in order to conquer an "earth-born hope" that she might continue living, rather than willingly accept death. Her beliefs are given conviction by the unshakable faith that the dead seem to have attained in heaven. That they "may not swerve, nor from your vows recede, / Nor of your faith make shipwreck" reveals that the speaker transfers her own desire for faith onto the figures of her vision. Ascribing to the dead the apparent ability to act likens them to the living for whom the problem of faith on earth is real and pressing. Despite our wish to see death at "a long vista of imagined years," our closeness to death appears with startling clarity, a consoling yet forceful reminder for Sigourney of our future heavenly existence.

Like many other poems of the period by sentimental writers that depict—

actually or symbolically—a woman's death, Sigourney's meditation evokes a woman's nostalgic desire to recapture the carefree life of childhood, ideally upon her mother's bosom. Two extraordinary examples of poems that idealize girlhood and a mother's sway are Elizabeth Akers Allen's "Rock Me to Sleep" and Sigourney's "Last Word of the Dying."[13] Having tired of flinging away the "soul-wealth" and of "sowing for others to reap," the speaker of Allen's poem begs her mother to return from death and take her into her arms again as if she were still an infant. Despite the passage of years, she longs for her mother's loving embrace to erase the pain of her burdensome adult life:

> Mother, dear mother! the years have been long
> Since I last hushed to your lullaby song;
> Sing, then, and unto my soul it shall seem
> Womanhood's years have been but a dream;
> Clasped to your arms in a loving embrace,
> With your long lashes just sweeping my face,
> Never hereafter to wake or to weep;
> Rock me to sleep, mother, rock me to sleep![14]

Allen's poem was enormously successful, even spawning another poem in response, spoken in a mother's voice, "Answer to Rock Me to Sleep." Given women's frequent admission of forced self-denial, "Rock Me to Sleep" provides a platform from which Allen could offer other women a momentary respite, a fleeting escape. Remarkable for the speaker's wish both to regress and to die, the poem offers only modified satisfaction for the expectations of women's lives. Indeed, its powerful regression—"Backward, turn backward, O Time, in your flight" (l. 1)—and blunt admission of unhappiness make it exemplary in expressing the dissatisfaction of women's lives.

Sigourney also suggests that the strong bond between a woman and her mother promotes a desire for reunion, especially among the dying. In "The Last Word of the Dying," the speaker depicts a woman who, unable to speak, instead spells out the word "Mother" in sign-language. This last act prompts the speaker to wonder if the dying woman perceives her mother's ghostly presence ("She, whose soft hand did dry thine infant tear, / Hovereth she now, with love divine / Thy dying pillow near?" [ll. 34–36]) or if she can barely bring herself to relinquish her hold over her children ("Those three fair boys, / Lingers thy soul with them, even from heaven's perfect joys? / Say—wouldst thou teach us thus, how strong a mother's tie?" [ll. 53–55]). For Sigourney, as for Allen, a woman's wish to return to her mother's arms in heaven is almost as strong as her desire to protect her own children, a desire that recurs in elegies in which women seek the shelter of a mother's arms in heaven.

In "The Dream," Elizabeth Oakes Smith similarly portrays the way a visionary state brings us a changed perspective in life:

> I dreamed last night, that I myself did lay
>   Within the grave, and after stood and wept,
>   My spirit sorrowed where its ashes slept!
> 'T was a strange dream, and yet methinks it may
>   Prefigure that which is akin to truth.
>   How sorrow we o'er perished dreams of youth,
> High hopes and aspirations doomed to be
> Crushed and o'ermastered by earth's destiny!
>   Fame, that the spirit loathing turns to truth—
> And that deluding faith so loath to part,
> That earth will shrine for us one kindred heart!
>   Oh, 't is the ashes of such things that wring
> Tears from the eyes—hopes like to these depart,
>   And we bow down in dread, o'ershadowed by Death's wing![15]

Rather than imagine that the grave offers consolation, Oakes Smith imagines that it represents the end of earthly hopes or fame. Life is a mournful and never-ending remembrance of the "perished dreams of youth / High hopes and aspirations." Oakes Smith's poem precisely indicts the grave's ability to preserve our fame. The speaker consigns to "dreams" both "fame" and the deluding "faith" that "one kindred heart" will be enshrined on earth. Rather than address the actual "ashes" of the dead, the speaker turns at the end of the poem to the unfulfilled aspirations of her life, a more serious subject to mourn.

The curt aphorisms and biting refrains of Puritan gravestones, whose death's-heads promise that the reader will come to the same end as the dead, were an apt model for Dickinson's own revisions of cultural beliefs about death and mourning. Whereas mid-nineteenth-century women's elegies sought to soften the realization of death and redress the disappointments and griefs women often suffered, these inscriptions typically adopt the voice of the dead to remind the reader of his fate. Jackson's essay contains a number of epitaphs that serve as apt comparisons to Dickinson's own lyrics. A popular motto invokes the language of economic loss and gain, so evident in elegies within the Puritan tradition:

> Death is a debt to nature due,
> Which I have paid and so must you.
> (207)

Like a promissory note that has reached maturity, death is a "debt" that must be paid with exactly the price of life. As Jackson notes, "A business-like view of such events must have been a family trait throughout that community, for they found nothing more tender and solemn to say of her" (207).

Another epitaph enjoins the reader to pause and contemplate the scene, reminding her of her eventual end:

> Reader, behold and shed a tear;
> Think on the dust that slumbers here;
> And when you read the fate of me,
> Think on the glass that runs for thee.
>
> (206)

The first-person speaker enjoins the reader to consider that his or her fate will be similar. Although epitaphs often record some information about the deceased, they adopt many stock funerary conventions: the invitation to stop, the injunction to meditate on one's fate, and the envoi (or send-off). The tripartite structure of the epitaph enjoins the reader to look upon the deceased's grave and to sympathize ("Reader, behold, and shed a tear"), to ponder the remains of the dead ("Think on the dust that slumbers here"), and to equate his or her own fate with the deceased's ("And when you read the fate of me, / Think on the glass that runs for thee"). The verbs of perception, such as "behold," "think," and "read," and the direct address actively engage one's attention and foretell the similar outcomes of one's life. As Debra Fried points out, the act of reading an epitaph itself aptly summarizes and predicts the death of the reader:

the epitaph's repetitions suggest that the pair, stranger and gravestone, doubly represents both the before and after, so to speak, of both living and dead. Epitaphs make us see ourselves as doubles—perhaps incomplete or imperfect doubles—of the dead, as living dead, as readers awaiting our epitaphs.[16]

The epitaph, like the tombstone, becomes a figure for the reader, who will eventually, following the inexorable logic of the epitaph, be turned into an inscription, a read text. As Fried trenchantly notes, "to be dead is to be read" (617). Yet the consoling fiction that the dead could speak also reverses this formula, for reading the epitaph is also imaginatively to exchange places with the dead, to become so enamored of mourning as to become almost dead ourselves: to read is to be dead.

Besides mirroring the position of the reader of the inscription, epitaphs serve another function distinct from other types of poetic tributes: they create a posthumous persona. As Jonathan Culler has argued, apostrophe, or the figure of voice created through direct address in a poem, can seem to animate the natural world and to create in nature an interlocutor:

We might posit, then, a third level of reading where the vocative of apostrophe is a device which the poetic voice uses to establish with an object a relationship which helps to constitute him. The object is treated as a subject, an *I* which implies a certain type of *you* in its turn. One who successfully invokes nature is one to whom nature might, in its turn, speak.[17]

If apostrophe and the "O" that signals the creation of poetic voice can posit a constitutive relationship with the world, then epitaphs can perhaps be said to perform the reverse: they create a persona by addressing a reader who is real, but willed into silence by the speaker's voice. Indeed, the formula of the epitaph does more than create a receptive listener: it forces the reader into dead silence, as if it replicated the stillness of the tomb. Epitaphs of the "Pause, Traveller!" variety enjoin the reader to give over the moment to identifying with the speaker, who aptly foretells for the reader a future identical to his own. As Fried argues, "epitaphs predict the collapse of reader and poem and a consequent proliferation of more epitaphs" (616).

Dickinson transforms the epitaphic tradition into a ghostly reversal of living and dead that casts doubt on the apparent comfort that Victorian mourning conventions sought to offer. The dead appear unwilling to communicate, as in this brief lyric:

> Endow the Living—with the Tears—
> You squander on the Dead,
> And They were Men and Women—now,
> Around Your Fireside—
>
> Instead of Passive Creatures,
> Denied the Cherishing
> Till They—the Cherishing deny—
> With Death's Etherial Scorn—
>
> (J, 521)

2. squander on] spend upon—

This poem suggests that the living to whom one denies cherishing will scorn cherishing once they are dead. Rather than "squander" our tears in regret, we should instead hold dear the living while they are able to return our care; once "Death's Etherial Scorn" is set on their faces, they will be unresponsive to our tears, having been "Denied the Cherishing / Till They—the Cherishing Deny—." In characterizing the silence of the dead as willful, Dickinson ascribes life and agency to the dead in a way that profoundly criticizes nineteenth-century habits of mourning. The ambiguous syntax of "And they were Men and Women—now" implies that the mourners might have been to blame for the dead's disappearance. The speaker's blaming of the living for the dead's fate—and the equally ambiguous implication that the dead might be revived if the mourners are affectionate to the living—is the crux of the poem: death has the power to confer "Etherial Scorn," both celestial and impalpable. Just when the mourners would most like to "Cherish" their loved ones, the dead seem most distant and outrightly elude their grasp. In contrast to their portrait as "Passive Creatures," who can only suffer the grief of the mourners, the dead in this final image appear vengeful, willfully rejecting our attentions.

Another poem suggests that our close attachment to the dead allows us to deceive ourselves that they may return to life, until we belatedly find that our preoccupation with them has made us more dead than alive:

> The distance that the dead have gone
> Does not at first appear;
> Their coming back seems possible
> For many an ardent year.
>
> And then, that we have followed them,
> We more than half suspect,
> So intimate have we become
> With their dear retrospect.
>
> (J, 1742)

4] For many a fruitless year. / That first abandoned
year. / That first absconded year.

That the dead almost palpably live on is reinforced by the variants of the last line of the first stanza: "ardent" might be replaced by "fruitless," both words that signify the passion or gestation left unfulfilled due to the dead's disappearance. "That first abandoned year" rather than "For many an ardent year" limits the recurrent act of mourning for the dead over a number of years to the period immediately following their death; "absconded" for "abandoned" further implies that the dead are temporarily removed from sight, hidden away only for the moment. Our memory of the dead leads us to become, so the poem argues, nearly dead ourselves. Not only does "their dear retrospect" invoke our act of reviewing their lives in our minds, but it proves to be the vantage point to which the living mourner, who literally moves closer to death over time, has progressed by the poem's end.

Although Dickinson also evokes the appearance of the dead in a dreamlike vision, she discounts the comforting promise of a reunion after death. The speaker of the following poem implies that the dead appear to us only while we are in a visionary state and delude us with their reality:

> Of nearness to her sundered Things
> The Soul has special times—
> When Dimness—looks the Oddity—
> Distinctness—easy—seems—

The Shapes we buried, dwell about,
Familiar, in the Rooms—
Untarnished by the Sepulchre,
The Mouldering Playmate comes—

In just the Jacket that he wore—
Long buttoned in the Mold
Since we—old mornings, Children—played—
Divided—by a world—

The Grave yields back her Robberies—
The Years, our pilfered Things—
Bright Knots of Apparitions
Salute us, with their wings—

As we—it were—that perished
Themself—had just remained till we rejoin them—
And 'twas they, and not ourself
That mourned.

(J, 607)

8. The] Our

Like the kindly figures in Sigourney's "Dream of the Dead," the "Shapes" of stanza two seem "Familiar" or home-like, well acquainted with the "Rooms" they once inhabited. To the speaker, these shadowy figures appear completely untouched by death, "Untarnished by the Sepulchre." Yet the "Mouldering Playmate," wearing a "Jacket" "Long buttoned in the Mold," takes on in Dickinson's elegiac meditation a reality that travesties the consolatory myth that portrayed the dead's more natural existence in heaven. Sympathetically evoking the image of a child whose jacket might have been buttoned by a parent in life, the jacket "Long buttoned in the Mold" also comments ironically on the supposed immortality of the body: unlike the buttons, the body has steadily decomposed. While in Sigourney's "The Dream of the Dead" the deceased infant appears natural and human in its "material vestments," in Dickinson's poem the child has been steadily decaying, thus differentiating the actual contents of the grave from the speaker's visionary perception of the dead "Shapes." "Divided—by a world—," living and dead exist side by side, and their proximity echoes Sigourney's claim that we walk a tightrope between life and death. Dickinson undercuts the popular contention that we can take comfort in the vision of the dead in heaven as untouched and lifelike.

Although the dead child seems to return to life, the speaker's vision proves a merely psychological event, frightening in its realism and ultimately delusive. In the first stanza, "sundered Things" appear to the "Soul" at "special times," although this new angle of perception gives only a superficial clarity to the speaker's recollected thoughts. We might understand "Oddity" to suggest that, in the daily course of events, "Dimness" characterizes the speaker's perception of the spiritual world. Moreover, the "Distinctness" with which the speaker can discern these spirits only "easy—seems—," an all-too-tentative assertion of the speaker's actual insight. This falseness of discrimination, however, goes unnoticed by the collective adult speaker through the final two stanzas when the dead return to life. In imagining that the "Grave" yields up "her Robberies" and the "Years" return "our Pilfered Things," the poem alludes, as in the "sundered Things" of the first line, to the popular characterization of the child as a precious object stolen away by death.

Yet the wished-for reunion of living and dead that the speaker of Sigourney's poem finds consoling proves merely a fiction. "Bright Knots of Apparitions" are "nots" of being, as this pun hints. While the welcoming "Salute" of the spirits, possibly even a toast to our health, promises good will (etymologically deriving from "to preserve or wish health to"), their greeting is anything but wholesome for those who meet them. The last stanza describes a reversal between the living and the dead that allows us to experience the dying of those who have already died, and its formal oddity reflects our necessary suspension of disbelief: the pentameter line with a feminine ending, which breaks the tetrameter format, parallels our wish that we might join the dead. But our desire is cut short in the last two lines, in which the child angels who have apparently exchanged positions with us seem to be themselves the living and mourning beings. The poem suggests that the visions of the dead that were popular in nineteenth-century funerary verse provide an illusory sense of consolation, as doubtful as the consolation offered to mothers in poems on the loss of children. The dead allow us to forget our distance from them only momentarily.

Dickinson reverses the consoling expectation that we will be joined by the dead. The following lyric points to the delusory wish to substitute the memory of the dead for the companionship of the living:

> You'll find—it when you die—
> The Easier to let go—
> For recollecting such as went—
> You could not spare—you know.
>
> And though their places somewhat filled—
> As did their Marble names
> With Moss—they never grew so full—
> You chose the newer names—
>
> And when this World—sets further back—

> As Dying—say it does—
> The former love—distincter grows—
> And supercedes the fresh—
>
> And Thought of them—so fair invites—
> It looks too tawdry Grace
> To stay behind—with just the Toys
> We bought—to ease their place—
>
> (J, 610)

8. names] times—

The poem addresses the power of memory to recall the dead by adopting an important epitaphic convention: that the dead could speak. The lyric describes our wish to choose the "newer names," to substitute the living for the dead. By literalizing the voice of the dead as epitaphs on their own tombstones, whose grassy "places somewhat filled— / As did their Marble names / With Moss" (ll. 5–7), she counters the fiction of voice developed in the epitaph: that the dead could speak as if they had a voice.[18] Dickinson discusses the normal human tendency to remember the dead and contends that the memory of the dead is a welcome incentive. Normally the prospect given by the epitaph's posthumous speaker, the shift in perspective in this poem is voiced by the living speaker, who recounts the change that takes place in the dying. Indeed, as we grow older and closer to death, the "former love" of the long dead seem to beckon us to join them, and life on earth without them looks "too tawdry Grace" (l. 14). When one places this poem in the context of the elegies on children, moreover, one sees that the "Toys / We bought—to ease their place—" might refer to children or young people who substitute for those who have died as well as to the trivial aspects of life. By the end of the poem, the speaker's perspective shifts to take in not only the inviting prospect of joining the dead but also the newly vilified life on earth.

The iconography of mourning increasingly promoted the myth that the dying embodied supernatural sensitivity and virtues beyond the normal. Funerary portraits and scenes of mourning in verse and fiction grew increasingly formulaic in their representations of weeping willow motifs toward mid-century. In Judd's novel, *Margaret* (1845), the heroine and Isabel carry an uncomplaining crippled boy, appropriately named Job, to his home. There they encounter his mother and notice a decorative sampler that epitomizes the conventional mourning pictures of the era:

The bright sunlight streamed into the room, quite paling and quenching flames and coals in the fireplace. A picture hung on the walls, an embroidery, floss on white satin, representing a woman leaning mournfully on an urn, and a willow drooping over her.

The woman did not appear to be at all excited by her boy's misfortune, only the breeze of her prevailing sorrow, that sometimes lulled, seemed to blow up afresh a little, as she resumed her seat after attending to his wants. (1, 237)

An embroidery that features the popular triptych of mourning maiden, funeral urn, and weeping willow captures the home's atmosphere of melancholy resignation, one which mothers of dying children were destined to accept as their own. Barton Levi St. Armand characterizes this tearful maiden, a "veiled figure" of classical origins, as "'Woman Weeping,' in contrast to Emerson's galvanic and frankly masculine image of 'Man Thinking.'"[19] He notes that "as an allegory of unalloyed remorse, of inconsolable and perpetual grief in the pagan manner, Woman Weeping was Christianized and romanticized until she took on a Madonna-like calm" (46). Indeed, we might extend the portrait to the actual circumstances of Job's awareness of his impending death and to the description of his mother, who is "a wan, care-worn, ailing looking woman, yet having a gentle and placid tone of voice" and whose own sickly appearance and religious resignation was typified by the weeping willow motif. A widow, Mistress Luce supports her son alone through domestic handiwork, a common occupation for women with little education or other training. Brought on perhaps by the added burden of domestic chores and the care of her ailing children, her illness attests to the strain of household cares for women of the working classes in the nineteenth century.

Remarkably resigned though saddened by her son's illness, she describes Job in a way that parallels the willow's growth from sapling to mournful tree:

"He gets worse and worse," she sighed,—"we did all we could."

"Won't he grow straight and stout?" asked Margaret.

"Alas!" she answered, "a whipporwill sung on the willow over the brook four nights before he was born;—we had him drawn through a split tree, but he never got better."

"Whipporwills sing every night most at the Pond in the summer," said Margaret.

"I have heard them a great many times," added Isabel. "Ma says they won't hurt us if we are only good."

"I know, I know," responded the woman, with a quick shuddering start.

"Ma says that they only hurt wicked people," continued Isabel.

"I always knew it was a judgment on account of my sins."

"What have you done?" asked Margaret anxiously.

"I cannot tell," answered the Widow, "only I am a great sinner; if you could hear the Parson preach you would think so too. I just read in my Bible what God says, 'Because you have sinned against the Lord, this is come upon you.'"

"I saw Job at the Meeting one day," said Margaret; "he recited the catechism so well. Do you know what it meant?" she continued, turning to the boy.

"If I do not, Mammy does," replied the latter. "But I know the whipporwill's song."

"Do you?" asked Margaret; "can you say it?"

"No, only I hear it every night."

"In the winter time?"

"Yes, after I go to bed."

"Do you have dreams?"

"I don't know what it is," replied the boy, "only I hear whipporwill. It sings in the willow over the urn, and sings in here," he said, pointing to his breast. "I shall die of whipporwill."

"O Father in heaven!" groaned the mother bitterly, yet with an air of resignation, "it is just."

"It sings," added the boy, "in the moonshine, I hear it in the brook in the summer, and among the flowers, and the grasshoppers sing it to me when the sun goes down, and it sings in the Bible. I shall die of whipporwill."

(1, 237–39)

The mother's story about her struggle to cure her son's illness reveals a crossover between folk wisdom and orthodox religion that was eventually combined into a new icon of sentimental mourning by the mid-nineteenth century. Although she heeds the dictums of folklore—hearing a whipporwill sing brings tidings of death, while drawing a child through a split tree wards off illness—she also relies on the minister's interpretation of the Bible to mean that her own sins are to blame for her son's frail nature. Even the gentler influences of gradualism and evangelical Christianity, whose exponents believed feeling was evidence of salvation, could not completely erase the awareness of sin and its consequences: "They are plainly told that all whom the heavenly Father hath not been pleased to plant as sacred trees in his garden, are doomed and devoted to destruction."[20]

Like his mother, the dying boy imitates the conventional mourning attitudes represented in consolatory lithographs of the period. The hanging embroidery recalls, as I have noted, the actual moment of the mother's first awareness that her son was fated to die, and Job also acquires his foreboding knowledge of death from the needlework's suggestion. Although he learns the catechism by means of rote memorization, he knows "whipporwill" instinctively, almost as if it were a language. Moreover, this doleful music has many manifestations for him in the natural world, yet he points first to the picture within his home as evidence of the song's pervasive presence. Mother and child thus so thoroughly have internalized the conventions of grieving represented by this mourning artifact that their behavior is dictated by its represented attitudes.

Another poem suggests that despite the illusory sense of progress the dead make toward heaven, their ultimate goal is uncertain:

> These tested Our Horizon
> Then disappeared
> As Birds before achieving
> A Latitude.

Our Retrospection of Them
A fixed Delight,
But our Anticipation
A Dice—a Doubt—

(J, 886)

Dickinson's use of optics and geography suggests that our assurance of the dead's ultimate arrival in heaven depends largely on our sense of perspective. Furthermore, the discourse of scientific inquiry reflects the speaker's desire to fix heaven as a spot in the calculable universe, where the dead test the horizon to prove that it exists. "Latitude" points to the birds' disappearance before rising above the horizon; it suggests a fixed point on a grid, a desire to locate and to predict a point in space. Given the difficulty Dickinson personally experienced in justifying the existence of heaven, "Retrospection" of the dead as they were in life provides a reassuring view of our own futures, a "fixed Delight." Yet this backward glance, though predictable and reassuring, also transfixes us as we remember the beloved dead. Similar to the image of the dead's disappearance, the last line increases our doubts exponentially. In "Anticipation" of meeting the dead, we find "A Dice—a Doubt—," as much security as in a game of chance. Moreover, the multiplication of dots on dice implies the many possible combinations in each throw, none of which can be predicted with certainty. Much as the doubled die puns on the deaths of the reader and those who have disappeared from sight, our lives are doubly circumscribed by a morbid fondness for the dead and the fear that no afterlife exists.

Dickinson partook of her era's monumentalization of the dead in "Alabaster Chambers" (J, 216) that more resemble a house than a tomb, yet her terse rejection of the mourning practices suggested in the elegies of sentimental writers reveals that she was closer to the acerbic wit of the Puritan graveyards than to the mawkishness of the nineteenth-century elegy. She criticizes the ability of tombstones to memorialize the dead, partly because of the mourners' short memories and partly because fame is itself a rhetorical construct. Often writing lyrics that themselves might have been inscribed on tombstones, she invokes the cemetery setting with its artful monuments to play on the supposed "naturalness" of the dead's resting place. Indeed, her use of the epitaph to portray death's ultimate reversal was more closely related to Puritan wit than to the Christian gradualism of her era. Included in a letter written in June 1877, perhaps on the third anniversary of her father's death, the elegy beginning "Lay this Laurel on the One" (J, 1393) is most likely devoted to him, as she notes in the accompanying letter to Higginson that his death has magnified the importance of living: "Since my Father's dying, everything sacred enlarged so—it was dim to own" (*Letters* 2, 583). Later in the letter she refers to Higginson's poem, "Decoration," which had appeared in June 1874 in

Scribner's Monthly. Higginson sent a copy of Dickinson's lyric to Mrs. Todd in 1891, while she was preparing the second series of *Poems*, and he remarked that it was the "condensed essence of [the original] & so far finer."[21]

The considerable differences between the two poems suggest how Dickinson revised epitaphic conventions. Full of clichéd sentiments, Higginson's "Decoration" ostensibly concerns a speaker's memorialization of an anonymous dead soldier to whom he cannot adequately pay tribute:

DECORATION.

"Manibus date lilia plenis."

Mid the flower-wreath'd tombs I stand
Bearing lilies in my hand.
Comrades! in what soldier-grave
Sleeps the bravest of the brave?

Is it he who sank to rest
With his colors round his breast?
Friendship makes his tomb a shrine;
Garlands veil it; ask not mine.

One low grave, yon tree beneath,
Bears no roses, wears no wreath;
Yet no heart more high and warm
Ever dared the battle-storm,

Never gleamed a prouder eye
In the front of victory,
Never foot had firmer tread
On the field where hope lay dead,

Than are hid within this tomb,
Where the untended grasses bloom;
And no stone, with feign'd distress,
Mocks the sacred loneliness.

Youth and beauty, dauntless will,
Dreams that life could ne'er fulfill,
Here lie buried; here in peace
Wrongs and woes have found release.

Turning from my comrades' eyes,
Kneeling where a woman lies,
I strew lilies on the grave
Of the bravest of the brave.

The typical encomium given to the dead soldier, "the bravest of the brave," and the tribute to his valour are thoroughly conventional; like Longfellow, Higginson attempts to achieve catharsis by putting the pain of death into common language. Yet though the speaker's language invokes the traditional praise for the dead soldier, he dismisses the need for a poetic or floral tribute—"Garlands veil it; ask not mine" (l. 8)—and turns instead to the actual object of praise, a woman whose duties within the home and grief perhaps due to the death of a loved husband or brother in battle have gone unrecognized. In contrast to the garlanded tomb, the woman's "low grave" "wears no wreath." Despite the lack of ornamentation, the implicit comparison is between the woman's survival and a soldier's valor on the battlefield. But the speaker acknowledges that an inscription could not give voice to the speaker's sorrow, making silence more appropriate: "And no stone, with feign'd distress, / Mocks the sacred loneliness." Ultimately, the speaker's recollection of the dead woman modifies the reader's expectations about the "Dreams that life could ne'er fufill"; at the end of the poem, he strews lilies, symbolic of resurrection, on the grave as a tribute.

Dickinson's poem, too, concerns the impossibility of communicating the glory of the dead. Creating posthumous speakers who threaten to exchange places with the reader, she often reverses the roles of living and dead, mourner and mourned, as in the following lyric:

> Lay this Laurel on the One
> Too intrinsic for Renown—
> Laurel—vail your deathless tree—
> Him you chasten, that is He!
>
> (J, 1393)

The laurel or bay leaf, traditionally used to crown poets and military victors, promises immortality. But the two addressees—the reader and the laurel tree—reverse one's expectations. As in the traditional epitaph, the speaker enjoins the reader to stop and ponder the remains of the dead and enforces on the reader an awareness that he or she is "chastened" by their example. "Too intrinsic for Renown—" implies that the dead soldier needs no external recognition and hence renders the use of monuments unnecessary, for he is complete within himself. Addressing the laurel, whose open display of immortality embarrasses the speaker and prompts her wish that it might be shrouded, the speaker conveys the sense that poetic immortality is perhaps the only true guarantee of remembrance after death. In invoking the images of a veiled trunk, Dickinson naturalizes the graveside scene and symbolically preserves an image of the body, itself draped in a coffin. Like the marble columns half-draped with cloths populating many Victorian cemeteries, the veiled tree modifies the Romantic image of a curtain separating life from death, the fathomable from the unknown. Rather than openly portray the dead in their monuments, the Victorians symbolized the passage from life to death with a curtain, thus preserving its secrecy and displaying the heightened theatricality surrounding death. In the light of her portrayal of the unostentatious tribute to the dead, the last line proves ambiguous: "Him you chasten" might refer to the dead soldier, or to the speaker of Higginson's poem, for whom "youth and beauty, dauntless will, / Dreams that life could ne'er fulfill" are quashed by early death, despite his wish to enhance these virtues. Finally, and perhaps most importantly, "He" applies to the reader who feels "chastened" by the example of the deceased. Dickinson adapts the epitaph in her poetry in order to modify our expectation of fame, implying that not only the deceased but also the mourner are subject to the same, moderating experience.

The laurel tree also evokes a traditional symbol in funerary iconography that combines images of celestial and earthly existence: the tree of life. At least as early as Sumerian times, the tree signified the lives of human beings: "The righteous shall flourish like the palm tree: he shall grow like a cedar in Lebanon" (Psalms 92:12). A symbol of spiritual values for many cultures, the tree of life represented for the Puritans the power of God's word to regenerate human souls, just as a twig can be replanted and grow into a new plant. As Edward Taylor writes, "Yet I shall stand thy Grafft, and Fruits that are / Fruits of the Tree of Life thy Grafft shall beare."[22] Often carved on gravestones with branches cut off to signify the number of dead or hung with anthropomorphic disks, representing the souls that have taken flight, trees symbolized the lives of the deceased as well as the promise of everlasting life from the fruit of God's word. Later, the image of the tree underwent two further transformations: first in the eighteenth century as palms (signifying victory and the garden), and second in the mid-nineteenth century as the weeping willow (which represented the regeneration of the soul, the tearful remembrance of the dead, and the belief that trees planted in cemeteries might drain hazardous swamp-filled areas).[23]

Trees also figure prominently in Victorian funerary sculpture. Cut trees, stumps, logs, and natural crosses, made of granite or white marble, naturalized the remains of the dead. Often draped with ivy signifying remembrance or sheaves of wheat symbolizing human life, these sculptures promoted the fiction that the dead were similarly felled in a natural and unremarkable way. The frequent anonymity of these graves is an important reminder that all would join in one mighty sepulcher after death. Popular in this era, too, "natural" monuments marked the spots where soldiers were killed in battle during the Civil War, though these monuments are often curiously unable to convey the significance of the loss. In Herman Melville's "An Uninscribed Monument on One of the Battle-Fields of the Wilderness," for instance, a tree or other natural landmark, "though tableted," can never convey the din of battle as well as the quiet of the wood and the silence to which the reader is condemned at the end of the poem.[24] Dickinson also contends that the gravestone's inscription cannot adequately pay tribute to a dead soldier:

> Step lightly on this narrow spot—
> The broadest Land that grows
> Is not so ample as the Breast
> These Emerald Seams enclose.
>
> Step lofty, for this name be told
> As far as Cannon dwell
> Or Flag subsist or Fame export
> Her deathless Syllable.
>
> (J, 1183)

Recalling the injunction common in funerary inscriptions to pause to consider the deceased, the poem encourages the reader to "step lightly" on the ground above the dead. Rather than extol the life of the dead person, however, the speaker emphasizes the unreadability of the gravesite. She contrasts the valour of the soldier—his "ample" "Breast"—with the "narrow" space in which the body is interred, suggesting that his courage could not be contained by the grave. Only "Emerald Seams" distinguish the grave as a site. Rather than serve as a pompous memorial to the dead, this simple grave registers the impossibility of summarizing the significant events of the dead person's life.

Furthermore, Dickinson points to the power of sound to memorialize the dead. "Step lofty" enjoins the reader to rise above the grave and its small, mundane concerns. By casting the event in the realm of the hypothetical and using the subjunctive "be" rather than "is," she suggests that the soldier's fame is sustained by the repeated remarks of others. The cannon and flag "dwell" and "subsist," almost as if they lived and carried on his name in his place. "Deathless Syllable" also connotes vocality or music, since fame exists whenever the soldier's name is pronounced. In fact, "syllable" hints at the way sound as well as sense convey the soldier's fame: it calls up both the discrete sounds of words and the "bell" of a funerary procession. Although the soldier's body is buried in the "narrow spot" of the grave, his name transcends its confines and ultimately reminds us that celebrity depends upon the poem and other verbal and written tributes, rather than on the actual monumentalized grave site.

Another poem of Dickinson's combines cemetery iconography and epitaphic conventions to undercut the professed grief of the mourners. Writing to Higginson in 1877, Dickinson explicitly referred to the following poem as "an Epitaph," and Mills Campbell states that "her notion of the stone as 'confiding' is directly related to her own style of writing and that style is directly related to the convention of the speaking monument.[25] According to Mills Campbell, every linguistic gesture is a type of "speaking monument," since it attempts to claim as fully present a moment that has already been lost. At its best, poetry expresses language's "Constancy," its ability to testify to the absence of the speaker, especially in the face of our inconstant emotions toward the dead:

> She laid her docile Crescent down
> And this confiding Stone
> Still states to Dates that have forgot
> The News that she is gone—
>
> So constant to it's stolid trust,
> The Shaft that never knew—
> It shames the Constancy that fled
> Before it's emblem flew—
>
> (J, 1396)

Cosmological figures, such as the sun, stars, and moon, depict constellations representative of heaven on gravestones; more specifically, the sun represents the flight of the soul heavenward.[26] "Crescent" thus may represent the trajectory of life toward the celestial sphere. Like the marble shafts of the antique and quaint cemetery described in Judd's novel or the cut or broken marble columns scattered throughout most Victorian cemeteries, the "Shaft" of the gravestone records with "stolid trust" the life of the dead, and it exposes the less reliable "Constancy" of the living, who forget the dead woman while the stone itself still stands. A worksheet draft of the poem reveals several changes that emphasize the way the tombstone speaks as deliberately uncertain: "subjunctive" for "confiding" conveys the idea of hypothetical or contingent action, much as the eternal stone memorializes one in a less than secure state; alternately, "mechanic" for "confiding" conveys the way the formulaic rendering of the inscription prevents the full expression of emotion. The tombstone still records the "News" of the woman's death, although its "Dates" have been forgotten by most. Far from simply recording the facts of this woman's life, Dickinson indicts the culture and the family for their short memories and erects her poem as a monument, a tribute to the beloved dead.

Moreover, the lyric's presentation situates it in the context of pictorial art and furthers its critique of the epitaph's memorialization of the dead.[27] Dickinson pasted two clippings from newspapers above the poem: in the upper lefthand corner, a crescent moon with a star between the horns, and at the right, slanting tombstones with an undecipherable inscription.[28] The crescent moon and slanting tombstones might represent Islamic and Christian powers respectively and thus undermine the preeminence of a single system of belief. Placed in the context of funerary sculpture, however, these illustrations create a visual text, an "emblem" to be interpreted. Indeed, perhaps part of the point is that both pictures instill even more obscurity into our awareness of the dead's fate. Finally, if one considers that Dickinson performs by adorning her poem with illustrations the same action the speaker describes (laying down a crescent, remembering the dead), then the poem becomes an artifact that pays tribute to the dead. Like a tombstone, which combines visual and written elements, the lyric and its arrangement on the page visibly symbolize the idea that death may be recorded yet not understood.

Dickinson invokes the common fiction that the dead are only sleeping and enjoins a peaceful silence on them, even at the Apocalypse:

> Ample make this Bed—
> Make this Bed with Awe—
> In it wait till Judgment break
> Excellent and Fair.
>
> Be it's Mattress straight—
> Be it's Pillow round—
> Let no Sunrise' yellow noise
> Interrupt this Ground—
>
> (J, 829)

Sent to Thomas Niles in 1883 and entitled by the poet "Country Burial," this lyric alludes indirectly to the epitaphic convention of posthumous speech, but rather than portray the dead predicting the demise of the living or instructing the reader in holy living, Dickinson softens the expectation that the dead will rise on the last day to a comforting wish that they might be undisturbed in death. While the speaker wishes that the dead might be comfortable as they anticipate the second coming of Christ, she exaggerates the image of an "Ample" bed by invoking death's sublime sense of "Awe." According to St. Armand, Dickinson's poems reflect a celestial day in which each time of day reflects a different state of the soul.[29] The possibility of salvation is reflected in perhaps the most important cosmological image in her poems: the sun. Anticipating the arrival of the Son of God on the dawn of the Day of Reckoning, the speaker lays the emphasis on the ecstatic and hence indescribable nature of death. Punning on "Judgment Day" in "Judgment break," the speaker implies that sunrise brings with it the end of night as well as the justice of paradise. "Excellent" derives from "to rise out of" and hints etymologically at the rising of the dead from their graves as well as the outstanding good of the light of salvation. Moreover, her off-rhyme "Fair" does not conform either to the tidy rhythms of Isaac Watts's hymns or to the comforting pictures of heaven as a wholly merciful and beautiful place provided by other elegists. In the synesthesic "Sunrise' yellow noise," Dickinson combines the wish that the dead might be left undisturbed by the blaring trumpets of the resurrection and voices and peals of thunder predicted in Revelations (4:1, 5) with the arrival of the sun-god. Even "Interrupt" implies that death is a continuum whose silence is better left undisturbed. Far from embracing the joyful awakening of the dead, Dickinson wishes a peaceful silence that contradicts the popular image of the dead's resurrection.

Adapting the symbols of funerary sculpture and gravestones in her lyrics, Dickinson displays both the inconstancy of human beings' affections and the inability of epitaphs to memorialize the dead. Consigning the dead to a trenchant silence, her poems tell us again and again instead how the memorialization of the dead foreshadows our own terse-lipped quiet in the grave. In one of the four conclusions she wrote to one of her best-known poems beginning "Safe in their Alabaster Chambers" (J, 216), Dickinson adopts the images of the "Crescent," "Arcs," and "Firmaments" to depict heaven and the crown, so often found on New England tombstones, to describe immortality.[30] Pointed, fluted, layered, ribbed, banded, beaded, and pierced, crowns signified the righteousness of God's elect: "Henceforth there is laid up for me a crown of righteousness, which the Lord, the righteous judge, shall give me at that day: and not to me only, but unto all them also that love his appearing" (2 Timothy 4:8). Given the apocalyptic imagery, it is also likely Dickinson meant to invoke the elders in Revelations (4:10) who cast down their crowns as a form of obeisance before the throne of God. Rather than give voice to their worshipful chorus, however, these "Doges" are silent. Like an abstract expressionist painting, which evokes a mood through the use of color rather than form, her lyric concludes with the color white, reminiscent of "Snow," the white marble of tombs, and the emptiness of a blank page:

> Safe in their Alabaster Chambers—
> Untouched by Morning—
> And untouched by Noon—
> Lie the meek members of the Resurrection—
> Rafter of Satin—and Roof of Stone!
>
> Grand go the Years—in the Crescent—above them—
> Worlds scoop their Arcs—
> And Firmaments—row—
> Diadems—drop—and Doges—surrender—
> Soundless as dots—on a Disc of Snow—
>
> (J, 216)

Using the epitaphic conventions popular in graveyard poetry and inscriptions, Dickinson reverses the expected formula that we should wait patiently to see the dead by showing them anticipating our arrival. Nineteenth-century American women poets, like Sigourney and others, often portray heaven as a utopia where women can reunite with female friends, mothers, and children.

Epitaphs similarly posit the existence of the dead, creating the fiction that they live on in posthumous voices. Far from rejecting these notions outright, Dickinson partakes of and enriches epitaphic conventions in her elegaic meditations. Whereas other women writers romanticize the possibility of a reunion after death, Dickinson opens the epitaph to a wide range of speakers and questions the easy consolation promised in the Victorian period.

"ANCESTOR'S BROCADES"

Chapter 5

"Paradise Persuaded"
Dickinson, Osgood, and the Language of Flowers

The expression of this divine passion ought to be divine also, and it was to illustrate this that flowers were ingeniously made emblematical of our most delicate sentiments; they do, in fact, utter in "silent eloquence" a language better than writing; they are the delicate symbols of the illusions of a tender heart and of a lively and brilliant imagination.
—Frances Sargent Osgood, *The Poetry of Flowers, and Flowers of Poetry*[1]

Language of flowers. They like it because no-one can hear.
—James Joyce, *Ulysses*[2]

You ask me what my flowers said—then they were disobedient—I gave them messages.
—Emily Dickinson (*Letters* 2, 333)

"Let me thank the little Cousin in flowers, which without lips, have language—," wrote Emily Dickinson to Eugenia Hall in 1885 (*Letters* 3, 881). For Dickinson, as for her contemporaries, flowers were repositories of cultural meaning and communicated emotions privately. During the 1840s and 1850s, popular female writers were adding to a growing fund of literature: the language of flowers. "Little study is necessary in the science here taught; nature has been before us," writes Frances Sargent Osgood, who combines a floral dictionary, poetry, and botanical treatise in her book, *The Poetry of Flowers, and Flowers of Poetry* (1841) [25]. Creating dictionaries that codified floral meanings and often appending botanical treatises, these writers developed flowers into a linguistic system that, though probably never used, reflects the popular consciousness of the Victorian period. Of course, such communication depended on the ethic of privacy cultivated by genteel men and women who preferred to express their emotions in private acts rather than public displays,

129

in letters rather than conversations. Because women especially were expected to embody piety and domesticity and were limited to these topics in public, their passion needed to be mediated through a rhetoric of "silent eloquence"—a language of gesture that implied meaning through a series of codes rather than through overt statement. I take this phrase from a passage by a popular verse writer who also penned her own dictionaries, Frances Sargent Osgood, for it embodies the language of gesture and implied meaning through which women communicated to each other without reserve feelings that were unacceptable to a reading public and staked out new emotional territory for themselves.

For nineteenth-century women, who were frequently encouraged to shy away from the harsh light of self-revelation and public scrutiny, floral symbolism afforded a private way to express their thoughts to friends, lovers, and acquaintances. Fearing for her friend, Thomas Wentworth Higginson, who was at the time leading a Union regiment during the Civil War, Emily Dickinson alluded to the pervasive floral rhetoric: "I trust the 'Procession of Flowers' was not a premonition—" (*Letters* 2, 424). Her reference to Higginson's nature essay, which appeared in the *Atlantic Monthly* in December 1862, reminds us that seasonal change is associated with death. Part of the naturalist tradition, Higginson's essay displays the nature worship of a neo-Romantic sensibility imbued in the transcendentalist belief in the traces of the divine. Indeed, even his imagery is Emersonian, as in this allusion to "Circles": "Not in the tropics only, but even in England, whence most of our floral associations and traditions come, the march of the flowers is in an endless circle, and, unlike our experience, something is always in bloom."[3] Higginson's essay encompasses a clinical examination of plants with a more sentimental rendering of their importance as harbingers of our own impermanence. "Men are perplexed with anxieties about their own immortality," he writes,

but these catkins, which hang, almost full-formed, above the ice all winter, show no such solicitude, but when March wooes them they are ready. Once relaxing, their pollen is so prompt to fall that it sprinkles your hand as you gather them; then, for one day, they are the perfection of grace upon your table, and next day they are weary and emaciated, and their little contribution to the spring is done. (*ODP*, 320–21)

Transitory and fragile, the catkins emblematize for Higginson the course of a human life. His description also captures the moment of sexual release: the plants are "ready when March wooes them" and, "once relaxing," they disgorge their pollen, "which leaves them weary and emaciated," spent forever after a brief moment of perfection.

Redolent of change, loss, and sexuality, Higginson's essay would undoubtedly have appealed to Dickinson, for she lived in an era saturated with nature writing whose authors often did not distinguish between—or saw no reason to view as mutually exclusive—scientific observation and nostalgic reverie. She was exposed to nature writing not only through essays and journal articles, like Higginson's, but also through two other works in her family's library: Mrs. C. M. Badger's *Wild Flowers Drawn and Colored From Nature* (1859) and Edward Hitchcock's *Catalogue of Plants Growing Without Cultivation in the Vicinity of Amherst College* (1829). Given that these books were written, moreover, for male and female audiences, they show that the sexes were indoctrinated with proper behavior through floral handbooks. Badger's and Hitchcock's books demonstrate that reverie and observation were two competing, though perhaps not contradictory, approaches to the natural world in nineteenth-century America: one scientific, rational, and exploratory, the other sentimental, aesthetic, and poetic. Hitchcock's book serves as a compendium for indigenous American plants that grew in and around Amherst and lists both Latin and common English names for plants. In his preface, Hitchcock names as his audience "young gentlemen, whose disposition to promote the interests of science appears so favourably in the publication of this catalogue"; he adds that through this book "they may have a pretty complete list of the plants growing in their vicinity," and further that it also "may serve as a very convenient index to an Herbarium."[4] Dickinson notes to Higginson in 1877 that every winter Hitchcock's treatise gave her much needed consolation about the continuation of natural life: "When Flowers annually died and I was a child, I used to read Dr Hitchcock's Book on the Flowers of North America. This comforted their Absence—assuring me they lived" (*Letters* 2, 573).

With its beautifully hand-colored illustrations accompanied by poems that convey the meaning of each flower, *Wild Flowers* enforces the emblematic and didactic nature of flowers. Unlike Hitchcock's catalogue of plants' names, Badger's book conforms to the type of floral compendium frequently written and read by American women in this period. Presented to Dickinson by her father, Edward Dickinson, in 1859, the book suits his desire for her to embody traditional feminine virtues even as he remembered his daughter's fondness for flowers. Badger's book embodies the tradition of women's floral writing in its watchful care over women's moral behavior and deportment, even including an introduction and prefatory poem by Lydia Sigourney:

> —One fair hand, hath skill'd to bring
> Voice of bird, and breath of Spring,
> One fair hand, before you laid
> Flowerets that can never fade,—
> While you listen, soft and clear
> Steals her wind-harp o'er your ear,—
> While you gaze, her buds grow brighter,—
> Take the book, and bless its writer.[5]

Paula Bennett notes that Sigourney's poem captures the essence of women's floral writing, which sought to make every poem a living picture.[6] Although the pictorial representation of flowers accompanying these poems enlarges their meanings, Sigourney's poem also builds on the nineteenth-century rhetoric of flowers, proposing a secret language of seduction and "stealing" influence over the reader. Just as in Nathaniel Hawthorne's *The Scarlet Letter* (1850) the narrator plucks a rose and offers it to the reader "to symbolize some sweet moral blossom, that may be found along the track, or relieve the darkening close of a tale of human frailty and sorrow,"[7] Sigourney asks for the reader's sympathy for and acceptance of the author's efforts. More than most floral lyrics other than Dickinson's, Sigourney's poem engages the reader almost as if she were a lover and compares the act of reading to a kind of seduction: "stealing" over the ear of the listener and capturing her gaze, it encourages the reader to "take" the book—literally into her hands—rather than actual flowers. Although Sigourney adopts a submissive attitude appropriate for a woman writer in humbly asking the reader to "bless its writer," her poem initiates an erotic exchange in which Badger's book substitutes for actual flowers presented by the sender (writer) to the recipient (reader). To accept the book means to surrender oneself to its verisimilitude, to submit to the author's powers of seduction, and finally to agree tacitly to make the book come to life through one's own imagination. Furthermore, since blossoms often operate as a metonym for women, flowers symbolize the way women themselves could be traded between men and families through marriage. Sigourney's poem opens the possibility that Badger's "fair hand" offers not only "flowerets that can never fade" but, by extension, herself to other women as well as men.

Hitchcock's and Badger's books share an affinity for wild plants native to America, but their differences also suggest the ways women's floral handbooks are built on the inherent instability of language codes. Both Badger's and Hitchcock's books depict wild flowers, and both prefer native American species to European ones. They show an interest in preserving and exploring their own country's plant lore. Distinguishing American from European manners and legend was a crucial aspect of both, since most floral dictionaries began with an extended homage to floral legends abroad, especially in Europe.[8] But Hitchcock's book attempts to limit the number of botanical references and names of each plant, as the preface explains: "it presents [the reader] at once with an authority for each specimen, with the most important synonyms; and thus saves him the very great labour of comparing together the descriptions given by different writers: a work which severely tasks the powers of the most accomplished botanist" (iii). In contrast, Badger delights in the ambiguity of floral meanings, listing common names and adapting for her poems each plant's common association, habitat, or season. One can gather on the basis of her example that women's floral books adopted freely the variety of meanings and names attached to common wild flowers. Far from limiting women's writing, the multiplicity of meanings in floral dictionaries afforded women the opportunity to explore the cultural and social resonances of flowers.

Dickinson displayed a lively interest in observing nature, yet she differentiated herself from the women whose rhapsodic flights over flowers characterized much of the poetry in this period. She inquired in May 1845 of her childhood friend Abiah Root, "Have you made you an herbarium yet?" (*Letters* 1, 13), offering to send her specimens of local plants. In a September letter, however, Dickinson is tongue-in-cheek about preserving a bouquet for her friend: "I would love to send you a bouquet if I had an opportunity, and you could press it and write under it, The last flowers of summer. Wouldn't it be poetical, and you know that is what young ladies aim to be now-a-days" (*Letters* 1, 21). Distinguishing herself from these ladies, she criticizes their decorous behavior but also their desire to be "poetical" in their gifts of flowers, which had become faddish by the 1840s. Although she sent flowers to friends and relatives frequently throughout her life, she rejected the sentimental versifying that often accompanied floral missives. Writing to Dr. and Mrs. Holland in 1862, Dickinson shows her awareness of the way floral symbolism might easily substitute for written prose: "Now, you need not speak, for perhaps you are weary, and 'Herod' requires all your thought, but if you are *well*—let Annie draw me a little picture of an erect flower; if you are *ill*, she can hang the flower a little on one side!" (*Letters* 2, 413). Yet her attitude toward such communication is distinctly comical, as the lines that immediately follow these reveal: "Then, I shall understand, and you need not stop to write me a letter. Perhaps you laugh at me! Perhaps the whole United States are laughing at me too! *I* can't stop for that! *My* business is to love" (*Letters* 2, 413).

In the years immediately following her schoolhood letters to Abiah Root and others, Dickinson began to explore the connotations that flowers carried and their ability to signify human experience and emotion, as Higginson's description of the catkins suggests. In this chapter, I will explore the culture of flowers in nineteenth-century America to show how Dickinson wields this genre in her own floral poems. Many of her contemporary female poets, such as Frances Sargent Osgood, used the rhetoric of floral dictionaries. Their verses playfully adopt floral images to disclaim responsibility for their own capricious behavior or emotions. While they build on the image of women as childlike, they also implicitly enlarge the range of expression available to women through their indirect style and occasional parodies of stereotypical femininity. I will first provide a brief overview of floral dictionaries and then examine some of Osgood's floral poems, which I set against lyrics of Dickinson, exploring how she enriches floral diction. Placed in the larger social context of floral writing, Dickinson's poems not only overturn romantic conventions, but they also enlarge the range of sexual and emotional significances possible for women.

Although the language of flowers culminated in the nineteenth century, it originated much earlier. The cultural anthropologist Jack Goody writes in *The Culture of Flowers* (1993) that the symbolic use of flowers in the West was predated in China and Japan by many years.[9] Among the first Western poets to use flowers symbolically, Dante used the rose as a mystical symbol for Christ. The tradition of assigning meanings to individual flowers continued among the Elizabethans and seventeenth-century English poets, such as Herrick and Marvell. Interest in the language of flowers peaked in the nineteenth century. Inspired by Madame de la Tour's *Les Langages des Fleurs*, Victorians codified and refined the significances assigned to flowers, and a vast number of floral dictionaries appeared in the 1840s and 1850s.[10] Sarah Josepha Hale's *Flora's Interpreter, and Fortuna Flora* (1850) and Frances Sargent Osgood's *The Poetry of Flowers, and Flowers of Poetry* (1841) are only two American examples.[11] Additionally, Almira H. Lincoln's *Familiar Lectures on Botany*, one of Dickinson's textbooks, contained an appendix, "Symbolical Language of Flowers," that proves the poet had direct access to floral associations.[12]

Written primarily for and by women, these dictionaries reflect the heightened sentiment and tearful "melting" popular among the Victorians. Like the Romantics, Victorian writers saw nature as a book that could be interpreted symbolically. They thought plants were emblematic of a range of emotions. Dorothea Dix, who was later to become famous as an advocate for the mentally ill, wrote in an early work that flowers were part of a language of nature: "Oh! flowers, flowers,—we may well think them 'the alphabet of the angels.' But how coldly do we look on them; how often are we regardless of their charms here; while in other lands they almost subserve the use of writing,—expressing by a blossom, joy, grief, hope, despair, happiness, devotion, piety, and almost every other sentiment that fills the mind."[13]

But the leisured Victorians used a rigid codification of floral meanings to reaffirm their class status and to maintain their high morals. Not only does floral symbolism serve as a language of sentiments, but flowers can also inculcate the viewer with virtue, as Dix reveals: "A virtuous character is likened to an unblemished flower. Piety is a fadeless bud that half opens on earth, and expands through eternity. Sweetness of temper is the odor of fresh blooms, and the amaranth flowers of pure affection open but to bloom forever" (26). Moreover, unlike their European counterparts, who used flowers purely for decoration, Americans tended to stress their didactic value. A journalist, novelist, and poet, Sarah Josepha Hale writes in her *Flora's Interpreter* (1850) that her intent is to improve the moral standing of her readers: "May it inspire our young women to cultivate those virtues which only can be represented by the fairest flowers; and may our young men strive to be worthy of the love that these fairest flowers can so eloquently reveal."[14] In comparing women to flowers, Hale implies that they should cultivate virtues while they remain passively rooted and unresponding to events outside the home. Sometimes, to stress these virtues, the meanings of flowers were often toned down in America: the red rose signifies "volupté" or voluptuousness in French dictionaries, but in American ones is often translated as "I have seen a pretty girl." In *The Culture of Flowers*, Jack Goody notes that "While it is unlikely that the Language of Flowers would have originated in a country that paid them so little attention at that time, Americans seem to have taken it more seriously, more morally, than Europe, stressing its use to promote virtue, to stimulate education and to define the values of the new nation."[15]

The language of flowers was considered a woman's genre, as the prefaces and introductions to these works reveal. In the preface to an 1843 floral dictionary, the writer tells a number of anecdotes illustrating the use of floral language in Turkey, India, Spain, and Italy—but all the stories depict women. After a short list summarizing the meanings of flowers, the writer concludes with the hope that the book may "furnish a pleasing exercise for the ingenuity of our fair readers," a remark surely directed to women.[16] Flora, the goddess of flowers, was frequently depicted in illustrations accompanying the text or referred to in poems. Authors of nineteenth-century floral dictionaries upheld the belief that women's poems and flowers were interchangeable. Hale writes in her dictionary that since "the expression of these feelings has been, in all ages, the province of poetry," then poetry must provide a "philology of flowers" (iii).

Whatever their value as literature, floral dictionaries echo the prevailing critical discourse surrounding women's poetry in the nineteenth century. Stemming from the popular portrayal of women's writing as natural and spontaneous, women's poems and flowers were often considered interchangeable both by male critics and female authors. For instance, an anonymous 1852 reviewer of Alice Cary's *Lyra and Other Poems* in *Harper's* writes that her verse "displays a rich luxuriance of imagery; all the flowers of the season woven into the elegaic wreath; but it is too artificial, too curiously wrought for the subject."[17] Indeed, when Higginson wrote the 1890 introduction to Dickinson's posthumous *Poems*, he remarked that "In many cases these verses will seem to the reader like poetry torn up by the roots, with rain and dew and earth still clinging to them, giving a freshness and fragrance not otherwise to be conveyed."[18] Rather than compare her verse to "a lily grown in a cellar," as one writer in 1878 did the poetry of "Saxe Holm" (Helen Hunt Jackson), no doubt imagining that it was Dickinson's,[19] Higginson refers instead to their "found" quality in comparing them to wild flowers, thus absolving himself of responsibility for presenting them to the public. Given that women's verse was frequently described as unpremeditated, Higginson recognized her verse's power yet attributed its originality to "extraordinary grasp and insight, uttered with an uneven vigor sometimes exasperating, seemingly wayward, but really unsought and inevitable" (vi). Indeed, the very chapter titles of his edition of

Dickinson's poems in 1890 reflect his desire to fit her poetry to the conventional topics of women's writing: "Life," "Love," "Nature," "Time and Eternity" (Dickinson, *Poems* [1890]).

One need only glance at the titles of some popular literary works from this period to assess the pervasiveness of this floral rhetoric and plant lore in America: Elizabeth Stuart Phelps's *The Last Leaf From Sunnyside* (1854), Fanny Fern's (Sarah Parton) *Fern Leaves From Fanny's Portfolio* (1850), Laura Greenwood's *The Rural Wreath; or, Life Among the Flowers* (1853), Lydia Sigourney's *The Voice of Flowers* (1846), and, perhaps most significant, Walt Whitman's *Leaves of Grass* (1855). A mere portion of the collections in this era whose titles allude to plants, flowers, or weeds, these literary works are imbued with textual and visual puns on "leaves" as pages of a book and on "flowery" or "gemmy" prose as metaphorical. Furthermore, they associate images of nature with textuality and femininity. The title page of Walt Whitman's *Leaves of Grass*, for example, depicts the twining tendrils and sprouting leaves common in women's books of verse. Helen Hunt Jackson's 1870 *Verses* also contain emblems of sacred and secular love: a hand plucking petals from a daisy, a triptych displaying the nativity scene, decorative flowers, and twining roses. Indeed, the expression "flowers of rhetoric," as metaphorical language came to be known, epitomized the belief that figurative language is ornate and decorative, and the very vocabulary of bookmaking has continued to display its roots in floral discourse well into the twentieth century. The term "fascicle," generally the division of a book, derives from floral rhetoric, and the hand-sewn packets that Dickinson made of fair copies of her poems are also termed fascicles, which are described by Hale's floral dictionary as "flowers on little stalks variously inserted and subdivided, collected into a close bundle, level at the top" (viii). "Anthology," too, comes originally from the Greek "anthologia," meaning a collection of flowers, thus pointing to the close connection between flowers and rhetoric.

The language of flowers operates according to a series of codes that is itself open to change and interpretation.[20] Their meanings derived partly from legends and partly from arbitrary assignment, flowers could therefore have many meanings. A floral handbook published in 1913 (which is still in print), contains eight meanings for daisy and thirty-nine for rose alone.[21] Moreover, there were instructions about how to present flowers, since their meanings often depended on how they were placed. For example, a flower inclined to the right indicated the first person; to the left, the second person. An upright flower expresses a thought; upside down, its reverse. Placed upon the head, a flower signifies a thought; upon the heart, love; upon the breast, ennui. The same definitions for each flower rarely appear in any two dictionaries, except in cases where generic associations are made or the same works are reprinted in a new edition. The anonymous writer of *The Language of Flowers* in 1843 attests

that the expressive power of flowers is due largely to the variety of their meanings: "Yes, flowers have their language. Theirs is an oratory, that speaks in per-
fumed silence, and there is tenderness, and passion, and even the lighthearted-
ness of mirth, in the variegated beauty of their vocabulary. To the poetical
mind, they are not mute to each other; to the pious, they are not mute to their
Creator."[22]

The authors of floral dictionaries link femininity and flowers. In the introduction to her floral dictionary, *The Flowers of Poetry, and Poetry of Flowers*
(1841), Osgood belittles her work and asks the reader's indulgence, a ploy
common in women's literature: "Only Fancy and Feeling have woven a wreath
which may yield neither bloom nor sweetness, unless the sunshine of Indulgence, and the kindly dew of Sympathy, be suffered to play on its leaves."[23]
Women's writing was thought to be natural and unpremeditated, as the language of flowers was also thought to be natural and beyond instruction. For
Osgood, each creature and plant reveals God's inspiration, a thought that can
best be expressed by women due to their sensitivity and piety: "The expression
of this divine passion ought to be divine also, and it was to illustrate this that
flowers were ingeniously made emblematical of our most delicate sentiments;
they do, in fact, utter in 'silent eloquence' a language better than writing; they
are the delicate symbols of the illusions of a tender heart and of a lively and
brilliant imagination" (23). The idea of the language of flowers as a fund of
"silent eloquence" conveys not only the privacy of this language, but also its reliance on tacit assumptions rather than on explicit discussion of emotions. Furthermore, by writing poems that expressed their thoughts, nineteenth-century
women wrote a new, radical poetry. As I will show, women used the language
of flowers to express ideas not otherwise considered acceptable.

When he made his first visit to Dickinson at her Amherst home in 1870,
Higginson was unaware that her offering him "two day lilies" (*Letters* 2, 473)
as her "introduction" was a calculated act, since according to the language of
flowers, day lilies signifies, among other meanings, "Coquetry." If her gift was
an intentional act of self-presentation, she meant to offer the flowers as her
metonymic substitute. Rather than reveal all to Higginson during his visit, she
meted out as much of her mind as she pleased. Dickinson thus transformed the
common habit of enclosing flowers in a note or presenting them to others into
a more complex mode of self-presentation. Given the common editorial discourse that asserted women's poems and flowers were interchangeable, she
collapses the distinction between them. Like the answer to a riddle, flowers are
often the unstated subjects of her lyrics, hinted at but not fully explained.
Dickinson draws on the associations about flowers in order to undercut the tradition of romantic courtship, and her floral lyrics exult in secrets, silence, and
deferral of meaning, rather than its full expression.

In assessing Dickinson's appropriation of these forms, we might consider

more closely the work of another poet who seems to combine both the sentimentalism of her era and the growing dissatisfaction that women expressed
about their lives—Frances Sargent Osgood. Cheryl Walker has written that
"Frances Osgood is undoubtedly one of the most alluring women poets before
Emily Dickinson."[24] Praising Osgood for her wit and humor, she notes her
"pointedly arch and Millayish" persona, which was "anything but naïve."[25]
Similarly, in her groundbreaking *The Poetry of American Women from 1632 to
1945*, Emily Stipes Watts says of the period from 1800 to 1850, "Osgood is
simply the best poet of all the women who wrote during these years."[26] Recently, critics have pointed out Osgood's wit and reliance on sentimental conventions and have thrown her more rebellious, irreverent poems into bold relief when compared with less original versifiers.[27] In fact, Osgood surpasses
many of her contemporaries in her ability to play off the conventions of
women's versifying and still retain a satiric tone about the relations between
men and women. As Joanne Dobson has noted, Osgood wrote a number of
witty salon verses, which have remained unpublished perhaps due to the author's awareness that they diverged from the predominant image of women as
pious and docile beings.[28] Addressed to the worldly and sophisticated New
York society of the 1840s, these lyrics question the limits of women's sexual
lives and allow their speakers to transgress, if momentarily, the image of idealized feminine behavior. Steeped in the conventions of what Barton Levi St.
Armand has termed the "sentimental love religion"—the popular fiction that in
death lovers would be reunited—Osgood manipulates in her lyrics the possibilities for satiric points of view concerning men's and women's love relations,
as Dobson notes: "What the 'sentimental love religion' allows her here is an
imaginative arena for indulgence in playful erotic posturing."[29]

Osgood wittily adopts in her verse floral images to disclaim responsibility
for women's capricious behavior or emotions. While these images build on the
characterization of women as childlike, they also implicitly enlarge the range
of expression available to women through their indirect style and occasional
parodies of stereotypical femininity. Osgood herself publicly conformed to the
image of a poetess in the authorial portrait to her 1850 *Poems*: clad in a classical décolleté gown and facing the viewer with a full-eyed expression, she typifies the ideal, otherworldly poetess. Though by 1850 she had acquired enough
stature to be pictured authoritatively above her stamped signature on the facing title page of her *Poems*, her first collection of verses, which appeared in
1846, set a more domestic and utopian tone with the illustration of a thatched
cottage half hidden in a wood and its summary legend: "Happy at Home." A
devotee of floral poetry, she published a number of works whose titles evoke
the language of flowers: *A Wreath of Wild Flowers from New England* (1838),
Flower Gift: A Token of Friendship for All Seasons (1840), *The Poetry of
Flowers, and Flowers of Poetry* (1841), *The Floral Offering; A Token of*

Friendship (1847), and *The Flower Alphabet in Gold and Colors* (1845). Given Osgood's independent lifestyle and wit, it is perhaps not surprising that her floral poems define a range of positions taken by women with their lovers—seduced, imploring, betrayed, cast off—while they maintain decorum for the nineteenth-century reading public. In fact, Osgood surpasses many of her contemporaries in her ability to play on the conventions of women's versifying and still retain a pointed, satiric tone about the relations between men and women.

In her 1846 *Poems*, Frances Sargent Osgood includes the following adaptation from the language of flowers:

> A cold, calm star look'd out of heaven,
>   And smiled upon a tranquil lake,
> Where, pure as angel's dream at even,
>   A Lily lay but half awake.
>
> The flower felt that fatal smile
>   And lowlier bow'd her conscious head;
> "Why does he gaze on me the while?"
>   The light, deluded Lily said.
>
> Poor dreaming flower!—too soon beguiled,
>   She cast nor thought nor look elsewhere,
> Else she had known the star but smiled
>   To see himself reflected there.[30]

Written perhaps as a response to Edgar Allan Poe, Osgood's literary mentor and possibly her lover, "The Lily's Delusion" epitomizes Osgood's witty, rebellious use of floral language. Close in form and sentiment to Poe's "Evening Star," written in 1827, the poem may have been meant to comment sarcastically on her betrayal by Poe, who sought to improve his own reputation through placing her poems near his by-line.[31] The Lily's semi-consciousness hints that, not yet fully initiated into the deceptions of love, she must undergo a romantic betrayal. Furthermore, the lily symbolizes death, resurrection, and purity—the woman's eventual fate. Innocent and flattered by the "fatal smile" of a "cold, calm star," the Lily does not see the vanity of the flower until too late.

Best known as Poe's literary protégée, Frances Sargent Osgood led a short but active life as a professional writer. Born in 1811 to a Boston merchant and his second wife, she spent her childhood in Hingham, Massachusetts. The family included a brother and older half sister, Anna Maria Wells, who herself became a popular New England poet. Her engagement and eventual marriage to the American portrait artist, Charles Stillman Osgood, was no doubt founded on her love of romance, which he amply satisfied when she sat for her portrait in 1834 by telling her exotic adventure stories culled from his youth. After marrying in October 1835, they moved to England, where Frances enjoyed the literary society that would end their marriage. Summering in Provincetown in 1845, Osgood met Edgar Allan Poe, who proved to be the most enduring influence on her career. She had become estranged from her husband the year before, after nine years of marriage that produced two daughters. Sexually as well as economically independent, she lived a free life, which, coupled with her apparent infatuation with Poe, has given rise to the theory that she became his lover and may have had by him her third daughter, Fanny. Poe proved to be a powerful advocate for her in the popular press, writing a number of very complimentary reviews of her poems.

Osgood's more conventional use of floral imagery offers a touchstone for women's writing about flowers, since she combines both the sentimentalism of her era and the dissatisfaction that women increasingly expressed about their lives. Although many of her lyrics propose conservative values about women and do not radically alter poetic conventions, other poems display the dissatisfaction she must have felt with woman's position. Although "Caprice" echoes the traditional view of women as flighty, moody creatures, it also claims their right to decide their own fates without explanation:

> Reprove me not that still I change
>> With every changing hour,
> For glorious Nature gives me leave
>> In wave, and cloud, and flower.

> And you and all the world would do—
>> If all but dared—the same;
> True to myself—if false to you,
>> Why should I reck your blame?[32]

Osgood builds on the myth that women were closer to nature than men as well as on the transcendental belief that whim is a legitimate expression of the soul. Nature's mutability gives the speaker permission to act, and so she divests herself of responsibility for her actions, even if that freedom comes at the expense of being called "capricious." She accepts the stereotype of the flighty woman, but she also calls "caprice" women's "only right":

> Be less—thou art no love of mine,
> So leave my love in peace;
> 'Tis helpless woman's right divine—
> Her only right—caprice!
>> (*Poems* [1850] 214, ll. 45–48)

The resonance of the word "only" suggests a seriousness below the poem's "helplessness": Osgood's speaker insists that women lack all other rights except one—whim—then turns this natural "right" to her advantage and uses it to excuse her behavior.

Just as flowers signified emotions and thoughts that were only expressed covertly, gems were taken by many poets to signify the metaphorical use of language. Densely metaphorical prose was frequently described as "gemmy"; hence, they were associated with rhetoric in much the same way as flowers. Osgood makes this connection explicit in her poem, "The Flowers and Gems of Genius," whose otherwise forgettable rhymes and maudlin tone might encourage us to dismiss it as yet another attempt to rend unearned tears from the reader. The poem is interesting, however, when we consider that once again Osgood addresses the subject of why women write: suffering underlies their poetry, and "gems" and "flowers," that is, metaphors, hide its origins in pain.[33] In another poem, "The Language of Gems," Osgood alludes to the way the language of flowers has overtaken the older common cultural language of gems. Many of the gems she mentions are Dickinson's favorites—the ruby, chrysolite, emerald, opal, amethyst, and, most important, the diamond and pearl.[34] Like the conservative writers of floral dictionaries, however, Osgood encourages women to wear interior gems of virtue, rather than outward displays.

An anonymous article in the March 1861 issue of the *Atlantic Monthly* proves that Dickinson had contact with materials that would have strengthened her associations between jewel, flowers, and poetry. In "Diamonds and Pearls," the author recounts the story of a pearl diver who drowns in search of an exquisite specimen, then includes a poem to a lady who is begged not to wear another pearl, "the flower of gems."[35] The pearl typifies purity and virginity, and the lady in the poem would nullify the diver's sacrifice if she were to wear another. In a poem that Thomas Johnson dates from around the same year, Dickinson uses a similar subject to describe her attachment to Mary Bowles:

> Her breast is fit for pearls,
> But I was not a "Diver"—
> Her brow is fit for thrones
> But I have not a crest.
> Her heart is fit for *home*—
> I—a Sparrow—build there
> Sweet of twigs and twine
> My perennial nest.
> (J, 84)

The speaker establishes a ground for female attachment by distinguishing between the traditional offerings of men and her own gifts. Unlike the "'Diver'" who represents active exploration, or the noble who can offer her a "crest," she extols the nest of the lowly sparrow, who constructs a shelter out of remnants of more lofty constructions—"twigs and twine"—love and perseverance. Dickinson thus offers to build in Bowles's heart a "perennial" shelter, one that promises the return of love with each returning season, rather than a single tribute to her extolling the class or bravery of her male lover.

As this poem suggests, Dickinson found in another woman's heart a suitable place to build her "perennial nest," where she might cherish the sentiments and affections of those closest to her geographically and emotionally, just as she drew from the floral rhetoric of her era in order to create her own poetics of poverty. Her poems, like those of other nineteenth-century American women writers, were fashioned of domestic materials, threads, scraps, and other left-overs, yet they provided a virtual treasure house of images that she returned to again and again. She partook of the common rhetoric of flowers that created a distinctly "feminine" style in this period, yet in her poems sent to friends and relatives she expanded these images to play on the very limits of expression, to put into words emotions previously unspoken. Women in this period addressed one another in loving terms, and this erotic strain pervades especially Dickinson's relationship with her sister-in-law, Sue Gilbert.[36] As Carroll Smith-Rosenberg points out, demonstrative language had become stylized by the middle of the nineteenth century; not only homosexual but also heterosexual women learned to value sentimental, emotional relationships with other women, for they created an outlet for emotions otherwise repressed by Victorian society.[37]

Given her way of addressing Sue as "Darling" and "dear little bud" (*Letters* I, 209–10), Dickinson's affection for her sister-in-law reaches beyond merely stylized rhetoric and shows her profound love for her, which she expressed throughout her life and often imaged in floral tributes. During a stay in Cambridge about 1864 while under a physician's care for treatment of her eyes, the poet describes her love for Sue as central to her existence:

Sweet Sue—
There is no first, or last, in Forever—It is Centre, there, all the time—
To believe—is enough, and the right of supposing—
Take back that "Bee" and "Buttercup"—I have no Field for them, though for the Woman whom I prefer, Here is Festival—Where my Hands are cut, Her fingers will be found inside—
Our beautiful Neighbor "moved" in May—It leaves an Unimportance.
Take the Key to the Lily, now, and I will lock the Rose—

(*Letters* 2, 430)

Dickinson casts her imaginative encounter with Sue as a religious and super-vening event, a "Festival," in contrast to her lack of interest in the traditional forms of marriage and motherhood symbolized by the "Bee" and "Buttercup." Furthermore, she underscores the private communication between them through floral metaphors. As Smith argues, insofar as this letter uses floral images that carry the traditional associations about male-female courtship, Dickinson "appropriates the site of crucifying wounds to rewrite the biblical myth of human creation and tell a story about relations between two women who, like Adam and Eve, are flesh of one another's flesh, limbs of one another's limbs."[38] With its echo of the story of Saint Thomas who wished to verify Christ's resurrection through probing His wounds with his fingers, the description of her "cut" hands seems instead to suggest that Dickinson would subject herself to Sue's queries about the reality of her love. When one considers the vaginal and even masochistic associations of keeping open a wound, the passage suggests the twin pleasure and pain derived from her all-encompassing love for Sue. Given the traditional associations of the lily and rose, signifying purity and passionate love respectively, Dickinson may be suggesting that Sue should keep her virginity intact, while she "locks" up her own love away from the scrutiny of prying eyes.

Like other nineteenth-century American women, Dickinson frequently sent flowers to relatives and friends, often accompanying them with a letter or a poem. Yet in poems accompanying a flower, she collapses the distinction between poetry and flowers, thus enriching and complicating the act of self-presentation. Presented along with two more poems to Higginson after her first letter, this poem demonstrates a correspondence between flowers and poems:

> South Winds jostle them—
> Bumblebees come—
> Hover—hesitate—
> Drink, and are gone—
>
> Butterflies pause
> On their passage Cashmere—
> I—softly plucking,
> Present them here!
>
> (J, 86)

Sewall writes that this lyric "presented her poems to him as she frequently had presented them to others; that is, as flowers, things of nature that had come with no practice at all" (Sewall 2, 545). Surely, Dickinson was also drawing on the nineteenth-century critical discourse that portrayed women's poems as spontaneous and decorative outgrowths of a sensitive soul. For Dickinson, selecting and presenting her poems to Higginson was like culling flowers, since she presented them as unpremeditated, "found" things, thus diminishing her activity and responsibility. Yet their elusiveness is clear if we consider that they only sketch out an unmentioned topic. By omitting the actual subject of the poem—flowers—Dickinson only elliptically renders and "presents" them.

She instead depicts how the world acts on them: "South Winds," "Bumble-bees," and "Butterflies" appear for a moment or two and then vanish. The emphasis on movement and the fleeting passage of the wind, bees, and butterflies suggest that the object of description is constantly changing and that our perception of it relies on a partial view offered by the flowers' interaction with nature. Far from Amherst, "Cashmere" symbolizes transcendence; more importantly, its association with softness and lushness also parallels the speaker's act of "softly plucking" the flowers. When one considers that women's voices were commonly described as "soft" and low and that "plucking" suggests their musicality, the speaker implies that her poems are as elusive and reticent as her act of presenting them.

In sending letters to friends and relatives, Dickinson plays on the boundary between emotions that can be expressed and those that can only be implied. In a lyric sent with a flower to her cousin Eudocia Flynt in July 1862, she encodes a message about love and its ability to be articulated:

> All the letters I can write
> Are not fair as this—
> Syllables of Velvet—
> Sentences of Plush,
> Depths of Ruby, undrained,
> Hid, Lip, for Thee—
> Play it were a Humming Bird—
> And just sipped—me—
>
> (J, 334)

Previous interpretations of this poem have stressed its sexual innuendoes. In *Emily Dickinson's Imagery* (1979), Rebecca Patterson hints that Dickinson reverses the expected roles of writer and reader: by asking the reader to pretend that the flower is a hummingbird, she coyly sends a kiss.[39] But in conflating self and flower in the last two lines, she also conveys her wish to be kissed. Paula Bennett in *Emily Dickinson: Woman Poet* (1990) argues that it is an "invitation to cunnilingus."[40] Given the close association between female genitalia and flowers, Bennett's and Patterson's arguments are persuasive, yet such interpretations ignore the emphasis speech. The lyric flirts with the possibility of both telling and refraining from telling all about the speaker's feelings; it skirts the actual expression of desire by first anticipating the act, then casting it as a hypothetical exchange of emotions between two people, and finally relishing the supposed completion of the event. Contending that letters cannot compare in beauty to flowers, Dickinson describes the meaning hidden in the flower's "Syllables of Velvet" and "Sentences of Plush." Not only do "Velvet" and "Plush" recall the softness of human flesh, but they also point to the frequent characterization of women's voices as hushed. Likewise, "Depths of Ruby" may resemble the vagina, but it also suggests the mouth, organ of speech; these realms are as yet "undrained," promising the full expression of meaning. Yet they are also "Hid, Lip, for Thee": only to be relayed covertly to the recipient. Even the phrase "Play it were a Hummingbird," when "Play you were" or "Play I were" would have fit as easily, implies that the speaker is reluctant to name either herself or her interlocutor as participants in the exchange of emotion. In addition, the use of the subjunctive and past tense in the last two lines casts this event in the realm of fantasy and possibility rather than actual occurrence. Using the flower as a token of love, the speaker avoids actually confronting the recipient with the unrestrained expression of her feelings. Finally, she enlists the recipient's aid in encouraging her to imagine the full range of emotions represented by the hummingbird's act of tasting the nectar—with the sexual innuendo all the more fully developed as a result of including the reader's own imagination in the loving exchange proposed.

For Dickinson, letters as well as flowers prefigure death, since they disembody the speaker and rely on the absence of their interlocutor: "A Letter always feels to me like immortality because it is the mind alone without corporeal friend. Indebted in our talk to attitude and accent, there seems a spectral power in thought that walks alone—" (*Letters* 2, 460). Some lyrics treat the inability of flowers and letters to span the absence of loved ones:

> By a flower—By a letter—
> By a nimble love—
> If I weld the Rivet faster—
> Final fast—above—
>
> Never mind my breathless Anvil!
> Never mind Repose!
> Never mind the sooty faces
> Tugging at the Forge!
>
> (J, 109)

Sewall notes that about this time Dickinson was sending flowers and letters to both Samuel Bowles and his wife, Mary, and this lyric may well have recorded the sense of strain and uncertainty about Bowles's lukewarm response to the poems she submitted to the *Republican* (Sewall 2, 498). Nevertheless, the central issue is faith—the conviction that the ultimate *peine forte et dure* of death will result in heavenly "Repose." Like an infernal blacksmith, the speaker "weld[s] the Rivet faster—," until it is soldered permanently in heaven, yet the "sooty faces" which are "tugging at the Forge" suggest the underworld upon which immortality rests. For Dickinson, staving off the absence of friends and loved ones through an exchange of loving sentiments could only temporarily defer the threat of mortality.

Sent to Samuel Bowles in 1858, the following lyric declares that the speaker has little to do with tradition:

> If she had been the Mistletoe
> And I had been the Rose—
> How gay upon your table
> My velvet life to close—
> Since I am of the Druid,
> And she is of the dew—
> I'll deck Tradition's buttonhole—
> And send the Rose to you.
>
> (J, 44)

Cheryl Walker contends that, when read against the normative responses of other women, like Helen Hunt Jackson, to the publishing world, this lyric might well be addressing the whole generation (of which Bowles was one) that misjudged her poems.[41] Dickinson was perhaps also commenting on tradition and possibly marriage, when she juxtaposes midsummer and midwinter blooming plants with historical and traditional connotations. According to Osgood's floral dictionary, mistletoe signifies "I surmount all Difficulties" and rose, "Beauty."[42] Perhaps she was also hinting at her affection for Bowles, since the speaker says she would have found it "gay" to decorate Bowles's table, yet the belief that she might die there just as strongly rejects the possibility. Characterizing herself instead as "Mistletoe" and Mary as the "Rose" in contending that she is of the "Druid" and Mary is of the "dew," Dickinson prefers to adorn "Tradition's buttonhole" with her challenging and unexpected literary revisions. "Druid" carries religious connotations, for Celtic priests performed rituals to herald the spring every year. Such pagan rites perhaps involved sacrifice as well as gathering of plants, suggesting the martyrdom of women such as Mary to religious and cultural beliefs. Moreover, given that a buttonhole is normally adorned with a flower in man's dress, the speaker implies that she favors adopting a man's free life and rejects the decorative functions common for women. In comparing her older, wilder spirit to Mary's younger, gentler one, Dickinson relinquishes the desire to be bound by socially defined roles and embraces instead the act of redefining women's lives.

For Emily Dickinson, as for Thomas Wentworth Higginson and others of their generation, flowers are the harbingers of the divine, fragile symbols of God's presence. Higginson believed that nature's processes parallel the progress of human life. Yet his nature essays also betray the pantheistic leanings that characterized much writing of the age, and throughout they evoke the tragic sense that writers have failed to capture the poetry of nature. Just as Whitman received as a call-to-arms Emerson's injunction to find a new poet in

his essay "The Poet," Dickinson might well have taken Higginson's characterization of the state of nature writing in American letters as her *point d'appui*.
In his essay "My Out-Door Study," Higginson, an amateur naturalist, encourages an aspiring writer to mirror in his prose the complexity and detail of nature, to depict like a landscape artist the shadings and monochromatic changes
in the hues of the universe:

If one could learn to make his statements as firm and unswerving as the horizon-line,—
his continuity of thought as marked, yet as unbroken, as yonder soft gradations by
which the eye is lured upward from lake to wood, from wood to hill, from hill to heav-
ens,—what more bracing tonic could literary culture demand? (*ODP*, 255)

In studying the details of Higginson's essay, Dickinson must have sympa-
thized with his anti-sentimental call for a masculine and "bracing tonic" to literature, but she also was of an era that allied nature and piety with little self-
questioning in women's writing. "Beauty and fragrance are poured abroad
over the earth in blossoms of endless varieties, radiant evidences of the boundless benevolence of the Deity," writes Frances Sargent Osgood in the introduction to her *The Poetry of Flowers* (1848) [7]. Like the transcendentalists, Osgood sees evidence of God's plan rather than natural selection in the almost
infinite variety of species in the plant and animal worlds. Not surprisingly,
women might easily substitute for flowers in her description, since they perform the same function in uplifting the human soul and preserving virtue:
"They are made solely to gladden the heart of man, for a light to his eyes, for a
living inspiration of grace to his spirit, for a perpetual admiration" (7). Higginson's and Osgood's essays reflect the simultaneous reverence for and investigation into the processes of nature, which underlie Dickinson's subtle alter-
ation of the pious notions embedded in the discourse of flowers.
   One poem combines religious fervor with sexual ecstasy:

> Come slowly—Eden!
> Lips unused to Thee—
> Bashful—sip thy Jessamines—
> As the fainting Bee—
>
> Reaching late his flower,
> Round her chamber hums—
> Counts his nectars—
> Enters—and is lost in Balms.
>
> (J, 211)

According to the language of flowers, one of the meanings of Spanish "Jes-
samine" is sensuality, and Dickinson's fondness for jasmine was well known

by those who visited her conservatory. Undoubtedly aware of the meanings attached to this flower, Dickinson portrays the arrival in heaven as a sexual consummation, where the "fainting Bee," worn out from his flight, arrives late, and is "lost in Balms." In contrast to the niggardly act of counting his "nectars," the bee is "lost" in the fragrant, healing oil. Invoking the Garden of Eden, she uses the intrusion of death and sexuality in order to define heaven as a place where the pleasures of human life can be enjoyed.

In contrast, Dickinson elsewhere draws on the theme of deferred consummation in love to argue for the sanctity of heaven:

> Did the Harebell loose her girdle
> To the lover Bee
> Would the Bee the Harebell *hallow*
> Much as formerly?
>
> Did the "Paradise"—persuaded—
> Yield her moat of pearl—
> Would the Eden *be* an Eden,
> Or the Earl—an *Earl*?
>
> (J, 213)

According to the language of flowers, the harebell or bluebell signifies grief and submission, and it is the second meaning that illuminates for us both the poem's romantic narrative of a refusal to consummate a love affair and its larger theological implications. Rebecca Patterson notes that this lyric "describes the poet as a beleaguered flower or a pearl-moted Eden refusing to admit the impetuous bee-earl."[43] The speaker argues that the bluebell loses the respect of the bee if she gives in to his sexual advances. The Old Testament language of "hallow," "Paradise," and "Eden" hints that the poem fundamentally concerns the denial of earthly satisfaction in exchange for an afterlife. Indeed, if we take this poem in its theological context, then we can see that Dickinson retells the fall from the Garden of Eden in such a way that sexuality is a necessary precursor to salvation. Surely, Dickinson also had in mind the pearl as a sign of virginity as well as the "pearl of great price," the kingdom of God promised to the elect (Matthew 13:46).[44] "Paradise" derives etymologically from a garden, thus situating the poem's narrative within the botanical realm. The speaker seems to ask the question: if paradise were to yield the gate of "pearl," then wouldn't it lose all value as a utopia, as a threshold of new, unending, and never-tasted pleasures? Yet our awareness that Eve was "persuaded" suggests that within the garden a constitutive element existed that produced pain and sexuality as well as the opportunity for salvation, a *felix culpa*. Dickinson implies that the familiar courtship struggles between men and women—the characteristic pursuit and chase—precisely define women's and men's roles.

Another poem uses the image of the "Heart's Ease" or pansy to convey the speaker's faith and steadfastness in love:

> I'm the little "Heart's Ease"!
> I don't care for pouting skies!
> If the Butterfly delay
> Can I, therefore, stay away?
>
> If the Coward Bumble Bee
> In his chimney corner stay,
> I, must resoluter be!
> Who'll apologize for me?
>
> Dear, Old fashioned, little flower!
> Eden is old fashioned, too!
> Birds are antiquated fellows!
> Heaven does not change her blue.
> Nor will I, the little Heart's Ease—
> Ever be induced to do!
>
> (J, 176)

This lyric develops a narrative of loyalty and affectionate attachment which aptly draws on the pansy's most common significance according to the language of flowers: "Think of me."[45] According to a popular floral lexicon of 1869, "pansy" is a corruption of the French "pensez-a-moi," and it is fittingly also called "Heart's-ease, a sure result of a confident assurance that those whom we love are not unmindful of us when present or absent; not so unmindful, that is, to be careless and thoughtless of those claims we have upon their regard and affection."[46] Adapting the romantic associations of pansies as signifiers of a beloved's remembrance, Dickinson's lyric casts the theme of religious faith in secular terms and interprets Christ's injunction that he will remember in heaven those who were faithful to Him as the basis for the pansy's steadfastness in love. Indeed, if we place this poem in the context of others concerning the Garden of Eden, we see that Dickinson rejects the patristic tradition that portrayed women, specifically Eve, as treacherous, greedy creatures. The speaker's childlike voice counters God's righteous anger, his "pouting skies," and constructs a syllogism concerning the advent of heaven: why should the flower refrain from blooming even in the face of God's negligence? Indeed, the male bee's cowardice makes the pansy more resolute, as she realizes that no one will speak on her behalf an apologia, a formal argument of the type the Christian forefathers made in explanation of their faith. Characterizing Eden as an "old fashioned" place and birds as "antiquated fellows," the speaker of the third stanza affirms that the pansy's faith will be rewarded. Unlike the tempests to which flowers and human beings are subject on earth, heaven remains "blue," serene and loyal to its faithful. Not to be misled by fatuous arguments, as was Eve, the pansy asserts that she will never be "induced" to give up her faith—and by implication her constancy to her lover. Dickinson thus counters the characterization of women as flighty, moody creatures through her adaptation of floral rhetoric.

Another lyric sent to Susan Gilbert Dickinson about 1875 celebrates the arbutus for its human virtues of humility and constancy, but the flower's apparent meekness is actually a type of boldness:

> Pink—small—and punctual—
> Aromatic—low—
> Covert—in April—
> Candid—in May—
> Dear to the Moss—
> Known to the Knoll—
> Next to the Robin
> In every human Soul—
> Bold little Beauty
> Bedecked with thee
> Nature forswears
> Antiquity—
>
> (J, 1332)

Blooming for roughly two to three weeks from about the middle of April to the middle of May in northern New England, the arbutus or "pink" is one of the earliest and most ephemeral of spring flowers and hence a "punctual" herald of the season; its nature as a creeping vine also symbolizes its "low" and humble attitudes. In his essay "April Days," Higginson comments on the arbutus's potent fragrance: "the May-flower knows the hour, and becomes more fragrant in the darkness, so that one can then often find it in the woods without aid from the eye" (*ODP*, 227). Unlike the gentian, another of Dickinson's favorite flowers, the arbutus does not carry an awareness of death but undergoes instead a series of changes that play on one's expectations of women's roles. It begins the season as "Covert," then "Candid," until recognized and cherished both by plants and human beings alike.[47] Dickinson's use of the dactyl throughout underscores the plant's development and highlights its proximity to its neighbors: each plant and animal and their love of the arbutus are accentuated by each line's two primary stresses. Late in the season, however, this humble flower, like a woman primped for admiration, becomes a "Bold little Beauty." Adorned by this humble flower, nature is led to renounce its dull appearance and "forswears / Antiquity." Indeed, if we consider that "forswear" connotes perjury, we see that Dickinson shrewdly adopts one facet of stereotypically feminine behavior: women are untrustworthy and lead men to ruin. For Dickinson, as for Osgood, such flowers supported the normative Christian understanding of human character in which humility and lowliness are elevated, yet their images also masked their playful and questioning attitudes about the traditional modesty of women.

One of her most striking poems makes the lilac a symbol of the sunset, against which she tests the observer's faith in the existence of God:

> The Lilac is an ancient shrub
> But ancienter than that
> The Firmamental Lilac
> Upon the Hill tonight—
> The Sun subsiding on his Course
> Bequeathes this final Plant
> To Contemplation—not to Touch—
> The Flower of Occident.
> Of one Corolla is the West—
> The Calyx is the Earth—
> The Capsules burnished Seeds the Stars—
> The Scientist of Faith
> His research has but just begun—
> Above his synthesis
> The Flora unimpeachable
> To Time's Analysis—
> "Eye hath not seen" may possibly
> Be current with the Blind
> But let not Revelation
> By theses be detained—
>
> (J, 1241)

7] To spectacle, but not to Touch   20. detained]
profaned—

According to Osgood, lilacs trenchantly symbolize "First Emotion of Love," and their monochromatic hues of light violet to deep purple signified a naturally artistic visual spectacle: "The gradation of colour, from the purple bud to the almost colourless flowers, is the least charm of these beautiful groups, around which the light plays and produces a thousand shades, which, all blending together in the same teint, forms that matchless harmony which the painter despairs to imitate, and the most indifferent observer delights to behold."[48] For Dickinson, purple connotes royalty as well as the blood of Christ; when set against the horizon in the sunset, this color dramatically renders His death for the entire world to bear witness. If we consider the poem's floral imagery, moreover, we see that Dickinson uses highly technical and botanical details to describe a sunset as a flower with a precision hardly equalled in contemporary literature. We know that she was exposed to the botanical names and definitions of plants and flowers through one of her textbooks, Almira H. Lincoln's 1838 *Familiar Lectures on Botany*. Lincoln's volume has a copious listing of parts of flowers, including "calyx," "corolla," "seeds," "sepal," and "petals," all joined under the general category "organs of reproduction, or parts of fructification."[49] Like many scientific texts that sought to provide a Christian answer to the advances of science, Lincoln's book argues throughout that nature is simply the manifest thought of divinity and offers a lesson about the immortality of the soul: "How impressively is the reanimation of the vegetable world urged by St. Paul, as an argument to prove the *resurrection from the dead!* The same power, which from a dry and apparently dead seed, can bring forth a fresh and beautiful plant; can assuredly, from the ruins of our mortal frame, produce a new and glorious body, and unite it to the immortal spirit by ties never to be separated" (103). Dickinson believed such a revelation to be evident through the natural world, accessible in its minute detail rather than the theories of faith. "Corolla"—petals—derives from "crown," pointing to royalty as well as to Christ's crucifixion. While the "Capsules" or seedcases enclose "burnished Seeds" or the stars, the "Calyx" or sepal is the earth, an opposite and fitting receptacle for the play of light. This lyric conjoins religion and science to cast doubt on science as a method of spiritual investigation. "The Scientist of Faith," the spiritually doctrinaire, may conduct research on flowers, fragile and transient plants, but the "Flower of Occident" will continue "unimpeachable" forever. The Son-sun pun implies that Christ's final death and resurrection is mirrored in the heavenly display. Like the purely intellectual flower in Emerson's "The Rhodora," Dickinson's "Firmamental Lilac" is given "to Contemplation—not to Touch," and only the "Blind" in soul would need more empirical proof of God's existence in the face of such a magnificent display as the sunset: "But as it is written, Eye hath not seen, nor ear heard, neither have entered into the heart of man, the things which God hath prepared for them that love him" (1 Corinthians 2:9).

Dickinson was imbued with the sentimentalism and high "feeling" of the Victorians who were reluctant to name love and other emotions outright, instead preferring a language of gesture and innuendo. Emblems of fragile innocence, flowers bore religious and cultural significance. For Dickinson, flowers were tokens of sympathy that could be sent to friends and relatives, yet they also allowed the poet to revise many of the romantic positions women assumed in nineteenth-century verse. Among her floral poems, the lyrics depicting the rose and the daisy in particular show how Dickinson established a more mature poetic voice. Among many possible floral associations, the rose probably is the most significant, signifying in Osgood's lexicon "Beauty" and for other writers "Passionate Love." Osgood's "The Dying Rose-bud's Lament," for instance, characterizes a rosebud on the verge of blooming as an allegory of a woman's life:

> Ah me! ah! wo is me!
>   That I should perish now,
> With the dear sunlight just let in
> Upon my balmy brow!
>   (*The Poetry of Flowers*, 234)

This lyric captures the moment when the speaker, into whose young life love had just entered, is tragically dying. Dickinson laments, although more originally, the same fate of a nameless rose who embodies loyalty in the face of indifference:

> Nobody knows this little Rose—
> It might a pilgrim be
> Did I not take it from the ways
> And lift it up to thee.
> Only a Bee will miss it—
> Only a Butterfly,
> Hastening from far journey—
> On it's breast to lie—
> Only a Bird will wonder—
> Only a Breeze will sigh—
> Ah Little Rose—how easy
> For such as thee to die!
>
>   (J, 35)

As Martha Dickinson Bianchi comments in an unfinished manuscript from the 1930s, Dickinson's garden was replete with roses of various types and shades, including the tiny Greville roses, hedgehog roses, blush roses, cinnamon roses, and calico roses, whose exuberant variety parallels the range of significances contained within references to a single flower. Associated with marriage and brides, roses had a privileged place not only in their multiple plantings but also in their central placement draping the garden-house: "In my grandmother (Emily Dickinson's mother)'s day the same little flagstones led down to the garden path that ran through plots of blossom on either side, under honeysuckle arbors to a summer house thatched with roses."[50] For Dickinson, the continuance of flowers was a crucial aspect of their pleasure, as noted in Bianchi's recollection of the poet's words: "'In childhood I never sowed a seed unless it was a perennial—and that is why my garden lasts'" (2). Thus the rose's death in this poem seems all the more evocative of the anonymous "pilgrim," who lives out her life with little notice from others except members of the same mute, neglected sisterhood, with which Bianchi associated the poet:

"'I was reared in the garden, you know,' my Aunt Emily Dickinson wrote her cousin Louisa Norcross; her mother loving and living in it a hundred years ago. And as far as inheritance goes with people like that same little Emily, who grew up a poet and mystic, her mother's love of flowers came down to her intensified only by her own spirit sisterhood with every bird and flower" (1).

Another early lyric about the rose portrays nature worship as an alternative to Christianity:

> A sepal, petal, and a thorn
> Upon a common summer's morn—
> A flask of Dew—A Bee or two—
> A Breeze—a caper in the trees—
> And I'm a Rose!
>
> (J, 19)

Like many of her nature lyrics, this poem reveres nature as an alternative to Christianity. Yet the poem also defines the ease of transformation for the speaker, who, in a nearly heretical way, becomes herself the embodiment of Christ. The association of the Holy Trinity and the triple parts of a flower—"A sepal, petal, and a thorn"—suggests that a flower prompts her to take nature as her object of worship. Indeed, the speaker stresses the transformative aspects of her imagination: a "common summer's morn" can change quickly into something extraordinary with the addition of a "flask of Dew" and other natural elements. The end and internal rhyme, moreover, emphasize the ability to change one's character rapidly and at will, especially when such changes are considered in light of the unrhymed last line. The last line points to the performative aspect of the act of self-transformation: read as a declaration of her identity ("I'm a Rose!") and as a causal explanation for becoming a rose (the "And" implies "And *so* I'm a Rose!"), the speaker depends both on the creatures around her and on her own power of imagination to transform herself. Whereas Osgood's rose poems use flowers to situate women within a moral universe in which they are often victims, Dickinson's fanciful poem revels in the speaker's ability to change identity and so to evade the most traditional associations about the self, identity, and womanhood.

Osgood uses the language of flowers to conform to the dictates for women's expression, but her poems also raise the issue of what could and could not be said in women's verse—a central preoccupation of hers. In "The Daisy's Mistake," for example, she portrays a Daisy who arises before the spring to show off its beauty, despite the knowledge that it is too early. Like a debutante, the daisy is dressed "for the show" (l. 9); the other flowers resemble *grandes dames* ("The Cowslip is crown'd with a topaz tiara! / The Crocus is flaunting in golden attire" [ll. 21–22]). The daisy's vanity dooms her. Lured by the sunbeam and zephyr's promise of outings and flattery, she blooms early, even though "Instinct" counsels her to be cautious:

> Then a still, small voice, in the heart of the flower,
>   It was Instinct, whisper'd her, "Do not go!
> You had better be quiet, and wait your hour;
>   It isn't too late even yet for snow!"

> But the little field-blossom was foolish and vain,
>   And she said to herself, "What a belle I shall be!"
> So she sprang to the light, as she broke from her chain,
>   And gaily she cried, "I am free! I am free!"
>   (*Poems* [1850] 329, ll. 33–40)

This daisy, of course, is a representation of a woman, as we can tell both from Osgood's use of the feminine pronoun and from the mention of "Instinct," which was believed to be more strongly developed in women than in men. The "still, small voice" alludes to I Kings and affirms the popular belief that women's natures were more moral and pious than men's: "And after the earthquake a fire; but the Lord was not in the fire: and after the fire a still small voice" (19:12). Rather than "be quiet" as Instinct cautions her, she forsakes the feminine virtues of restraint and modesty, imagining herself too much a "belle" to hold back any longer.

"The Daisy's Mistake" turns quickly into a parable about careless girls. After the daisy symbolically frees herself by sprouting, the wind and the sun turn against her. Osgood's speaker remarks that the wind "scolded" (l. 52) the daisy as if she were a child—a girl "brought out" too soon into the social world. In fact, one might imagine a mother trotting out a similar story to convince her daughter that entering too hastily into fashionable society has dire consequences. Exiled from the ground, she laments her fate in the last stanza:

> And so she lay with her fair head low,
>   And mournfully sigh'd in her dying hour,
> "Ah! had I courageously answer'd 'No!'
>   I had now been safe in my native bower!"
>   (*Poems*, 331, ll. 57–60)

Through the allegory of the daisy, Osgood depicts women as vain and moody creatures who are punished for their faults, but she also hints that women have little choice in what happens to them. The logic by which the zephyr and sunbeam encourage the daisy to shine is a double bind: she is "either too bashful or lazy" (l. 32), not brave enough or too indolent, if she does not appear. Innocent or coquette, Osgood's daisy occupies an untenable position that constrains her behavior no matter how she reacts.

Dickinson also wrote a cluster of poems in which the speaker styles herself as "Daisy," and the innocence that this flower traditionally connotes allows her to develop a range of positions for speakers who challenge the traditional concept of womanhood. Floral images in her poems overturn accepted doctrines of romantic place, for they provided a fund of traditional associations about womanhood and courtship against which she could subtly question these commonly held values. In a lyric probably sent to Austin about 1859, Dickinson characterizes him as "Caesar" and herself a mild "Daisy," who seeks admission into his presence:

> Great Caesar! Condescend
> The Daisy, to receive,
> Gathered by Cato's Daughter,
> With your majestic leave!
> (J, 102)

If Dickinson meant to send a flower with this poem, she playfully anticipates and reverses the expectations Austin might have had for refusing to accept it. She styles herself as Portia, the daughter of Cato, a Roman general and enemy of Caesar. In Shakespeare's *Julius Caesar*, Portia, in order to discover the reason for her husband Brutus's moodiness, declares herself more resilient than the average woman: "Think you I am no stronger than my sex, / Being so fathered and so husbanded?" (II.i.296–97). By styling herself as a woman with a "man's mind" (II.iv.8), as does Portia, Dickinson both asserts her independence from traditional gender stereotypes and plays on the expectation that a woman would be received gallantly by any man. Given that Cato was Caesar's opponent, a flower as a gesture of reconciliation or love from his daughter would have been rejected. Yet a flower—or the woman who presents it— would undoubtedly be allowed into his presence. Furthermore, she may allude in a more radical way to herself as the descendent of a female tradition: just as Austin as Caesar is the offspring of a line of male rulers, she hails from "Cato's Daughter," an opposing and female line. Dickinson thus plays on the romantic conventions in this period that would have made it difficult for a man to reject a woman's offering, while she elevates her brother as Caesar and casts herself in the role of the lowly and modest Daisy.

Another poem describes an indolent housewife who is made fully indolent by death until she is laid in "Daisies" at the end:

> How many times these low feet staggered—
> Only the soldered mouth can tell—
> Try—can you stir the awful rivet—
> Try—can you lift the hasps of steel!

Stroke the cool forehead—hot so often—
Lift—if you care—the listless hair—
Handle the adamantine fingers
Never a thimble—more—shall wear—

Buzz the dull flies—on the chamber window—
Brave—shines the sun through the freckled pane—
Fearless—the cobweb swings from the ceiling—
Indolent Housewife—in Daisies—lain!

(J, 187)

The poem depicts a housewife who seems lazy in giving up her home duties, thus contrasting with poems by other nineteenth-century American women poets in which women happily perform their duties. By addressing the reader directly, Dickinson highlights not only the woman's life of domestic toil but also the reader's impotence in the face of death. In the first stanza, the woman's mouth, "soldered" in death, prevents her from betraying its secrets. Given the improvements in funerary technology in this period, the "awful rivet" and "hasps of steal" of the coffin aptly convey to the reader the permanence of death. Furthermore, the editors' substitution of "can" for "care" in the sixth line in the published version of her *Poems* (1890) lessens Dickinson's under-stated emphasis on the general indifference over the woman's welfare and instead points to the reader's incapacity to wrest the woman from death, despite the reader's pity.

In contrast to the reader's impotence, Dickinson reveals in the last stanza the woman's own seeming willful indolence. The room, grown untidy due to the housewife's disappearance, gradually reveals in its disarray the woman's assertiveness: although "dull flies" buzz, suggesting death and corruption, a cobweb "Fearless . . . swings" from the ceiling, and the sun shines "Brave" on the pane "freckled" with dirt. The characterization of the housewife as "Indo-lent" is twofold, meaning both lazy and, etymologically, free of pain. In contrast to the inability of the speaker to wrest the housewife from death, the housewife seems to languish in bed, rather than in a coffin. Unlike Osgood, who uses the daisy to teach a lesson of moral rectitude, Dickinson undercuts the expectation that women perform their duties with pious and uplifted spirits.

A subservient speaker prostrates herself before a powerful "Master," the sun, in the following lyric, but she seems to assert herself by approaching him:

The Daisy follows soft the Sun—
And when his golden walk is done—
Sits shily at his feet—
He—waking—finds the flower there—
Wherefore—Marauder—art thou here?
Because, Sir, love is sweet!

> We are the Flower—Thou the Sun!
> Forgive us, if as days decline—
> We nearer steal to Thee!
> Enamored of the parting West—
> The peace—the flight—the Amethyst—
> Night's possibility!
>
> (J, 106)

Echoing the "Sir" with which the heroine of Charlotte Brontë's *Jane Eyre* (1847) addressed her beloved Rochester, the Daisy adoringly follows the sun, shortening the distance between them. Rather than affirming her dependence on him, her approach asserts her presence, as she embraces "Night's possibility." As Margaret Homans also has shown, the daisy derives from "day's-eye," a term that reflects the phototropic flower's dependence on and resemblance to the sun.[51] A mere reflection of the sun's presence, the daisy is described by the third-person speaker as "soft" and "shy" in the first stanza, but she assumes the role of speaker in the second stanza and subtly reverses the expectations about the passive/feminine behavior of women in the eyes of the active/masculine "Sun." According to most floral dictionaries, the "Daisy" typifies innocence, and Badger writes in *Wild Flowers* that the daisy is "a troublesome weed to farmers, but a favorite flower with children" (v). Indeed, this flower represents naiveté and a childlike purity, which Dickinson adopted in many of her poems. Following the sun during his daily "golden walk," the daisy "shyly" turns her face toward his warmth in a way that seems to confirm her passivity. Yet his characterization of her as a "Marauder" correctly reveals that she also skillfully renegotiates her position and assertively presses forward, as "steal" hints in the second stanza. Adopting a generalized first-person plural speaker, Dickinson allows the reader and the flower to form an "I-Thou" relationship with the "sun," thus solidifying the daisy's relationship with the reader and setting both against the masculine sun. Echoing Isaac Watts's hymn "Nearer My God to Thee" in the daisy's plea for forgiveness, Dickinson not only rewrites a more conservative scriptural intention but also reverses the expected roles for men and women by allowing the daisy actively to approach her adored lover.

Although the path of the "enamored" daisy is toward the "parting West," the poem's final lines also point to a liberating "flight," an escape from the strictures of responsibility in the realm of "Night's possibility." "Enamored" of the sunset, the daisy desires a union with her lover that inevitably also promises death. Yet the night is also defined as the absence of the sun, a time when the daisy is freed from the expectations that keep her firmly in an inferior position during the day. Recalling the deepening purple of sunset, "Amethyst" connotes royalty and points to her accession to power. In approaching her lover, the sun, the daisy not only seems to approach him more assertively but also opens herself to a realm of freedom.

Floral imagery covertly expresses the physical side of Daisy's love:

> I tend my flowers for thee—
> Bright Absentee!
> My Fuschzia's Coral Seams
> Rip—while the Sower—dreams—
>
> Geraniums—tint—and spot—
> Low Daisies—dot—
> My Cactus—splits her Beard
> To show her throat—
>
> Carnations—tip their spice—
> And Bees—pick up—
> A Hyacinth—I hid—
> Puts out a Ruffled Head—
> And odors fall
> From flasks—so small—
> You marvel how they held—
>
> Globe Roses—break their satin flake—
> Upon my Garden floor—
> Yet—thou—not there—
> I had as lief they bore
> No Crimson—more—
>
> Thy flower—be gay—
> Her Lord—away!
> It ill becometh me—
> I'll dwell in Calyx—Gray—
> How modestly—alway—
> Thy Daisy—
> Draped for thee!

(J, 339)

Dickinson might have had Samuel Bowles in mind as the recipient of this poem, since Johnson dates it from "early 1862," approximately the same time that the Bowleses sailed to Europe (Sewall 2, 526). Indeed, the poem seems to be addressed to a lover who is gone, the "Bright Absentee," while the speaker's garden blossoms. The poem concerns the domestic and housewifely duties of tending a garden. In light of the opening reference to sewing, the pun on "Sower" alludes both to the planting of seeds in a garden and the stitching of a housewife. Yet, as it progresses, Dickinson describes the speaker's sexual desire through the floral images as revealed in a dream. It is appropriate that this poem takes a dream as the setting for expressing pent-up longings, unraveled and exposed in sleep. The "Coral Seams" might represent a panoply of bodily and social functions, which "rip" and are reconstructed during sleep. Might Dickinson have meant by "Coral Seams" the mouth's lips? the vagina's? or housewifely duties and tasks? Like Penelope's weaving, such tapestries are broken down every night and must be reconfigured during the day.

Both the colors and the physical descriptions of the flowers point to the speaker's sexual desire. Dickinson uses a variety of flowers in an almost hallucinatory way, revealing the speaker's concern with self-exposure and gender inversion. Nearly all the flowers are red or pink and suggest some sort of sexual violation: geraniums "tint—and spot"; the cactus "splits"; carnations empty their "spice"; a hyacinth exposes a "Ruffled Head." Despite the many references to pollination and growth, the strength of the speaker's desire surprises even her, as she "marvel[s]" at the volume of perfume held by such small "flasks." Of course, odors might refer to bodily smells as well as to perfume, and even the gender confusion of "My Cactus—splits her Beard" suggests that, in the throes of the dream, the differences between men and women are conflated.

Finally, the speaker's remark in the last stanza that she "modestly" waits for her lover in nunlike "Calyx—Gray—" ironically understates the vivid, impressionistic description of the garden. Dickinson's use of archaisms such as "lief" and "becometh" associate the speaker with an old-fashioned modesty that is perhaps required by the "Lord" who may return. The speaker seems to be saying: why should my garden bloom and I be happy while my lover is absent? Yet she only pretends to shroud herself in somber hues by day, since her thoughts in sleep reveal an impatient and surging passion, contradicting the modesty and innocence that the daisy connotes.

By considering a sentimental poet like Osgood, we can see that Dickinson absorbed the conventions of nineteenth-century American women's writing, while transforming these norms in her own idiosyncratic verse. Like more conservative women writers, she sent flowers to relatives and friends in order to commemorate holidays or as tokens of friendship. Yet she complicates this tradition by writing poems that not only present flowers to a recipient but also play on the common association of poetry and flowers. Far from the formulaic rendering of feelings by Osgood and other sentimental poets, Dickinson's poems transmute floral meanings in order to comment more profoundly on change, mortality, and the afterlife. In addition, she transforms the sending of flowers to a loved one from a simple social gesture to a more significant act of self-presentation. Recovering nineteenth-century American social and literary traditions, such as the language of flowers, allows us to see Dickinson's reliance on the genteel conventions of her age as well as her originality as a poet.

Chapter 6

"Fame of Myself"

Dickinson, Jackson, and the Question
of Female Authorship

A very subtle analysis upon a very few truths pushed to their extreme
application; the morbidness, improbability, quaintness and shrinking which
would result from a lack of the sun's ripening influences, like a lily grown in
a cellar. All these lead us to the conclusion that the author may be a person
long shut out from the world and living in a world of her own; that perhaps
she is a recluse.

—"Who Is Saxe Holm?" (1878)[1]

Travel increaseth a man. But, next to going bodily, is to wander, through the
magical power of print, whithersoever one will. A good book of travel is a
summer's vacation . . . Every one is in itself a gem. Brilliant, chatty, full of
fine feminine taste and feeling,—just the letters one waits impatiently to get,
and reads till the paper has been fingered through. It has been often
observed that women are the best correspondents. We cannot analyze the
peculiar charm of their letters. It is a part of that mysterious *personnel*
which is the atmosphere of every womanly woman.

—Anonymous review of Helen Hunt Jackson, *Bits of Travel*[2]

Most she touched me by her muteness—
Most she won me by the way
She presented her small figure—
Plea itself—for Charity—

Were a Crumb my whole possession—
Were there famine in the land—
Were it my resource from starving—
Could I such a plea withstand—

Not upon her knee to thank me
Sank this Beggar from the Sky—
But the Crumb partook—departed—
And returned On High—

I supposed—when sudden
Such a Praise began
'Twas as Space sat singing
To herself—and men—

'Twas the Winged Beggar—
Afterward I learned
To her Benefactor
Making Gratitude
—Emily Dickinson (J, 760)

8. plea] face   10. this] the   20. Making] paying

In a letter of March 1885 to Helen Hunt Jackson, Dickinson expressed her admiration of her correspondent's novel: "Pity me, however, I have finished *Ramona*. Would that like Shakesphere, it were just published!" (*Letters* 3, 866). Much as for her Shakespeare was "just published," Dickinson strove for eternal fame that would keep her poetry perpetually alive. Some critics have ascribed Dickinson's high praise of Jackson to flattery or to the poet's own misguided taste for sentimental writing.[3] Yet that Dickinson read and enjoyed much women's verse, including Jackson's, suggests that she had wide-ranging and eclectic tastes. In an 1871 letter to Thomas Wentworth Higginson, she remarks on the eternal quality of Jackson's writing: "Mrs. Hunt's Poems are stronger than any written by Women since Mrs—Browning, with the exception of Mrs Lewes—but truth like Ancestor's Brocades can stand alone—" (*Letters* 2, 491).

Although Dickinson began her correspondence with Jackson about 1868, when she was already a fully mature poet, she responded almost as intensely to her as she had to Higginson after the publication of his essay, "A Letter to a Young Contributor," in the *Atlantic Monthly*, seven years earlier. If Higginson was Dickinson's literary counselor and aesthetic soul mate, Jackson was a lively correspondent and appreciative reader who demonstrated both the pleasures and perils of entering the literary marketplace. Most importantly, Jackson was the only contemporary of Dickinson's to recognize her greatness, and her appreciative inquiries about the status of her friend's "portfolios" probably encouraged Dickinson to meet with her twice and to correspond with her for the rest of her life (*Letters* 3, 841). Jackson thus characterized her friend's verse as part of the sentimental tradition of women's verse writing, and even her most thoughtful support carried with it the belief that it was a woman's responsibility to perform acts of selfless charity, as she remarks sententiously to Dickinson in mid-May, 1879: "To be busy is the best help I know of, for all sorts of discomforts" (*Letters* 2, 639).

Even though she praised Jackson's talent, Dickinson refuted both the commercialism of the popular press and the stereotypical role to which women writers were expected to conform. The duality of a nineteenth-century American woman writer's life—personal freedom and professional constraints, radical poetry and conservative beliefs—was nowhere more present than in Jackson's. To extrapolate from one of Dickinson's mid-1860s poems to Jackson's life, Jackson embodied the "Winged Beggar" whose demure, pious, and even mute approach enlisted "Charity" from editors and critics, only to allow her to sing more loudly "To herself—and men—" (J, 760). Like her views on home and the family, her correspondence with Dickinson and with her editor, Thomas Bailey Aldrich, reveals a complex relation between what she wished to express and what she was able to say according to the prescribed modes of speaking for women writers. Moreover, her *Verses* (1870), which acquired considerable praise from critics and other writers, resembles other women's works both in its use of initials to identify the author and in its physical design with emblems (located at the beginning and end of the volume and directly over the table of contents) representing Christian faith, secular love, and the decorative arts. Nevertheless, her poems often undercut the accepted sentiment of women's writing, and thus clash with the more conservative illustrations for her book. To examine Jackson and Dickinson's correspondence and poems, then, gives us a privileged glimpse into not only the workings of the publishing world for nineteenth-century American women, but also the reasons why Dickinson chose not to exchange the "futile Diadem" of worldly renown for a longer lasting fame:

> Fame of Myself, to justify,
> All other Plaudit be
> Superfluous—An Incense
> Beyond Necessity—
>
> Fame of Myself to lack—Although
> My Name be else Supreme—
> This were an Honor honorless—
> A futile Diadem—
>
> (J, 713)

Jackson was one of few contemporaries to recognize Dickinson's talent, yet she was often unable to appreciate her meaning, a short-sightedness that must have confirmed Dickinson's belief that worldly fame was not to be. Around 1868, while Jackson summered in Amherst, they reestablished contact, and their subsequent correspondence lasted the rest of their lives. After Jackson married her second husband, William Sharpless Jackson, while vacationing in New Hampshire in 1875, Dickinson sent her wedding congratulations in the form of a one-line note and a cryptic poem:

Have I a word but joy?
                E. Dickinson

                Who fleeing from the Spring
                The Spring avenging fling
                To Dooms of Balm—
                      (*Letters* 2, 544)

Despite saying that she has only "a word," she feels the impact and qualifies the idea of marriage in the three-line lyric that follows. In fact, the poem might as easily concern Dickinson, as the positioning of her name above the poem implies. The seasons appear to "avenge" themselves on the poet, who avoids the rites of spring with their associations of marriage. Surely, the paradoxical expression "Dooms of Balm" suggests both the detriments and advantages of being single: she is condemned to life without a husband, yet she is promised the solace of poetry. Jackson responded by sending back the poem with a request for "interpretations" (*Letters* 2, 544); Dickinson withheld it, perhaps because she lacked confidence that Jackson was her best audience. Sensing that Dickinson had momentarily withdrawn her trust, Jackson asks her to write again "when it did not bore you" (*Letters* 2, 545); she further notes that she has "a little manuscript volume with a few of your verses in it," a common habit among nineteenth-century readers who transcribed or clipped and pasted their favorite verses into a book (*Letters* 2, 545). In one of her most far-reaching and noteworthy compliments in 1868, however, she adds that "You are a great poet—and it is wrong to the day you live in, that you will not sing aloud. When you are what men call dead, you will be sorry you were so stingy" (*Letters* 2, 545).

Jackson also made the mistake of thinking she could draw Dickinson into the type of social existence she had shared with other friends: "I hope some day, somewhere I shall find you in a spot where we can know each other" (*Letters* 2, 545). Higginson, too, had written her in 1869 asking her to come down to Boston, because "All ladies do" (*Letters* 2, 462); he characterized her as a literary "lady" author of the type that populated Boston and the Northeast. To his credit, however, he also recognized the originality and acuteness of her mind, which isolated her from her contemporaries:

It is hard [for me] to understand how you can live s[o alo]ne, with thoughts of such a [quali]ty coming up in you & even the companionship of your dog withdrawn. Yet it isolates one anywhere to think beyond a certain point or have such luminous flashes as come to you—so perhaps the place does not make much difference. (*Letters* 2, 461)

The physical and social existences which Higginson and Jackson lived were outside of her domain, and despite their wish to find a common ground for meeting their friend, her originality and intense privacy separated her from others.

Although she made one of the only serious attempts to convince Dickinson to publish, Jackson, like others of her generation, preferred the sonorous rhythms and discursive phrasing of the Victorians to the short, clipped lines of Dickinson's own more metaphysical poems. Jackson included in one of her letters a circular for the "No Name Series" to be issued by Roberts Brothers, her publisher, in hopes of convincing Dickinson to publish. As was so often the case, Dickinson turned to Higginson for advice in the matter, thus avoiding responsibility herself and deferring to his opinion. She mentioned that she told Jackson she was "incapable" of submitting her poems and begs him to "give me a note saying you disapproved it" (*Letters* 2, 563). Eventually, upon rereading Dickinson's verses, Jackson calls them "more clear than I thought they were" and agrees that "Part of the dimness must have been in me" (*Letters* 2, 565). Yet she remarks that "I like your simplest and [most direct] lines best" (*Letters* 2, 565), and she thanks her for writing "such plain letters" (*Letters* 2, 564). More complex than Jackson's poetry, Dickinson's lyrics struck her as obscure, much as the poet's life seemed abnormal. She notes the originality of Dickinson's writing and her life:

[I feel] as if I ha[d been] very imperti[nent that] day [in] speaking to you [as] I did,— accusing you of living away from the sunlight—and [telling] you that you [looke]d ill, which is a [mor]tal piece of ill[ness] at all times, but re[al]ly you look[ed] so [wh]ite and [mo]th-like[!] Your [hand] felt [l]ike such a wisp in mine that you frigh[tened] me. I felt [li]ke a [gr]eat ox [tal]king to a wh[ite] moth, and beg[ging] it to come and [eat] grass with me [to] see if it could not turn itself into beef! (*Letters* 2, 565)

Jackson uses language of transformation and of flowers and butterflies, so common in descriptions of women's verse, when she notes that Dickinson was "living away from the sunlight" and appeared "[mo]th-like." While Jackson is aware of Dickinson's originality, she also acknowledges implicitly the need for women writers to become "beef" to be consumed by others. As Betsy Erkkila argues, Jackson conformed to the dictates of the literary marketplace and compromised her artistic vision: "For all her national reputation as one of the most acclaimed writers of her time, Jackson was also in some sense both the product and the victim of popular taste."[4]

Despite Jackson's awareness of her friend's originality, she placed her in the "portfolio" tradition of other sentimental female writers. Jackson assumes that writers, perhaps especially women, have a duty to "sing aloud" for the good of others. Shortly before her death, Jackson thought of herself as part of an era that was fast becoming legendary: "It is a cruel wrong to your 'day & generation' that you will not give them light" (*Letters* 3, 841). Concerned with the status of Dickinson's works after her death, she offers to be the custodian of the fame that Dickinson so long and faithfully eluded: "If such a thing should happen as that I should outlive you, I wish you would make me your literary legatee & executor" (*Letters* 3, 841). Dickinson pointedly refused to answer. Jackson fully explains in this letter the ethic of feminine helpfulness that underlies her wish to see Dickinson publish:

Surely, after you are what is called 'dead,' you will be willing that the poor ghosts you have left behind, should be cheered and pleased by your verses, will you not?—You ought to be.—I do not think we have a right to with hold from the world a word or a thought any more than a *deed*, which might help a single soul. (*Letters* 3, 841–42)

For Jackson, a woman writer is duty bound to aid others with her words, much as any woman is expected to help others with her "deeds." Even the sentimentality of "might help a single soul" points to her belief that women were responsible for the moral welfare of others. Far from Dickinson's contention that Jackson's poetry resembles "truth," Jackson's argument as to why her friend should put forth her works in print adheres to the doctrine of feminine helpfulness.

Although a highly successful poet, American Indian activist, travel writer, and novelist, Jackson expresses regret over exposing her work in print, a common remonstration in prefaces by women writers of this period. In a letter to Abigail May responding to a request that she speak before the New England Women's Club in the fall of 1873, for example, she writes that "I cannot conceive of, any emergency which could screw up my courage to the point necessary to enable me to 'make remarks,' or to read a paper of my own"; she adds, concerning her decision to publish, "It is often almost more than I can bear the slight publicity which I have brought upon myself by saying,—behind the shelter of initials, and in the crowded obscurity of print—a few of the things I have felt deeply."[5]

No mere modest gesture, Jackson's engagement in social issues, especially the American Indian's plight, as well as in her career and an energetic social life, would seem to contradict her reluctance to voice her opinions publicly.[6] From about 1881 to 1883, she was organizing the background information she needed in order to write *Ramona*, and she published several articles in support of the Indian cause during this time, such as "Father Junípero and His Work" and "The Present Condition of Mission Indians in Southern California."[7] Such political sentiments were also genuinely felt and commonly expressed by her counterparts. Women writers supported temperance, abolition, suffrage, and revivalism, among other movements, and their political activism loosened the bonds of social conformity. Many worked toward social change, speaking publicly, lobbying legislators, holding office in male organizations, and crossing the barriers of race in the service of a higher cause, but at the same time they accepted the conventional view that women should embody the virtues of restraint and modesty. According to social historian Carroll Smith-Rosenberg, "It is significant that most of these women remained rooted within a bourgeois world of marriage and motherhood."[8]

Despite her interest in bettering the world, Jackson adhered to the values of family and home. In the same 1873 letter to Abigail May, she writes:

> But I thank you most cordially—and through you, the committee—for this invitation. It touches me to the heart, and gratifies me more than I can say that I should have been thought worthy to speak on that sacredest of all themes—"Little children." I should disagree with you utterly in regarding "Home and private life" as a "narrower field" than those you have previously discussed.—It is to me the one sublime point, from which the lever rightly poised, can heave the whole world:—the only point from which the world ever will be moved. All these reforms seem to me trivial, dilatory, ineffective. Give the world one generation of good just, loving, clear headed, well educated mothers,—and the men and the measures which the world needs, will follow. (A-134, May-Goddard Collection)

Like Lydia Huntley Sigourney and other nineteenth-century American women poets, Jackson was conservative about the place of women in the home and their role as protectors and teachers of their children. What might be taken for two competing interests—women can struggle to achieve real change in society or they can nurture their husbands and children in the home—are reconcilable. Bringing up children for the larger good is the "lever" by which power relationships are destabilized and new social bonds established. Although "men and the measures" may ultimately accomplish the work, Jackson clearly believed that women were the source of monumental change by educating, prodding, and guiding their children. According to Susan Coultrap-McQuin, Jackson's belief in feminine helpfulness and the desire to effect social change was not contradictory: "Though True Womanhood and individuality seem almost wholly contradictory to our contemporary thinking, for Jackson they were not. In fact, her paradoxical beliefs in True Womanhood and in her expression of individuality seem to have given her an effective approach to a marketplace in transition from the ideals of the Gentleman Publisher to those of the Businessman Publisher" (150).

Jackson's poetry received high recommendation in the literary world.

Fig. 5. Emblem, Helen Hunt Jackson's ("H.H.") *Verses* (Boston: Roberts Brothers, 1875), viii.

Emerson included five of her poems in his anthology, *Parnassus* (1874), and writes in the preface that her poems "have rare merit of thought and expression, and will reward the reader for the careful attention which they require."[9] In his journals, he further praises her for "originality, elegance, and compression" and especially admires her "Thought" and "Ariadne's Farewell."[10] According to one anecdote, he was asked to name the best woman poet in America and replied, "Jackson," adding "Why not drop the word *woman*?"[11] The abstractness and mythological references of her poems must have appealed to him, and the emblems that frame the text of her 1875 *Verses* reflect the dichotomy of holy and secular love, an issue with which Emerson was himself concerned. Two illustrations immediately following the preface—a hand holding grapes above a chalice (which appears directly below the table of contents) and a triptych of Christ with the shepherds and Magi (placed above the first poem of the volume, "A Christmas Symphony")—have Christian resonances: one recalls the sacramental wine, which, in the Christian community, becomes the blood of Christ through the rite of transubstantiation, and the other evokes the birth of Christ, whose passion and death appear symbolically in the wreath of thorns surrounding the Christ Child's picture (Figs. 5 and 6). Yet the figure also evokes wine as a source of forgetfulness and love, since "Vintage" is listed in the table of contents directly above the illustration. Rather than invoking Christian themes, "Vintage" associates wine with a mythic place:

> Before the time of grapes,
>   While they altered in the sun,
> And out of the time of grapes,
>   When the vintage songs were done,—
>
> From secret southern spot,
>   Whose warmth not a mortal knew;
> From shades which the sun forgot,
>   Or could not struggle through[12]

Emerson's "Bacchus" also describes an oxymoronic "remembering wine" that issues from a secret place:

Fig. 6. Illustration, Helen Hunt Jackson's ("H.H.") *Verses* (Boston: Roberts Brothers, 1875), 9.

> Bring me wine, but wine which never grew
> In the belly of the grape,
> Or grew on vine whose tap-roots, reaching through
> Under the Andes to the Cape,
> Suffer no savor of the earth to scape.[13]

While Emerson uses wine to revive inner-consciousness, Jackson refers to wine as a symbol of a woman's love:

> Soul of my soul, the shapes
>   Of the things of earth are one;
> Rememberest thou the grapes
>   I brought thee in the sun?
>
> And darest thou still drink
>   Wine stronger than seal can sign?
> And smilest thou to think
>   Eternal vintage thine?
>   (*Verses*, 190, ll. 13–20)

"Wine stronger than seal can sign" alludes to the Song of Solomon—"Set me as a seal upon thine heart, as a seal upon thine arm: for love is strong as death; jealousy is cruel as the grave" (8:6)—and possibly to Revelations, where a book is "sealed with seven seals" until the Lamb of God reveals it to human beings (5:1). Despite its biblical context, Jackson's verse emphasizes the secularity of love and the arbitrariness of its external signs. "Soul of my soul" suggests that her outlook is romantic rather than religious, and "the shapes / Of the things of the earth are one" implies that it is far from everlasting. Love is perilous, and when based on "things of the earth," doomed to fail. Finally, the series of rhetorical questions ending the poem underscores the ambiguity of love's outcome: the beloved's sureness of "Eternal vintage" may be based on the "sign" of love and its covenant, but that sign may be misinterpreted, much as the "shapes" of earth are delusive and based on appearances.

Other reviewers considered her a poet of genuine vision and insight, yet their assessments conform to the standards by which women's poems were commonly judged. Higginson praised her work for "an intensity of feeling un-surpassed by any woman since Elizabeth Barrett Browning"; nonetheless, he disliked their compactness and their metrical roughness—features that now make Jackson seem modern.[14] Similarly, an anonymous reviewer for *The Nation* remarked an "intenseness of feeling, or rather a tension of feeling, which is incompatible with prettiness."[15] By and large, critics disliked the metrical ir-regularity that conflicted with the sheer "prettiness" of her poems, although they praised her, as did the writer of this review, for "evidences of poetical feeling" and genuine insight (183). Underlying the vague criticisms of these reviewers was the belief that the best women's poetry was sweet and "smooth," while the worst was intellectual and "harsh": "The merely pretty things that may be found in it are very few, for, in truth, H.H. appears to be not only too ready to use—perhaps as seeming more intellectual—somewhat involved and harsh modes of expressing her thoughts and feelings" (183–84). Yet her enor-mous popularity was undeniable. Magazines so valued her work that Josiah Gilbert Holland, a friend of the Dickinsons and the editor of *Scribner's Magazine* and *The Century*, reputedly considered giving over one number entirely to Jackson's writing, a proposal that was finally dismissed only because it might have been thought too sensational.[16]

Many of Jackson's *Verses* (1870) look forward to the imagistic concision and literary experimentation of early Modernist writers such as Amy Lowell and H.D. Often employing the theme of Christian piety and self-denial com-mon among female poets, Jackson's didacticism and moralizing are worthy of other, less inventive sentimental women writers. Yet she differs from other prominent women poets, especially those who wrote in the early to middle part of the century, in depicting moral irresolution and criticizing women's do-mestic alienation. Her poetry displays more realism than those of many of her contemporaries, perhaps prompting critics to disparage her poems as too rough and unmusical. In the era immediately preceding the literary experimentation and the changing attitudes toward women's lives of the 1880s and 1890s, Jack-son registers a discomfort with social norms, both in her conflicted relation-ship with her editors and in her frequently troubled attempts to resolve ques-tions of faith or a woman's place.

First published in 1870 and subsequently reissued with additions, Helen Hunt Jackson's 1875 *Verses* and 1910 *Poems* contain illustrations that reaffirm the dictates of women's poetic expression.[17] Her *Verses* resembles other women's works both in its use of initials to identify the author and in its design, with emblems representing Christian faith, secular love, and the decorative arts (located at the beginning and end of the volume and directly over the table of contents). The title page of the 1875 edition shows a woman spinning thread, and this image reappears in the second poem, "Spinning," whose "blind spinner" valiantly confirms the speaker's faith against the passage of time and the blindness of fate. Placed at the head of this volume, the illustration hints that the female poet, like Jackson, "spins" out words for money. For a woman poet, writing amounted to a type of domestic endeavor. A "spinster" was a woman who remained single beyond the traditional age for marrying, perhaps employing herself by making thread for others. "Distaff" refers to the staff on which flax, thread, or yarn is wound and alludes to feminine toil. Jackson was unmarried when she wrote this volume, and although she was not husbandless all of her life, she supported herself with the earnings from her book, much as a spinster might have lived on the wages she earned for her domestic labor.

Preceded by "A Christmas Symphony," a poem that conventionally assures the reader of an afterlife by celebrating Christ's birth, "Spinning" provides a counterpoint to the normative Christian standpoint and prepares us for the sets of opposites that form the rest of the book. Similar to Emerson's "Days," which depicts "hypocritic" time as a series of female figures, who are "Muffled and dumb like barefoot dervishes,"[18] "Spinning" depicts a speaker who, like a "blind spinner," passes her days in work without a definite sense of purpose or direction.

> Like a blind spinner in the sun,
>   I tread my days;
> I know that all the threads will run
>   Appointed ways;
> I know each day will bring its task,
> And, being blind, no more I ask.
>   (*Verses*, 14, ll. 1–6)

The spinner here resembles Clotho, who spins the thread of human life, one of the Fates, the trio of goddesses in classical mythology who were believed to determine the span of each human life. The speaker states that, "being blind," she resigns herself to the inevitable progression of "appointed" tasks in life. Although this poem contends that one should resign oneself with Christian faith to a new life in heaven, its invocation of a figure from Greek mythology supplements the purely Christian symbolism. The poem seeks to allay suffering with the promise of an afterlife, but, unlike other women's poetry, it diverges from the formulaic rendering of life as fulfilling and untroubled by combining Greek myth and Christian symbolism.

The aura of genteel sentiment that characterized women's poetry and lives did not prevent Jackson from pursuing her interests as a professional. Although she began writing as an outlet for her grief over her son Rennie's death, she considered publishing a way of making money: "I don't write for money, I write for love—I *print* for money."[19] Her life appeared to be full of the "secret sorrows" commonly thought to form the basis for women's poetry throughout most of the nineteenth century. Women were thought particularly capable of articulating these pitiful events, which more often than not included the deaths of their children. In particular, Jackson's very first published poems, "The Key to the Casket" and "Lifted Over," profited by a lucrative and growing call for child elegies, which provided consolation to the vast number of families who lost infants and young children.

For both Dickinson and Jackson, giving up poems to charities proved to be a problem, for they were requested with very little discretion. Jackson was judicious throughout her career in choosing where and when she would be published. Anxious to let only her best lyrics represent her in print, she was reluctant to send out poems for no pay to charitable causes. "A woman wrote asking me to send her a poem on the Arbutus for a subscriber's book—or chromo gallery or something I forget what," she wrote to Aldrich in 1884. "It is odd how people that would not dream of writing and asking you for $20—will calmly ask you to write a poem to order . . . I sat down & wrote three poems on the Arbutus! The first and second seemed to me quite too good for charity poems, & I meanly kept them, and sent her the worst!—" (23 February 1884; Aldrich, Ms. 2530). The genteel conventions of authorship placed the female writer in a double bind: women were supposed to contribute poems gratis to charities. Jackson wished to receive full pay for her poems, and she hoped to control where and when the best would appear, an important consideration for a poet who wished to present herself to the public in the best light possible.

Dickinson also resisted sending poems to a charity, although she probably saw the request as an imposition more on her privacy than on her pocketbook. The request was probably made by Joseph K. Chickering, a professor of English at Amherst College, who sought support for the Annual Sale of the Mission Circle, an event designed to aid children in India and Far Eastern countries. She wrote to Higginson several times concerning the proposed submission. The first time, in 1880, she tells him that "I have promised three Hymns to a charity, but without your approval could not give them—" (*Letters* 3, 680); she further notes "They are short and I could write them quite plainly" and asks if he would tell her if they are "faithful." But does she mean "faithful" to her own conception or sufficiently pious? Perhaps she was responding to a request for a poem on a religious topic, an appropriate choice considering that the charity was the Mission Circle, as evidenced also by her next letter to Higginson: "Grateful for the kindness, I enclose those you allow, adding a fourth, lest one of them you might think profane—" (*Letters* 3, 681). Of the four she included, the poem beginning "Dare you see a Soul *at the White Heat?*" (J, 365) might most easily have offended strictly orthodox sensibilities. In the letter's conclusion, she hints again at the religious dictates to which she felt these poems had to conform and to the almost pious "conviction" Higginson's criticism would engender in her: "Reprove them as your own—To punish them would please me, because the fine conviction I had so true a friend—" (*Letters* 3, 681). Rather than point to the ostensibly religious value of these poems, she commends Higginson for his devotion to her. For Dickinson, Higginson's criticisms would both prove his friendship and confirm the sanctity that she believed true poetry endows on the poet.

Although she expresses gratitude for Higginson's desire to help her and states that she will follow his advice "implicitly" (*Letters* 3, 681), her lukewarm response shows that she was not attracted to giving her poems to charity. In fact, she considered refusing Chickering's request, since it was impersonally delivered: "The one who asked me for the Lines, I had never seen—He spoke of 'a Charity'—I refused but did not inquire—He again earnestly urged, on the ground that in that way I might 'aid unfortunate Children'—The name of 'Child' was a snare to me and I hesitated—Choosing my most rudimentary, and without criterion, I inquired of you—" (*Letters* 3, 681–82). Rather than object to sending her poems to charity on the basis of a bad business venture, as Jackson did, Dickinson thought any submission of her poems as a kind of "publishing," a violation of the soul. Whereas in "Self-Reliance," Emerson condemns the "foolish philanthropist" for giving to "the thousandfold Relief Societies" when "there is a class of persons to whom by all spiritual affinity I am bought and sold,"[20] nineteenth-century American women were willing to submit poems for publication in service of a higher cause. In an era when female piety and charity were one, Dickinson might well have felt that Chickering was both intruding on her privacy as well as taking advantage of women's selflessness, a dilemma she finally resolved by deciding not to make her poems public.

In Jackson's *Poems* (1910), an illustration of the author departs from the presentation of women's sentimental verse writing. Judging from the motifs, illustrations, and designs, the editors clearly wished to place Jackson's volume in the Victorian era, but her portrait reveals a realistic and modern sensibility. The frontispiece displays Jackson's picture with her signature directly below, a common adornment that verifies the identity of the author. Although these portraits appear in works authored by men as well as women, the pictures in women's anthologies or collections of verse by a single author frequently are aimed at embodying the most prized female virtues. Frances Sargent Osgood's portrait in *Poems* (1850), for instance, is preceded by the illustrations of two figures from the poems—Zuleika, an Arabian maiden holding a rose, and an infant girl balancing a butterfly on her finger—both of which convey the

Fig. 7. Frontispiece, Helen Jackson's *Poems* (Boston: Little, Brown, and Company, 1910). "H.H." to ED: "What portfolios of verses you must have."

virtues of feminine innocence and purity. Osgood's portrait appears immediately before the poems along with a copy of her signature, and her beatific, full-eyed look suggests that she personally practices the virtues that she enjoins on her reader. Jackson's portrait seems to convey the feminine virtues of restraint and decorum, yet she appears in a much more realistic light than Osgood (Fig. 7). Rather than appear, like Osgood, in a classical-looking shoulderless tunic, which idealizes the poet by making her seem to be from some legendary time, Jackson is dressed as a conventional Victorian matron. Her eyes seem sharp yet amused, and her right hand is raised to her chin as if to suggest her meditation on the scene. Far from Osgood's tearful glance, Jackson's look conveys an acute mind that deals humanely and intelligently with the surrounding world.

Fig. 8. Illustration, Helen Jackson's *Poems* (Boston: Little, Brown, and Company, 1910), vii.

The illustration of a keepsake chest appearing directly above the table of contents, however, is squarely in the tradition of sentimental female versification, and it hearkens back to the mid-nineteenth-century portrayal of women's verses as private and untutored (Fig. 8). An ornately carved box, whose open lid reveals the initials "H.J." enclosed in a wreath, contains a protruding manuscript roll tied with ribbon, and surrounding the box are sheets of manuscript, presumably from Jackson's private cache. The roses placed behind the box correspond with the floral motif that appears elsewhere in the volume (as on the page entitled "Dedication," whose letters are interwoven with a budding rose and decorated at the bottom of the page by daisies). When coupled with manuscript rolls, the floral motif points not only to the decorative tradition of female verse, but also to the habit of enclosing pressed flowers in letters. In addition, a seal with the initials of the author suggests either that these manuscripts were included in her correspondence or that they were letters themselves, since only official documents or an envelope might be fastened with such a seal. As the designs in Jackson's volume attest, even in 1910 editors placed Jackson's verse in the prescribed categories by which women's verse was judged sixty years earlier, no matter how forward-looking it might be.

A holdover from the age of Victorian sentiment, the chest prefacing Jackson's book of poetry is synonymous with an era when women's poetry was thought to be nostalgic and sentimental. Since a chest or coffer was reserved for precious jewels, trinkets, and keepsakes, placing women's poems in a chest both elevates and trivializes them as sentimental tokens. Women's verses were popularly characterized as nostalgic trinkets or precious objects to be lovingly preserved. More generally, keeping one's poems locked away in a chest insured privacy, much as Dickinson herself placed fair copies of her poems, folded and sewn into packets, in a bureau drawer. An "Ebon Box" filled with letters and other mementos in one of Dickinson's lyrics recalls the chest filled with manuscripts adorning Jackson's book, but this chest also instills in the person who opens it an awareness of mortality:

> In Ebon Box, when years have flown
> To reverently peer,
> Wiping away the velvet dust
> Summers have sprinkled there!
>
> To hold a letter to the light—
> Grown Tawny now, with time—
> To con the faded syllables
> That quickened us like Wine!
>
> Perhaps a Flower's shrivelled cheek
> Among it's stores to find—
> Plucked far away, some morning—
> By gallant—mouldering hand!
>
> A curl, perhaps, from foreheads
> Our Constancy forgot—
> Perhaps, an Antique trinket—
> In vanished fashions set!
>
> And then to lay them quiet back—
> And go about it's care—
> As if the little Ebon Box
> Were none of our affair!
>
> (J, 169)

Not only do the trinkets in the "Ebon Box" recall the fleeting passage of time, but they also call up the memory of the beloved dead with a vividness that exposes the triteness of Victorian mourning conventions. The "Ebon Box" contains keepsakes popular in the Victorian era—a letter, a flower, a lock of hair, and a piece of jewelry—and betokens more than the popular consolatory habit of keeping mementos of the deceased, since it resembles a coffin as well as a chest filled with familiar objects from the past. Rather than simply memorializing the dead, the tokens themselves become signs of mortality: although the letter has "grown Tawny," its words, like "wine," once conveyed to the reader a hint of passion; the flower's petals resemble the "shrivelled cheek," perhaps of a suitor, whose "gallant—mouldering hand" plucked the flower at the distance of years; the curl reminds the speaker of the dead whom "our Constancy forgot"; and an "Antique trinket" is now set in "vanished fashions" of years before. Acts of politeness and gallantry are repaid with a lack of "Constancy" and inattention to the memory of the dead. Indeed, Dickinson's poem concerns the power of objects to evoke our remembrance of the dead, despite our wish to deny their continued relevance to our lives. Although we try to put aside the preserved and cherished mementos of the dead, "As if the little Ebon Box / Were none of our affair" implies that we cannot.

For Dickinson, the "Ebon Box" alerts its caretaker to the disturbing truth of mortality that putting these treacherous keepsakes in a box might be an effort to contain. As Barton Levi St. Armand explains, Dickinson revises the tradition of sentimental versifying that eventually elevated the dead into beloved objects, following from actual technological advances, as new methods of interment were developed and more sanitary cemeteries were built: "The loved dead themselves became keepsakes, as advances in embalming and the invention of waterproof tombs and airtight burial cases actually allowed sentimentalists to treat the corpse as the metaphorical gem, treasure, or idol it so often is in the lofty lamentations of mortuary verse."[21] Rather than convey a sense of the beloved dead's continued presence, keepsakes remind the reader of his or her own mortality. Dickinson placed the fair copies of her poems, folded and sewn into small packets, in a bureau drawer, and one might ask if poems placed in a chest or consigned to a drawer during the poet's life were as threatening as keepsakes: did they have the same explosive power to remind a reader years after the poet has died of the fact of human mortality?

For Dickinson, a word can infect its reader years after its author has died:

> A Word dropped careless on a Page
> May stimulate an eye
> When folded in perpetual seam
> The Wrinkled Maker lie
>
> Infection in the sentence breeds
> We may inhale Despair
> At distances of Centuries
> From the Malaria—
>
> (J, 1261)

2. stimulate] consecrate   4. Maker] Author

This lyric concerns the power of words to transmit meaning from dead author to living reader. Like a piece of paper, the "Wrinkled Maker" is "folded" and bound up, as if she were being mailed first-class to God. Even after its "Wrinkled Maker" has disappeared, a word transmits mortality's disease, "Despair." A word can live on and breathe out the "Malaria"—literally, "bad air"—as if it were the animated presence of its maker and remind us of death; we can later "inhale" it "at distances of Centuries." For Dickinson, poems have the power to "stimulate" the reader who carelessly happens upon them years later, much as keepsakes in the previous poem can convey a sense of mortality to their care-taker. In contrast to the image propagated by the publishing world that women's poems were sentimental tokens, Dickinson hints that poems can transcend the lifespan of the poet and convey the spectre of mortality to the reader years later.

Despite her early success, Jackson approached publishing carefully, and her manipulation of the publishing world is clear in her letters to her editor, Thomas Bailey Aldrich, and her mentor, Thomas Wentworth Higginson. Jackson's professional relationship with Aldrich was complex enough to allow her to express her business instincts, while she conformed to the prevalent self-effacing image. In many of her letters asking for his advice, she adopts a conventionally modest attitude toward Aldrich. She often feared that her verse was not good, asking Aldrich "Are either of these bits of verse lyrical?" (14 February 1884; Aldrich, Ms. 2529). Once she decided on writing as a profession, she adopted Higginson as her mentor. Early on, she had patterned her first prose efforts after his, parsing sentences and rewriting whole paragraphs from his *Out-Door Papers* in an effort to write more elegantly.[22] That she intended to flatter Higginson seems obvious, an intention not entirely lost on him. In the following anecdote concerning her first submission to *The Atlantic*, he notes her canny business sense:

It is certain that she was repeatedly urged to send something in that direction by a friend who then contributed largely to the magazine, but she for a long time declined; saying that the editors were overwhelmed with poor poetry, and that she would wait for something of which she felt sure. Accordingly she put into that friend's hands a poem called "Coronation," with permission to show it to Mr. Fields and let him have it if he wished, at a certain price. It was a high price for a new-comer to demand; but she was inexorable, including rather curiously among her traits that of being an excellent business woman, and generally getting for her wares the price she set upon them. Fields read it at once, and exclaimed, "It's a good poem"; then read it again, and said, "It's a *devilish* good poem," and accepted it without hesitation.[23]

Jackson modestly derides her own efforts in keeping with the belief that women should downplay their achievements, but in doing so she also secures herself a better reputation when she does send in her poem, having created an aura of interest about her work (the "friend" here who first asked Jackson to submit her poems was probably Higginson himself). Asking a "high price" for her first submission and being "inexorable" was at odds with her image as a genteel lady author, prompting Higginson to conclude that she comprised "rather curiously among her traits that of being an excellent business woman." Not expected to show an aptitude for business, Jackson's business sense appears even alongside a deferential attitude toward her publishers.

Despite her conventional attitude toward women's role in publishing, Jackson expressed herself openly with her editor, Thomas Bailey Aldrich, concerning the constraints placed on her poetry. Jackson's correspondence with Aldrich reflects many of the publishing conventions that applied to women writers in the nineteenth century. As editor of *The Atlantic Monthly*, Aldrich supervised the appearance of Jackson's pieces in his magazine from 1881 until her death in 1885. Their correspondence dates from the years when she had reached the peak of her popularity, having already published poetry, short stories, and travel pieces in *The Atlantic* and other magazines, as well as the capstone of her career, *Ramona* (1884). As an established writer, she conformed to the common image of women writers that encouraged them to ask meekly for the acceptance and encouragement of their editors. Yet she also resisted the criticisms of her proofreader when they differed from her own well-developed conception of her verse.

Although she used a self-belittling tone in sending Aldrich her poetry, Jackson sought to further her own interests by making sure that she would be published. She paid for the stereotype plates and publication of her first few volumes with Fields, Osgood and Company, until she moved to Roberts Brothers shortly afterwards. Despite a cordial relationship with her editors, she frequently felt the need to publish more often than they allowed to keep her name before the public, as she notes in sending Aldrich some unsolicited verses: "Look at the audacity of me—sending another bit of verse when you said you couldn't arrange for one more: but a sonnet doesn't take much room: and I don't want the Atlantic to go six whole months without hearing from me you know" (8 May 1882; Aldrich, Ms. 2500). Jackson expresses similar sentiments to Aldrich on at least two other occasions. She remarks on 16 October 1882, "I am always glad to have papers in the Atlantic at less rates of pay than I get elsewhere, because I consider the having them read by the Atlantic audience part of the pay" (Aldrich, Ms. 2504). In the same complimentary tone, on 22 February 1883, she again thanks Aldrich for the honor of being included in his magazine, and shows her interest in keeping her name before the public: "I consider part of the pay for an article in the Atlantic is, always, its being in the Atlantic:—at the same time, one must have some regard to one's 'market value'" (Aldrich, Ms. 2515).

Despite her desire to be remembered by the reading public, Jackson also recognized the dangers of publishing too much or too often. Successful writers were expected to turn out a great deal of publishable material for magazines. Like Lydia Sigourney, who acknowledged that churning out poetry for magazines ruined her career as a serious writer, Jackson feared that she might become a hack if she produced too quickly.[24] She responded testily to Aldrich in 1882 that she would not write to his or anyone's order: "I myself am sick of being asked,—or if not asked,—expected, to write 'magazinable' papers:—I am on the point of vowing not to write a word for magazines for a year" (29 November 1882; Aldrich, Ms. 2507). She remarks on another occasion that she dislikes the idea of being paid for each page of text she writes, although the proposal tempts her: "As for the so much per page plan, it is a vicious one—& if publishers could only see it is dead against their real interests. It is a million times easier to put your thing into twenty pages than into ten.—I confess, I wouldn't like to subject myself to the temptation of being paid by page or column" (22 February 1883; Aldrich, Ms. 2515). As a highly rated travel writer, Jackson could easily have stretched her copy for more pay. That she refused to do so is a tribute both to her skill and to her awareness of her "market value" as a well-known writer. Addressing Aldrich as her "Dear and Obdurate Editor," she nevertheless thanks him for his editorial comments, adding that his praise is worth more than money to her: "I would rather you send back a poem calling it, 'Lyrical & brook-like,' than accept it & send me a cheque silently" (14 February 1884; Aldrich, Ms. 2529).

Not only did Jackson reject the demand of publishers that she write to order, but she also ignored some of the corrections made by her proofreader. In several letters, she objects fervently to the vagueness and frequency of his comments:

And I wish you could tell the blue pencil man from me, that I think he ought to have some more colors in pencils—and let us understand the significance of them. He draws that doubtful blue line under a word—and I sit & rack my brain for half an hour to divine what he can possibly have seen to object to in that word, & then I suddenly discover—or think I do!—that all he meant by that particular blue line was that the word was not printed straight.— (4 November 1882; Aldrich, Ms. 2505)

Since the proofreader's corrections often amounted to little more than a plea for more legible handwriting, less repetitive phrasing, and the like, Jackson often found them tiresome, and sometimes agreed, sometimes ignored them. The issues underlying Jackson's dissension with her editor and proofreader varied, as did the tone she took toward them. Her arguments with her proofreader concern stylistic choices—repetitive phrases and word choice—while her discussions with Aldrich almost always refer to business negotiations—persuading him to take a piece, discussing pay scale, determining where and how frequently she would publish.

Jackson often bypassed the proofreader's stylistic comments by turning the authority for final editorial changes over to Aldrich. In another letter, for example, she refuses to yield to the corrections of the proofreader, disdaining even to call him by name: "If the underscoring came from your half of the blue pencil, I give right up: and you may put any other word in there you choose. But if it is 'the other fellow,' I stick to my (own) text" (15 January 1883; Aldrich, Ms. 2512). Concessions only went so far, and she was often unwilling to give in to another's opinion. Finally, when the recommendations of the "blue pencil man" were too abhorrent, she summarily rejected his criticisms without any attempt at conciliation: "I have not however heeded all the scornful underlinings of your Proof Reader.—Has he not a morbid aversion for the repetitions of a word? I have a liking for such repetitions in certain ways and places:—and have left some untouched, which he evidently expected me to hustle out of sight" (19 April 1881; Aldrich, Ms. 2482). The accusatory tone of "your Proof Reader" ultimately blames Aldrich for the criticism. Yet the proofreader, who is the safer object of satire and more responsible for the changes, receives all the insults. Persuade or deride: her attention to her editor's opinion and equally strong condemnation of her proofreader's comments indicates that she heaped her criticisms on the latter in order to preserve her good rapport with Aldrich.

In "The Way to Sing," Jackson testifies to a poet's need for independence of thought:

> The birds must know. Who wisely sings
> > Will sing as they;
> The common air has generous wings
> > Songs make their way.
> No messenger to run before,
> > Devising plan;
> No mention of the place or hour
> > To any man;
> No waiting till some sound betrays
> > A listening ear;
> No different voice, no new delays,
> > If steps draw near.
> > > (*Poems*, 37, ll. 1–12)

The indifference of the bird to whomever may be listening suggests that the poet must sing freely with little attention to audience or context. Jackson's literary career and public existence outside Amherst and Boston made her an attractive correspondent for Dickinson, for whom her flight from the East and unquenchable energy symbolized transcendence. Unlike the women of her sonnets, Jackson was not trapped by domestic circumstances. Upon hearing that Jackson had broken a leg, an injury that kept her infirm from January until her death from cancer in August of 1884, Dickinson made an analogy between poet and bird that conformed to the free bird image so popular among women poets: "I shall watch your passage from Crutch to Cane with jealous affection. From there to your Wings is but a stride—as was said of the convalescing Bird" (*Letters* 3, 840). Symbolizing personal freedom and the ability to transcend circumstances, the free bird contradicted the image of the caged bird, which represented the pressure of social and sexual constraints, like the parrot in a gilded cage at the opening of Kate Chopin's *The Awakening* (1900). When she alludes further to Jackson's injury shortly before her death in a letter to William Sharpless Jackson, Dickinson implies that her death provided an escape from life and a spiritual release: "Dear friend, can you walk, were the last words that I wrote her. Dear friend, I can fly—her immortal (soaring) reply" (*Letters* 3, 889). Not to be restricted simply to Christian imagery, however, she raises Jackson to classical and mythic proportions—"Helen of Troy will die, but Helen of Colorado, never" (*Letters* 3, 889). For the Dickinson of the letters, transcendence above a conventional woman's life and mutability were clearly Jackson's most admirable qualities late in her life.

Another poem of Dickinson's probably sent to Jackson conveys the same image of a bluebird's independent nature:

> Before you thought of Spring
> Except as a Surmise
> You see—God bless his suddenness—
> A Fellow in the Skies
> Of Independent Hues
> A little weather worn
> Inspiring habiliments
> Of Indigo and Brown—
> With specimens of Song
> As if for you to choose—
> Discretion in the interval
> With gay delays he goes
> To some superior Tree
> Without a single Leaf
> And shouts for joy to Nobody
> But his seraphic self—
>
> (J, 1465)

This relatively late poem of Dickinson's concerns our testing of the world with empirical hypotheses, which are proven to be perhaps too tentative in light of the bird's miraculous affirmation of self.[25] The arrival of a bluebird, which embodies independence and action, heralds the season and contrasts with the reader's belated acknowledgment of the season's arrival. We are provided "specimens," or examples, of songs that are representative of an entire class, genus, or whole, much as a scientist might provide examples of an animal or plant or a traveling salesman display samples of his wares. Indeed, "specimen" derives etymologically from specere, or *to see*; the bird, then, presents visual proof of spring. Littered with religious references ("God bless his suddenness," "Inspiriting habiliments," "seraphic self"), the description of the bird underscores the link between his sudden, gay appearance and the joyful and unforeseen existence of grace. Given that the reader foretells the appearance of the season only by "Surmise," his awareness precedes conscious thought— "before you thought of Spring"—and again implies that grace is unsought and preexisting. Finally, the words "as if for you to choose—," followed closely by "discretion," raise an interesting ambiguity: Is the speaker referring to the bird, who alights gingerly on the trees? Or is the remark directed to the reader, who may choose "discretion in the interval" rather than song? Like the bird, the reader has the opportunity to hold back from full expression, to engage in "gay delays" of singing, and perhaps withholding one's voice is evidence of freedom and independence of mind, much as the bird provides an overt vision of "Independent Hues." Given the common depiction of women's poetic voices as birdsong, this lyric may express Dickinson's attitude toward poetry and publishing her works in the literary marketplace: resisting the opinions of others and proclaiming its independence, the bird sets an example for his human counterparts as he "shouts for joy to Nobody / But his seraphic self—" (J, 1465).

Like most women of the period who published anonymously, Jackson signed her earliest pieces with initials. In her first published poem, "The Key to the Casket," she signed her name "Marah," an acronym of "Ma of Rennie Hunt," which fittingly evokes the poem's central event—the death from tuberculosis of her eight-year-old son only six weeks before. After publishing more poems under this pseudonym, including another tribute to her son entitled "Lifted Over," she began to use her initials, H.H., for all her poetry. "Saxe Holm" served as the pen name for a number of her novels and stories, prompting a series of articles aimed at deciphering the author's identity. To the end of her life, Jackson refused to acknowledge authorship, leading one columnist to speculate that perhaps she had co-authored the stories with Dickinson: "The two were intimate friends in early life and it is possible that the stories were the joint work of each, so that each could with truth deny that she had written them" (Leyda 2, 472). The so-called Saxe Holm controversy today seems a quaint exercise in the conventions of genteel authorship, yet the debate over the authorship of Jackson's writings underscores the common use of personae as a publishing strategy in nineteenth-century American women's writing. Throughout the nineteenth century, critics thought women used pseudonyms to increase their notoriety or to attaching themselves to a project that might fail, rather than to avoid the discrimination rampant in the publishing world. An anonymous 1875 article entitled "Another Woman Claims To Be Saxe Holm, Author" in *The Boston Gazette* disproves the claim of a Brooklyn woman that she was the real Saxe Holm, adding her story "is all very amusing to me, as I happen to know that the editor of Scribner's suggested these stories to the writer, who is a poet, and wrote under this signature fearing that they might not be successful, and dreading the effect of such a circumstance upon a name and reputation that already stood with the highest."[26] Reviewers like this one came to accept a woman writer's use of a pseudonym as a publishing strategy, much as they recognized her pen name as a persona—a fictional personality constructed for the benefit of the publishing community and the general readership and, ultimately, to sell more books.

Besides allowing an author to conceal her identity from the public, pseudonyms were part of constructed speakerly identities. An 1878 article called "Who is Saxe Holm?" published in *The Springfield Republican* and possibly written by editor Samuel Bowles (a close friend of the Dickinsons) implies that denying authorship is a posture agreed upon by both critics and writers: "The whole world of letters has seized upon this gospel of the new literary dispensation and circulated fibs with the most saintly countenance. It is this principle, no doubt, which has led our critics to believe that Helen Hunt could be Saxe Holm and deny it and be a very excellent woman all in the same moment. In fact, it has come to such a pass that denials of this sort are of no account whatever in the eyes of the reviewers."[27] Both acknowledging that such avowals and disavowals of authorship were only part of the publishing game and holding women to a higher moral standard than men were common among nineteenth-century critics. The writer sanctimoniously condemns the author for denying to be Saxe Holm, yet he admits that such pretense was common. Not merely a symptom of genteel reticence among women, this convention also allowed women to stimulate interest in their works among the reading public by coyly denying authorship and then creating controversy.

Furthermore, Saxe Holm's characteristics parallel those of Emily Dickinson's own personality. Bowles would have been aware of the poet's inclination early in her career to publish, and he might have hazarded a guess that she had turned to prose in the intervening years, submitting her work to be printed only under the shelter of a pseudonym. Although the writer contends that "H.H." is "open to the charge of sentimentality," he describes her primarily as a realist, "emphatically a woman of every day life," who deals in "practical home and society questions" (4). In contrast, he asserts that Saxe Holm is more imaginative, secretive, and less worldly. "The questions" that Saxe Holm "propounds," he writes, "are of a subtle, mysterious, way-side, we had almost said underground sort, so much do they smack of the cellar—questions which she gropes about with for some time and then abandons, leaving an uneasy conviction in the mind of the reader of something wrong" (4). The characterization of her poems as "way-side" and cellar-grown evokes the belief that she is beyond the pale of normal womanhood, much as Jackson's characterization of Dickinson as "moth-like" paints her as pale, timid, and abnormal.

Moreover, such characterizations might emanate from the many stories that revolved around Dickinson's life. While Jackson's poetry could flower in the full light of day, Dickinson's was most fit to be hidden away in a cellar or hothouse, too delicate to be exposed to the full light of public scrutiny. According to the author, Saxe Holm's abnormal thoughts derive from her unhealthy and reclusive living conditions:

A very subtle analysis upon a very few truths pushed to their extreme application; the morbidness, improbability, quaintness and shrinking which would result from a lack of the sun's ripening influences, like a lily grown in a cellar. All these lead us to the conclusion that the author may be a person long shut out from the world and living in a world of her own; that perhaps she is a recluse. (7)

Dickinson's habit of not admitting visitors certainly qualified her as a "recluse," and the description of Saxe Holm as "a lily grown in a cellar" suggests she is fragile and secluded from normal influences in keeping with the popular characterization of women as delicate flowers. The reviewer emphasizes the Poe-like morbidity of Saxe Holm—"always morbid, and morbid to the last degree . . . the ideal element of her poetry pushed to its extremity" (4). According to the reviewer, Jackson's writing varies from Saxe Holm's and their stylistic differences abound: Jackson's poetry is "sweet," sensitive, and pious; Saxe Holm's is "intense," jarringly emotional, and "reverent with the reverence of one stricken with admiration and awe" (5). Both these personae recall the obverse images of the sentimental and Gothic writers, and they suggest that they had largely become stylized performances, masks to be adopted and shed by the female writer depending on her intent. Saxe Holm, he writes, "seems to feel a kinship to the natural world, is as exquisitely sensitive to the feelings produced by birds and flowers and is as familiar with their ways and language as if she were, indeed, one of them" (5). Dickinson would surely have qualified as "morbid" in Bowles's mind, for he was very familiar with her secluded life and at least mildly aware of the elegaic tone of her writing, based on the few poems he had read. Furthermore, he places the writer in the class of sentimental female writers, who were described as sensitive, fearful, and lonely souls, and he calls her stories "weird and improbable" (4), comparing her poems to "strains of solemn music floating at night from some way-side church" (4). Neither her poems nor her stories, however, conformed to the dictates of Calvinism: "From the puritanical religion of New England's daughters, and especially from its cant, she is singularly free" (5).

Several more comments offer further proof that the writer probably had Dickinson in mind. The writer deems Saxe Holm's background privileged in many ways: "we may imagine her to be a member of one of those 'sleepy and dignified' New England families whom she has so vividly described; of a timid nature; separated from the outside world, devoted to literature and flowers" (7). Dickinson's family was the most distinguished in Amherst: her grandfather was a founder of Amherst College, and her father, a prominent lawyer, who served several terms in the Massachusetts State Legislature and one in Congress. Finally, the writer of the article supposes that Saxe Holm may, like Jackson, have been from Amherst, since "it may be stated in a general way that two persons capable of literary expression may have lived in the same town" (7).

The stereotypically feminine image of Saxe Holm as otherworldly, intense, and heterodox has profound implications for our understanding of Dickinson's choice of subject matter and style. Jackson's poetry is complex enough to embody the conflicting attitudes that led most nineteenth-century American editors to consider women writers saints or sinners, mothers and daughters or spinsters. The subject matter and presentation of her poetry reflect the fine line she maintained between accepting and resisting the standards for female expression: while conforming to the accepted topics of female verse—Christian love and self-denial—she reveals her dissatisfaction with these conventions. Jackson's uneasiness with the conventional role for women subtly resists the norms for women's expression, and this discomfort underscores Dickinson's more radical condemnation of women's roles. The decorative lettering and the final illustration offer a purely secular view of love. The first letter of each poem is capitalized and intertwined with flowers, which typifies Victorian floral design and makes no reference to Christian piety. The final emblem counterpoints the Christian design of a hand holding grapes over a cup. Appearing directly below the final poem, "Last Words," a pair of hands plucking a petal from a daisy points to the theme of worldly love (Fig. 9). This emblem implies that love is a game of chance, as does the poem "The Sign of the Daisy," which appears only two pages earlier. The speaker tells of a woman who, perhaps after an unhappy love affair, disregards the outcome of the children's game of plucking petals as a way of predicting affection, preferring to believe that "'One story no two daisies tell'" (Verses, 189, l. 6). After another summer, however, the woman has forgotten her suffering—"Her heart had lost its last year's pain" (Verses, 189, ll. 11–12)—and the speaker then remarks in the final stanza that self-deception is the daisy's real message.

> So never the daisy's sweet sign deceives,
>   Though no two will one story tell;
> The glad heart sees the daisy leaves,
>   But thinks not of their hidden spell,
> Heeds not which lingered and which fell.
>   "He loves me; yes, he loves me well."
> Ah, happy heart which sees, believes!
>   This is the daisy's secret spell!
>   (Verses, 189, ll. 17–24)

"The Sign of the Daisy" undercuts the interpretation of "signs" upon which both secular and religious love are based; while one is encouraged to "believe" without "seeing" according to Christian doctrine, the opposite dictum that

Fig. 9. Emblem, Helen Hunt Jackson's ("H.H.") *Verses* (Boston: Roberts Brothers, 1875), 191.

"seeing is believing" proves inapt in romantic love, where one might wrongly convince oneself of another's affection.

Given the disavowal of romantic love presented in "The Sign of the Daisy" (a critique reinforced by the emblem at the book's end), "Last Words" receives a different inflection due to its placement. The dying speaker reluctantly departs from life, enjoining her mourners to remember "that I am looking backward as I go, / Am lingering while I haste, and in this rain / Of tears of joy am mingling tears of pain" (*Verses*, 191, ll. 2–4). Her final words, however, are cast in doubt when juxtaposed with the emblem:

> And when, remembering me, you come some day
> And stand there, speak no praise, but only say,
> "How she loved us! It was for that she was so dear!"
> These are the only words that I shall smile to hear.
> (*Verses*, 191, ll. 11–14)

If we take seriously "The Sign of the Daisy"'s exposure of love as a fickle game, then the endearment hoped for in "Last Words" is less than secure. Expressing a conventional sentimental send-off, in which the plucked flower symbolizes mortality, the speaker wishes to obscure the humble traces of her existence ("Do not adorn with costly shrub, or tree, / Or flower, the little grave which shelters me" [*Verses*, 191, ll. 5–6]). But the placement of the poem immediately above the image of a hand plucking petals from a daisy, an emblem representing the fickleness of love, suggests that we cannot be sure of her affection or, if it is genuine, that she may not be able to trust those who have offered the same to her. By contrasting the redemptive powers of holy love with the trials and self-deceptions of its secular counterpart, Jackson implies that both are a part of her experience and perhaps of every woman's.

Dickinson found little comfort in the Victorian conventions of death, and her poems more radically critique women's roles than do those of other nineteenth-century American women poets. Her lyrics share themes of romantic and holy love, Christian self-denial, and ennobling renunciation with Jackson's, as the common use of the casket symbol shows. While Jackson's poetry was marketed as sentimental, she renounced the pressure on women's lives more strongly in her poetry than any other woman writer except Dickinson. Many of Jackson's poems embody features mentioned by Cheryl Walker and Emily Stipes Watts. Sorrow and suffering are characterized from a normative Christian standpoint as a type of richness. "My Legacy," for example, describes a fairy-tale scenario of a woman who fervently seeks a promised treasure, only to find that her inheritance is the privilege to share Christ's "sweet legacy of sorrow" (*Verses*, 18, l. 52). Jackson invokes extreme states of being and climatic conditions to describe the life of a woman who has been unduly neglected. "Found Frozen," for instance, adopts the conceit of a freezing traveler to depict a woman's slow death in her home, where her tribulations have gone unnoticed by her family. Other poems use the imagery of extreme landscapes and climates to represent the depths of passion, much as Dickinson's poems often depict a "tropic" or other exotic location to describe the experience of love. Finally, renunciation of love, food, and worldly ambition in Jackson's poems confers a royal status on the speaker, who will be rewarded with heavenly bliss for her sacrifices.

Famine in Jackson's poetry is often a metaphor for spiritual or emotional deprivation. Jackson depicts a speaker who laments the life of a woman deprived of her family's affection; that she has another woman defend the oppressed woman in her poem, rather than allowing that woman to speak, suggests that she felt too inhibited to criticize women's roles directly. Perhaps Jackson wished to prevent speculation on her own marriage, especially considering the attacks made against Saxe Holm. "In Time of Famine" defends a woman's stern behavior against the insults of a mocking crowd:

> "She has no heart," they said, and turned away,
> Then, stung so that I wished my words might be
> Two-edged swords, I answered low:—
>   "Have ye
> Not read how once when famine held fierce sway
> In Lydia, and men died day by day
> Of hunger, there were found brave souls whose glee
> Scarce hid their pangs, who said, 'Now we
> Can eat but once in two days; we will play
> Such games on those days when we eat no food
> That we forget our pain.'
>   "Thus they withstood
> Long years of famine; and to them we owe
> The trumpets, pipes, and balls which mirth finds good
> To-day, and little dream that of such woe
> They first were born.
>   "That woman's life I know
> Has been all famine. Mock now if ye dare,
> To hear her brave sad laughter in the air."
>   (*Verses*, 25–26)

The poem begins with the words of observers who misjudge the woman, claiming "'She has no heart'" and condemning her for not behaving as a stereotypical woman. Hoping her words might be "two-edged swords," the speaker recounts a story about the Lydians, who suffer a famine and devise games and musical instruments to fend off their hunger pangs. Lydia, an ancient trade center in Asia Minor, was well known for its riches (the wealthy Croesus was its last king, reigning from 560–546 B.C.). Lydians are said to have invented some musical instruments and to have made many innovations in music; that musical instruments and games resulted from a long period of famine clearly conveys the poem's theme: hunger is empowering. Rather than consider famine weakening, the speaker contends that "'long years of famine'" have made the woman stronger, concluding, "'That woman's life I know / Has been all famine. Mock now if ye dare, / To hear her brave sad laughter in the air'" (*Verses*, 26, ll. 14–16).

Hunger particularly evokes the care and attention the woman has been denied. In using direct discourse to recount the Lydians' words, Jackson gives voice to an ancient language still not fully understood, implying that the speaker has a special knowledge of their plight. Perhaps writing poetry was Jackson's response to deprivation in her own life: in discussing the instruments and toys the Lydians made, "'The trumpets, pipes, and balls which mirth finds good / To-day'" (*Verses*, 25–26, ll. 12–13), she alludes to the musical origin of poetry. Even the speaker's goading remark to those mocking bystanders that they should again deride the woman's "'brave sad laughter'" after learning her story reminds us that the woman expresses pain vocally. Tinged with bitterness, her cry exudes irony—she has experienced deprivation and can laugh in her total understanding. Finally, the speaker's "'I know'" hints that she is intimately acquainted with the woman's condition—perhaps she has experienced the same lack of care in her own life. Likewise, the speaker's sense of solidarity with the woman derives from shared experience, a response to the constraints on women's lives.

Especially through its association with love, the sonnet makes this form apt for Jackson, who comments on the lack of love between husbands and wives, parents and children. First, the sonnet afforded Jackson the opportunity to develop an analogy between a woman's domestic life and an extreme geographical setting in order to convey her sense of alienation. As Alistair Fowler has noted, far from imposing a difficult set of criteria to meet, formal or generic constraints such as those posed by the sonnet are often helpful to the author: "They offer room, as one might say, for him to write in—a habitation of mediated definiteness; a proportioned mental space; a literary matrix by which to order his experience during composition."[28] The idea of "proportioned mental space" to which Fowler refers also corresponds to a geographical location established in the poem. Like many of Jackson's sonnets, this one has an extended conceit in the octave (which here describes the freezing traveler), then a sestet in which this metaphor is applied to a woman's home life.[29] For Jackson, the orderly structure of the sonnet provided her geographic analogies with a habitation and a name.

Second, the sonnet allows Jackson to develop a woman's interior state of mind by comparison with external events and locales. According to Michael Spiller, one great achievement of the sonnet as developed by the *stilnovisti* and particularly Dante is that "the fourteen-line Sicilian sonnet, without in the least losing its capacity to argue, instruct, plead and also mock, acquires the further capacity to mirror the epiphanic moments of the inner self, the moments at which an inner transformation occurs through contact with the ideal."[30] Traditionally, the sonnet allows for moments of change in point of view, reversals of opinion, and the like. Jackson profits greatly from the dramatic unveiling and then reversal of the settings, and she mines the contemplative uses of the sonnet in portraying a woman's inner psychological landscape through references to the natural world. Finally, unlike other sonnet writers such as Shakespeare, Elizabeth Barrett Browning, Emerson, and Longfellow, Jackson consistently speaks as an observer who narrates another woman's unhappy life, either in defense, subtle agreement, or even acknowledgment that she shares her beliefs. Perhaps speaking for a woman who had no voice in the public sphere, Jackson expresses another woman's silent turmoil, even as she distances herself from actually speaking out against such suffering or admitting that the same may have happened to her.

Perhaps rejecting the sonnet after Elizabeth Barrett Browning's masterful use of the form in *Sonnets From the Portuguese* (1850), Dickinson found the lyric, with its metaphorical complexity and tighter format, more congenial. Jackson, on the other hand, was at ease with the more relaxed implied simile that formed the sestet. While Jackson uses the image of a freezing traveler to depict a woman's neglected life, Dickinson uses a freezing person as a metaphor for the psychic trauma of mourning, notably in the poem beginning "After great pain, a formal feeling comes—" (J, 341). She evokes the growing numbness that accompanies mourning, until the speaker reaches a state of sheer oblivion, which is remembered later as an "Hour of Lead" that comes "As Freezing persons, recollect the Snow—/ First—Chill—then Stupor—then the letting go—" (J, 341). Finally, Dickinson extends the central experience of the poem to the speaker herself; while Jackson's "I" operates on the margins of the poem, Dickinson's "I" fully explores a state of being.

In a lyric adopting images of snow, Dickinson comments perhaps on her decision not to make her poems available for publication:

> Through the strait pass of suffering—
> The Martyrs—even—trod.

Their feet—upon Temptation—
Their faces—upon God—

A stately—shriven—Company—
Convulsion—playing round—
Harmless—as streaks of Meteor—
Upon a Planet's Bond—

Their faith—the everlasting troth—
Their Expectation—fair—
The Needle—to the North Degree—
Wades—so—thro' polar Air!

(J, 792)

While it is impossible to document Dickinson's intent or state of mind, the poem accompanies a letter that Johnson surmises was sent in early 1862 to Samuel Bowles, who had by that time received a number of her poems to which he responded lukewarmly. Sewall, too, places the lyric in the context of her frequent exchanges with Bowles over her poetry (Sewall 2, 491). Bowles had printed anonymously on 4 May 1861, the lyric beginning "I taste a liquor never brewed" (J, 214); he gave it a new title, "The May-Wine," altered two lines to get an exact rhyme, and changed one line to create a more understandable metaphor. A second poem, "Safe in their Alabaster Chambers" (J, 216) was printed in *The Republican* as "The Sleeping," on 1 March 1862, with its punctuation, capitalization, and lineation regularized.[31] Dickinson may be insisting on the importance of her vision by refusing to submit her "Snow" to the publishers: "If you doubted my Snow—for a moment—you never will—again—I know" (*Letters* 2, 394). To extrapolate to a reading of her poem, she may be describing her decision to preserve her artistic vision against all external pressures. "The Needle—to the North Degree—" describes the direction that leads to the utmost height of the physical and celestial worlds, even while the phrase implies that the ascent through "polar Air" will be agonizing. Thus she figures poetic vocation as withstanding the physical demands of an extreme geographical locale, exactly the setting that other nineteenth-century American female poets used to convey a sense of alienation in the home.

In Jackson's "Found Frozen," for example, a freezing traveler portrays a woman's gradual death in her own home, which goes unnoticed by her family:

She died, as many travellers have died,
O'ertaken on an Alpine road by night;
Numbed and bewildered by the falling snow,
Striving, in spite of failing pulse, and limbs

> Which faltered and grew feeble at each step,
> To toil up the icy steep, and bear
> Patient and faithful to the last, the load
> Which, in the sunny morn, seemed light!
>   And yet
> 'T was in the place she called her home, she died;
> And they who loved her with the all of love
> Their wintry natures had to give, stood by
> And wept some tears, and wrote across her grave
> Some common record which they thought was true;
> But I, who loved her first, and last, and best,—*I* knew.
>   (*Verses*, 20)

A woman's slow demise is compared to a freezing traveler overtaken by growing numbness. Worn down by a burden "which, in the sunny morn, seemed light," the freezing traveler symbolizes a woman who perhaps began her youthful married life by easily managing her duties, only to find herself more and more estranged from her family. The second stanza provides an ironic commentary on the woman's death: she died "in the place she called her home" (*Verses*, 20, l. 9), alienated by the "wintry natures" of her family (*Verses*, 20, l. 11), who expeditiously weep "some tears" after she dies and compose an epitaph. Jackson hints dissatisfaction with the prescribed role for women when she writes that the woman's family erected "some common record which they thought was true" (*Verses*, 20, l. 13), implying that the typical encomium on the deaths of wives and mothers is not equal to the actual experiences of their lives. In contrast to the largely unrhymed lines of the rest of the poem, the final couplet enforces the speaker's awareness of the woman's plight both through its rhyme and repetition. By suspending meaning until the end of the line and adding an additional beat, Jackson forces us to reconsider the woman's plight not from a distance, but from the speaker's own perspective. She further joins in solidarity with the woman's plight when she repeats and emphasizes "I" in the last line: "But I, who loved her first, and last, and best,—*I* knew." In fact, "Found Frozen" might be a new epitaph for the woman's tombstone, since its title evokes many of the Victorian monuments of the dead, which provide a short poetic record of the dead's life or a caption of only a word or two, sometimes with no name.

Jackson's "Polar Days" uses a Lapp's waiting throughout the winter for the sunrise as an analogy for a lover's anticipation of a romantic union:

> As some poor piteous Lapp., who under firs
> Which bend and break with load of arctic snows
> Has crept and crouched to watch when crimson glows
> Begin, feels in his veins the thrilling stirs

Of warmer life, e'en while his fear deters
His trust; and when the orange turns to rose
In vain, and widening to the westward goes
The ruddy beam and fades, heartsick defers
His hope, and shivers through one more long night
Of sunless day;—
           So watching, one by one,
The faintest glimmers of the morn's gray light,
The sleepless exiled heart waits for the bright
Full day, and hopes till all its hours are done,
That the next one will bring its love, its sun.

(Verses, 127)

Evoking the imagery of many of Dickinson's lyrics, in which a speaker anticipates the appearance of a sun-god, "Polar Days" uses the dramatic setting and
wild imagery of Jackson's other love sonnets. A Lapp who anticipates the full
day and is disappointed is a metaphor for the lover who waits for the arrival of
his beloved. The extremity of the setting matches the intensity of the speaker's
feelings; the length of the winter above the arctic circle—six long months—in-
tensifies the lover's plight. Like the abandoned or deprived figures in Jackson's
other sonnets, the "sleepless exiled heart" here is figuratively banished to an
extreme geographical setting, even though the lover presumably exists in a setting much closer to what we know as home. Furthermore, the title, "Polar
Days," is at odds with the "full day" the lover anticipates in the second stanza;
this discrepancy implies that the "full day," which will come when all its hours
are done," may be heralded by the long-awaited sunrise or perhaps only by
death. In depicting a Lapp who waits for the sun that heralds the beginning of
summer, Jackson conjoins the time of day with the season; both the dawn and
summer symbolize awakening hopes and expectations.

Landscapes of extremes—arctic snow and polar seas, volcanoes and tropical
oceans—convey an inner, psychological landscape, in which the currents of passion are resolved only in death or the expiation of desire. "The Zone of Calms"
uses a dramatic geographical setting to convey the heights and depths of passion:

As yearning currents from the trackless snows,
And silent Polar seas, unceasing sweep
To South, to North, and linger not where leap
Red fires from glistening cones,—nor where the rose
Has triumph on the snow-fed Paramos,
In upper air,—nor yet where lifts the deep
Its silver Atolls on whose bosoms sleep
The purple sponges; and, as in repose
Meeting at last, they sink upon the breast
Of that sweet tropic sea, whose spicy balms

And central heat have drawn them to its arms,—
So soul seeks soul, unsatisfied, represt,
Till in Love's tropic met, they sink to rest,
At peace forever, in the "Zone of Calms."

(*Verses*, 21)

A note to Jackson's 1910 *Poems* reveals that "The Zone of Calms is the space comprised between the second degree north latitude and the second degree south" (20), a broad strip of land on either side of the equator spanning Asia and Africa. This poem draws an analogy between the power of nature and of human passions, depicting the convergence of waters from opposite ends of the earth in the "Zone of Calms," which symbolizes the satisfaction of desire. Passion is like a river, originating in "yearning currents" from desolate "Polar seas," flowing ceaselessly past volcanoes and over the high, bleak plateaus of the Andes. The volcano, "where leap / Red fires from glistening cones," and the rose, which "has triumph on the snow-fed Paramos," or plains, are symbols of subterranean passion and romantic love. Like the volcano, the "Atolls" are built up from the bottom of the earth and convey the idea of submerged passion; they resemble a conjugal partner, "on whose bosoms sleep / The purple sponges," until the currents, like exhausted lovers, "sink upon the breast" of the "sweet tropic sea," whose warmth and scent have "drawn them to its arms." Jackson embellishes the conventional perception of romantic love by depicting passion in all its raw energy and elemental attraction, which continues "unsatisfied, represt" until death.

Jackson's vocabulary echoes Dickinson's in its invocation of extreme climates and distant locales, as in "zone," "tropic," "torrid," and "polar," and one sees that nineteenth-century American women used such images to depict their alienation in the home. In "Dickinson's Mystic Day," St. Armand relates the hours, seasons, hemispheres, and colors in her poems to the speaker's nearness to death and salvation.[32] Dickinson uses "polar" to refer to exile, usually in the face of death, which in one poem presents a "Polar Expiation" (J, 532). Sometimes this withdrawal is self-imposed, as when the mind turns inward to face a more fearsome solitude than death, a "polar privacy," a "Finite Infinity" (J, 1695). In contrast, South America in particular represented a land of febrile heat and intense passion for Jackson and her contemporaries. Dickinson also refers to South America and other tropical locales as the stage for passion. In one poem, she equates "Brazil" with inestimable wealth, for which the speaker "offered Being" (J, 621). In another poem, she names a famed Ecuadorian mountain as an immense height, which perhaps symbolizes worldly obstacles to romantic union and which the speaker hopes she and her lover might scale together, "Taking turns—at the Chimborazo—," until they stand "Ducal" beside "Love" (J, 453). Italy, on the other hand, represents the land of romance and the home of her most beloved poet, Elizabeth Barrett Browning. In the poem beginning "Our lives are Swiss—" (J, 80), Italy represents the land of warmth and passion that stands beyond "the siren Alps," which "intervene" between the poet and her promised land.

For Dickinson, place names refer broadly to sumptuous luxury or physical striving without distinguishing one specific location from another. In "Emily Dickinson's Geography," Rebecca Patterson remarks that "Maps and geographical facts were of interest to her not for themselves but as she could use them symbolically to identify and order the more subtle elements of the mind's world."[33] Patterson further explains that places form "symbol clusters, in which all the differently named oceans mean the same thing, and all the warm countries—Italy, Africa, Brazil, for example—are the same heart's country, and all the mountain ranges and individual peaks are one and the same (except her volcanoes, which are a different kind of mountain and have their own unique function)" (141–42). Feminist critics have taken the volcano mainly to represent surging emotion, suppressed beneath the mild exterior of a woman's proper demeanor. In "Vesuvius at Home: The Power of Emily Dickinson," Adrienne Rich argues that the volcano often images the speaker's relation to her *daemon* or creative force.[34] Since patriarchal culture has used the language of heterosexual love or theology to convey a woman's relationship to her imagination, Dickinson dons a "mask, at least, of innocuousness and of containment" (169) and translates her struggle to express her conception in unorthodox and original poetry through a central metaphor, the volcano. Images of geographical extremes and volcanic mountains convey not only the depth of passion but also repressed expression:

> A still—Volcano—Life—
> That flickered in the night—
> When it was dark enough to do
> Without erasing sight—
>
> A quiet—Earthquake Style—
> Too subtle to suspect
> By natures this side Naples—
> The North cannot detect
>
> The Solemn—Torrid—Symbol—
> The lips that never lie—
> Whose hissing Corals part—and shut—
> And Cities—ooze away—
>
> (J, 601)

3. do] show   4. erasing] endangering   6. subtle] smouldering   12. ooze] slip—/ slide—/ melt—

The poem draws an analogy between outward existence and a seething volcano to convey a tumultuous but unspoken inner life. Reminiscent of the wild landscape of Frederick Edwin Church's *Cotopaxi* (1862), which depicts a famous volcano in the Andes, this poem also shows the repressed emotion of the speaker's life. The speaker alludes to nearby Pompeii, which conveys the same idea of repressed passion. Indeed, all of Dickinson's volcano poems allude to some deeply buried passion, only obliquely expressed and often misinterpreted by others: the oxymoronic "still—Volcano—Life—" and "quiet—Earthquake Style—" of this poem point to a composure that belies seething passion. As in Jackson's "Found Frozen," where the speaker blames the "wintry natures" of the abandoned woman's family for not recognizing her demise, this speaker hints that those around her do not suspect explosiveness beneath a mild demeanor, "too subtle" for "natures this side Naples" unaccustomed to the blistering heat of strong passion. The "Solemn—Torrid—Symbol—" suggests that the volcano must be interpreted, as if the speaker had already articulated her suffering but finds her words are constantly being misapprehended by those around her. Like the "uniform hieroglyphic" of Walt Whitman's "Song of Myself,"[35] "Symbol" implies that the volcano already stands as an object used to represent something else—hence, it is a sign that must be interpreted according to a system of belief. Furthermore, "the lips that never lie" underscores both the delights and dangers of honestly expressing one's innermost feelings. Like vaginal lips, her mouth resembles "hissing Corals," whose truth-telling wrecks everything in sight: "And Cities—ooze—away—." Both in the social world and in sex, giving voice to seething passion beneath a mild exterior is dangerous and ultimately can destroy.

Jackson's "A Woman's Death-Wound," in contrast, describes the effect of one biting remark on a woman:

> It left upon her tender flesh no trace.
> The murderer is safe. As swift as light
> The weapon fell, and, in the summer night,
> Did scarce the silent, dewy air displace;
> 'Twas but a word. A blow had been less base.
> Like dumb beast branded by an iron white
> With heat, she turned in blind and helpless flight,
> But then remembered, and with piteous face
> Came back.
>   Since then the world has nothing missed
> In her, in voice or smile. But she—each day
> She counts until her dying be complete.
> One moan she makes, and ever doth repeat:
> "O lips that I have loved and kissed and kissed,
> Did I deserve to die this bitterest way?"

(Poems, 205)

Like the other sonnets about women's lives, the speaker describes a woman who suffers throughout her life after she is psychologically "wounded" by a word; in fact, the poem might more appropriately be entitled "A Woman's Life-Wound," since she lives a slow death after perhaps a lover's rejection. After Freud, it is perhaps easy to imagine a woman's wound as the vagina. Yet even though the symbolic resonance of the "wound" may be less apt for a nineteenth- than a twentieth-century audience, the references to violence and verbal abuse suggest that the woman suffers at the hands of a lover as a sexual object. What is also striking in this poem is the hint at the woman's repressed emotion—she continues to exist in such a way that "the world has nothing missed / In her, in voice or smile" (*Poems*, 205, ll. 9–10). We are vaguely told that, after turning "in blind and helpless flight" (*Poems*, 205, l. 7), she "remembered," presumably her household duties, and "came back" (*Poems*, 205, ll. 8–9). Undoubtedly, Jackson refers to the doctrine that women should be serene, untroubled, and helpful at home. More likely than not, however, the woman is the victim of mental abuse: although we do not know the "single word" revealed, its impact is clear.

A parallel study of Jackson's "A Woman's Death-Wound" and Dickinson's "A Still—Volcano—Life—" (J, 601) reveals their syntactical and conceptual differences. Like most of her sonnets, Jackson's poem begins discursively, even conversationally: "It left upon her tender flesh no trace" (*Poems*, 205, l. 1). As the poem continues, however, the observer recounts a woman's suffering through an extravagant conceit or extended simile that emphasizes the depth of a woman's suffering: she has been mortally wounded in conversation by someone close to her. Although many of her descriptive phrases are trite and sentimental—"as swift as light" and "dewy air"—the octave develops a central idea expressed in normal syntax that strikingly conveys the woman's alienation. Repetition also highlights the key figure in the poem: "But she— each day / She counts until her dying be complete" (*Poems*, 205, l. 10–11). The initial spondee of this line arrests the reader's attention and the break in thought forces us to reassess the woman's happiness in light of her moment's pain. While her sonnets revert to a traditional notion of romantic love that supports an idealized notion of men's and women's relations, they also create a sense of implicit and political solidarity, as does "A Woman's Death-Wound," between the abused woman and the often female speaker, who recounts her tale and thus bridges the gap between her, the abused women, and, by implication, any reader.

Dickinson's lyric conveys a similar sense of extremity about women's lives, but she detaches herself from any connection with the subject, instead directing her gaze inward and emphasizing conceptual difficulty rather than the clarity of expression meant to convey meaning easily to others. In commenting on the poet's style in *Dickinson and the Strategies of Reticence*, Joanne Dobson observes that "Unlike Jackson, she does not find through her pain a connection with others; her metaphoric movement here is not a journey out into the world, but rather an exercise in conjecture."[36] Through ambiguity, paradox, and syntactical breaks, Dickinson's language offers her a privileged vantage point from which she can challenge the norms of expression for women while remaining aloof from their methods. Both lines, "A still—Volcano—Life" and "a quiet—Earthquake Style," describe through the use of paradox a woman's repressed existence, but they focus on her "style," both socially and linguistically, which allows her to subsist undetected. Unlike Jackson, Dickinson refuses to normalize her choice of adjectives and prefers combinations of noun pairs; in fact, she originally wrote "Volcanic" for "Volcano," then dismissed the choice. The use of infinitives "to do" and "to suspect" unattached to any particular subject create a sense of impersonality. Oddly, they also imply that the life and style actively escape the notice of others, rather than are simply overlooked, as the implied passive suggests. Rather than articulate her ideas in complete and coherent sentences, as do Jackson's lyrics, Dickinson's lines often lack a clearly defined grammatical subject. In fact, her stanzas often make sense only when the last line of the previous stanza is read with the one that follows: for example, "The North cannot detect / The Solemn—Torrid— Symbol—." By fracturing the sense of each stanza and forcing us to read the last line of one stanza as the beginning of the next, she undoes our expectations about the integrity of meaning inhering in the stanza form. The off-rhyme in the concluding line also opens the poem to new, radical interpretations and prevents easy closure. Reminiscent of the last line of Herman Melville's "Billy in the Darbies," "I am sleepy, and the oozy weeds about me twist,"[37] Dickinson's use of words like "ooze" reflects a wider range of lexical choices than Jackson's. Rather than appeal to the reader's sympathy or find in the expression of love an antidote to pain, Dickinson ends with the threat of destruction all the more strongly expressed for being implied in the last image.

Other poems of Dickinson's concerning volcanoes depict the power of speech to destroy. She uses Sicily's Etna to exemplify the belief that the female persona sways others more successfully through primping, caressing, and acting than aggression:

> When Etna basks and purrs
> Naples is more afraid
> Than when she shows her Garnet Tooth—
> Security is loud—
>
> (J, 1146)

In comparing the destructive force of a volcano's lava to a "Garnet Tooth," Dickinson calls attention to speech's power to disturb, dismay, and, ultimately, destroy. Rather than attribute to another the power to disturb a woman's life, the lyric presents speech as the guarantor of a woman's "Security"—the "loud" noise that is voiced and high in volume.

The following lyric, which Thomas Johnson dates as relatively late in Dickinson's career, images the power of repressed emotion as a seemingly dormant volcano, describing its power to erupt only in the final line:

> On my volcano grows the Grass
> A meditative spot—
> An acre for a Bird to choose
> Would be the General thought—
>
> How red the Fire rocks below
> How insecure the sod
> Did I disclose
> Would populate with awe my solitude
>   (J, 1677)

Like Jackson's "A Woman's Death-Wound," in which a woman suffers but presents a placid exterior to the world, Dickinson's poem uses the image of the volcano to symbolize repressed emotion whose power to destroy is revealed only in the last stanza. The first line calls attention to the location where the volcano lies, "a meditative spot"; it avoids any discussion of what lies below the earth and instead focuses on its benign appearance and location. Yet the geography of Dickinson's poem is highly personal and unspecific, as she chooses to describe a "spot" and "acre" of the type dismissed as being dangerous by the "General thought." Indeed, the image of the volcano embodies the duplicity of the woman's and the female writer's life: her pious and subservient appearance belies her tumultuous inner life, just as the land might shift due to subterranean pressures. Given that her lyric adopts strict pentameter rhythm for the concluding line, Dickinson suggests that the woman's speech has such explosive power that it can easily transcend the normal bounds of her tetrameter. While Jackson portrays a woman's constrained speech through the extended analogies of the sonnet, Dickinson breaks through her tightly reined tetrameter to hint at the power of woman's speech to destroy, rather than to conform to the dictates of expression.

Although Dickinson memorialized "Helen of Colorado" in her letters, Jackson applied very different standards to her own work than did other successful nineteenth-century American women poets. Jackson's poems treat acceptable themes for women—Christian love and self-denial, romantic attachment, and seclusion from the world outside the family—in a way that confirms the beliefs of the period. Yet her poems also disrupt these norms, especially underscoring the irony of a woman's role in the home and disclosing a feeling of solidarity with a deprived woman. Several other poems wrestle with faith or question its validity outright.[38] Although most of her poems do not explicitly criticize the place of women, Jackson frequently raises questions about the satisfactoriness of their lives.

Dickinson was similar to Jackson and other women writers in voicing conventional feminine themes—renunciation, piety, and self-sacrifice—yet she does not seek an easy resolution to metaphysical problems. Instead, she openly portrays moral irresolution, which Jackson registers only indirectly. Free from the need to girdle them to public taste, Dickinson did not wish to expose her innermost thoughts to public view. Instead, she created a personal mythology that partook of the norms for women's expression and privately explored the deepest elements of individual experience. Dickinson echoes the same indifference to worldly circumstance in a lyric sent to Jackson in the same letter in 1884, where a bird's reluctance to alight except where it is free clearly conveys its independence. In contrast to its search for "a Fence without a Fare," the bird "squandered" a "Note," the very excess of which signifies its inner liberty. Perhaps Dickinson's highest compliment to Jackson is Jackson's seeming unconcern for the reactions of others, yet the impact of her poems is undeniable:

> Upon his Saddle sprung a Bird
> And crossed a thousand Trees
> Before a Fence without a Fare
> His Fantasy did please
> And then he lifted up his Throat
> And squandered such a Note
> A Universe that overheard
> Is stricken by it yet—
>
> (J, 1600)

1. sprung a Bird] sprang the Bird,

7–8] A Universe's utter Art / Could not it imitate—

Chapter 7

Seeing "New Englandly"
Dickinson and Nineteenth-Century American
Women's Poetry

> A minor literature doesn't come from a minor language; it is rather that
> which a minority constructs within a major language.
> —Gilles Deleuze and Félix Guattari, *Kafka: Toward a Minor Literature*[1]

Dickinson was steeped in the culture and literature of nineteenth-century
America. She exploded many of the tropes and popular myths of nineteenth-
century poetry, while she made the boldest quest for poetic originality. As her
poems on volcanoes, tropic seas, and arctic wastes affirm, she used images of
geographical extremity that reflected her mind's alienated landscape. Her
lyrics, moreover, are illuminated by a comparative study of other nineteenth-
century women's poems, whose images, metaphors, and generic features trace
parallel lines of descent. Set against the editorial discourse that circumscribed
their verse, the reasons for Dickinson's refusal to succumb to what would have
been the indignity of publication are abundantly clear. Even though she far ex-
celled other poets of her age, the poetic careers of most nineteenth-century
American women writers reveal that they agreed to conform their verse to the
publishing dictates for women.

Emily Dickinson once said that her perspective differed from that of her
British contemporaries, since her way of seeing was "New Englandly":

> The Robin's my Criterion for Tune—
> Because I grow—where Robins do—
> But, were I Cuckoo born—
> I'd swear by him—
> The ode familiar—rules the Noon—
> The Buttercup's, my Whim for Bloom—

> Because, we're Orchard sprung—
> But, were I Britain born,
> I'd Daisies spurn—
> None but the Nut—October fit—
> Because, through dropping it,
> The Seasons flit—I'm taught—
> Without the Snow's Tableau
> Winter, were lie—to me—
> Because I see—New Englandly—
> The Queen, discerns like me—
> Provincially—
>
> (J, 285)

9. Daisies spurn] Clovers—scorn—

When Dickinson announces, "The Robin's my Criterion for Tune—," she acknowledges a profound affinity for the landscape and culture of New England, but she also underscores her decision to choose a standard for her verse that stands apart from the criteria used to judge other women's verse. While she adopts a common nineteenth-century trope for the female poetic voice as birdsong, her definitive control over both voice and poetic materials clearly sets her apart from most other poets. Commenting on the native materials that established the "criterion" by which she judged her verse, she asserts her affinity for things from New England rather than from England. Unlike the British Romantics, who were born in the land where the "Cuckoo" reigned supreme, she adheres to the native robin, buttercup, daisy, and "Snow's Tableau." Yet she readily admits that, based on the very accident of birth or social conditioning, we are subject to bias: we may perceive a false chronology about the passage of the seasons or associate times of the year with a certain display of nature, as suggested by "The Seasons flit—I'm taught—." Seeing "provincially" therefore applies not only to aspects of her daily, rural life but also to the individual's subjective perspective, leveling social distinctions and elevating the speaker: "The Queen, discerns like me— / Provincially—." The viewpoint expressed in seeing "New Englandly," as George Monteiro and Barton Levi St. Armand suggest, refers to a way of seeing, rooted in its culture and time: "For most readers it has come to mean in the broadest sense that her work should be interpreted in the context of and as part of New England's intellectual, religious, and literary history. But New England also has a social and cultural history, and it is of course only logical that Emily Dickinson should have her own place in that history, albeit an original one."[2]

This self-conscious "provinciality" drew widely on all available sources, and, as with many great writers, eclectically. In her second letter to Higginson in 1862, Dickinson mentions a number of British prose writers' and poets' works among her "Books," including those of Keats, Robert Browning, Elizabeth Barrett Browning, Sir Thomas Browne, and Ruskin. But she names as equally important her daily "Companions" in the woods and fields: "Hills—Sir—and the Sundown—and a Dog—large as myself, that my Father bought me—They are better than Beings—because they know but do not tell—and the noise in the Pool, at Noon—excels my Piano" (*Letters* 2, 404). She notes that nature's reticence is preferable to social interchange for her and indeed exceeds her own powers of expression. She later seeks information from Higginson and Susan Gilbert Dickinson regarding American novelists and poets, including Maria Lowell, Rebecca Harding Davis, and Harriet Prescott Spofford.

If Dickinson appropriated whatever came to hand, literary critics have been more fastidious. Despite the recent fine work by a number of critics who wish to reclaim a neglected tradition of American literature that includes these writers, "sentimental" writing still requires an apologia. Against the canonized Dickinson's poetry, nineteenth-century American women's poems, with their occasionally archaic diction and heightened emotion, occupy an embattled place in the on-going reconstruction of the American literary canon. Some critics have proposed a theory of reading practices in order to recuperate already extant nineteenth-century women's writing. Taking the point of view that literature should be read depending on how it is meant to move the reader, they argue that sentimental literature is rooted in institutional conventions and relies on a deeply entrenched set of communal values.[3] As Joanne Dobson has proposed, sentimental texts employ stock literary conventions to respond to human loss and grief: "Literary sentimentalism . . . is premised on an emotional and philosophical ethos that celebrates human connection, both personal and communal, and acknowledges the shared devastation of affectional loss."[4] Part of the critic's task, then, is to uncover the verbal codes and key gestures that act as cues to the reader's emotional responses and correspond to the social and behavioral norms of the period. Formalist criticism, currently out of fashion, might be used to expose the inner workings of texts, often reflecting the original use of language when filtered through their authors' idiosyncratic imaginations, and thereby secure their place in the literary canon. According to Dobson, "As a body of literary texts, sentimental writing can be seen in a significant number of instances to process a conventional sentimental aesthetics through individual imagination, idiosyncratic personal feeling, and skilled use of language, creating engaging, even compelling fictions and lyrics—as, for example, in works by Alice Cary, Harriet Jacobs, Frances Sargent Osgood, Lydia Sigourney, and Harriet Beecher Stowe, to name a few" (265).

The project of recovering and teaching nineteenth-century American women's writing has produced a self-critique that mirrors anxieties about how we assign cultural value. In "Commentary: Nineteenth-Century American Women Writers and the Politics of Recovery," Judith Fetterley notes that although the texts of nineteenth-century American women writers have been reprinted and several exemplary biographies have been written of novelists and short story writers, there is a general lack of critical biographies and literary studies. Indeed, critical studies and biographies of poets are comparatively absent. Fetterley has proposed several reasons why women's literature has continually been relegated to an aesthetically inferior and institutionally minor position. Among the possible reasons, she speculates that critical blindness spawned by current directions in literary theory has created "the sense of impossibility currently associated with the project of American literary history."[5] In addition, the feminist critique of the "literary" as a concept that privileges texts announcing themselves as literary over non-literary and, consequently, certain writers over others, has excluded a discussion of writers who define themselves as explicitly writing literature. Finally, according to Fetterley, the pronounced emphasis on the contexts in which these works were read denies the significance they may have for today's readers. Rather than argue for their aesthetic value, critics who have embraced aesthetic relativism in the interest of recovering women's literature have also risked sealing it off from any general audience, except one thoroughly familiar with the habits of nineteenth-century readers. The study of Dickinson and her contemporaries intervenes theoretically and pragmatically at a pivotal moment when scholars and teachers are searching for new ways to define the value of "minor" writers.

Except for Dickinson's crucial example, nineteenth-century American women's poetry was thought until only recently to be more conservative and less stylistically varied than the fiction, and intellectually dull. Even sensitive readers like Louise Bogan, who in her *Achievement in American Poetry, 1900–1950* (1951) delineated an "authentic current" of emotion and technical simplicity in the poems of Lizette Woodworth Reese (1856–1935), Louise Imogen Guiney (1861–1920), and Dickinson, considered sentimental poetry a backdrop against which the early twentieth-century writers needed to define themselves. Early twentieth-century critics and modernist writers divorced themselves from the exaggerated emotion and simple narratives about domestic life of the Victorian era and advocated instead restrained feeling and a highly imagistic style. The aesthetic criteria of the nineteenth-century editors who judged women's poetry—insisting that it speak about pious and domestic topics in a smooth-flowing, untroubled meter and with full, perfect rhymes—also prompted late nineteenth-century and early twentieth-century critics' vehemence against sentimental verse. Like Mark Twain's sentimental versifier, Emmeline Grangerford, the poetess became humorists' stock-in-trade.

In reaction to the period of high Victorian "feeling," the modern era ushered in an interest in the image and aesthetic restraint. As Paula Bennett has eloquently argued, however, the imagist poem finds its roots in late nineteenth-century women's nature poems, which often reflect "a movement . . . toward greater concrete detail, more ambiguous and flexible stylistic expression, and toward a much wider—and more disturbing—range of themes and voices than sentimentalism, with its commitment to religiously-based domestic and cultural values, allowed."[6] Male poets, like Edward Arlington Robinson (1869–1935), according to Bogan, were able to "twist the clichés of sentimental poetry to a wry originality" and heralded a new era in American poetry, revealing a heightened realism, laconic speech, and dry humor.[7] On the other hand, women poets, whose methods "proved to be as strong as they seemed to be delicate," were thought responsible for the important task of "revivifying warmth of feeling in the poetry of his time" (22–23). Bogan dates the beginning of this new era of genuine feeling and technical simplicity from the publication of Wilcox's *Poems of Passion* in 1886 and Reese's *A Branch of May* in 1887. Despite their achievement, however, she deems the high emotionalism and formulaic techniques of women's verse responsible for the drop in the quality of Victorian poetry:

Women, it is true, contributed in a large measure to the general leveling, dilution, and sentimentalization of verse, as well as of prose, during the nineteenth century. Their successes in the field of the sentimental novel had been overpowering; and their "poetic" ambitions were boundless. The American literary tradition, from the time of seventeenth-century Ann Bradstreet ("The Tenth Muse Lately Sprung up in America") had never been without an outstanding American woman "singer." Mrs. Sigourney had occupied this role over a protracted period—her life extended from the year of Washington's second Presidency to that of Lincoln's death—and she had successors. Women's verse of this popular variety reflected with deadly accuracy every change in the nation's sentimental tendencies. (23)

Although in many ways she belittled the quality of women's verse by inscribing it within a sentimental frame, Bogan also paid tribute to the first appearance of genuinely realistic and adventurous poets who were contemporaries of Dickinson: "It is all the more remarkable, in view of this redoubtable and often completely ridiculous record of sentimental feminine attitudinizing in verse, that true, compelling, and sincere women's talents were able to emerge. Sentimental poetry on the middle level was never destroyed—it operates in full and unimpeded force at the present day; but an authentic current began to run beside it" (24).

Rather than consign women's poetry to the dustbin of history, however, many critics are involved in the essential work of recovering and reading primary texts, which as Judith Fetterley has observed, "must precede the writing of literary history, biography, and criticism."[8] Considering the already extensive work done to reprint women's texts, write their critical biographies, pioneer new and more useful anthologies, and compile lengthy and inclusive encyclopedias, an examination of the assumptions brought to bear in the reading and teaching of nineteenth-century women's poetry has been largely ignored. Yet these presuppositions intersect with larger debates about the values underlying our pedagogical and critical approaches to authors and their works: as historical documents or aesthetic objects, close reading or thematic study, "major" or "minor" texts, subjects or socially constructed selves. Both theoretically and pragmatically, we need a critical assessment of the values by which women's verse has been judged, for these presuppositions intersect with larger debates about how we value literature and reflect how we teach literature generally. The critical disagreement about what constitutes "value" in literary works reflects the long-established divide between literature and American studies departments. Many critics have forsaken the idea of aesthetic standards and instead justify recovery of women's literature as a way of understanding the social, psychological, and political dimensions of women's lives. Like nineteenth-century editors and critics, who lauded the affective and spontaneous in women's poetical "effusions," twentieth-century debates about value reflect how closely our shifting aesthetic criteria correspond to changes in national and ideological orientations.

In attempting to recover a neglected tradition of sentimental literature, critics have suggested we examine the criteria by which women's work was originally judged. Engaging the reader in a heightened display of feeling, sentimental texts "work" when they succeed in moving the reader, although sometimes for reasons unintended by the author. In *Sensational Designs: The Cultural Work of American Fiction, 1790–1860* (1985), Jane Tompkins contends that, unlike modernist writers, who valued unique language, sentimental novelists used commonplace and conventional language to appeal to the reader's emotions. Rather than extol the works of Stowe and other female writers over those of their male contemporaries on aesthetic grounds, she contends that the neglected tradition of women's literature should be judged according to its political or moral objectives:

I will argue that the work of sentimental writers is complex and significant in ways *other than* those that characterize the established masterpieces. I will ask the reader to set aside some familiar categories for evaluating fiction—stylistic intricacy, psychological subtlety, epistemological complexity—and to see the sentimental novel not as an artifice of eternity answerable to certain formal criteria and to certain psychological and philosophical concerns, but as a political enterprise, halfway between sermon and social theory, that both codifies and attempts to mold the values of its time.[9]

Although Tompkins's work has been instrumental in grounding us in an appreciation of women's writing, to value sentimental literature only for its political objectives rather than its "psychological and philosophical concerns" threatens to ignore the already considerable intellectual complexity and psychological subtlety of women's writing and denigrates their artistic ability. One might read such works in order to excavate political and social values, but the works also yield pleasure based on rhetorical and linguistic complexity and stylistic eloquence, certainly objectives as important as their political motivation. Doing "cultural work," as Tompkins puts it, in a way that is not reductive or crassly materialistic means we must account for the rhetorical power and artistic achievement of texts when they are precisely grounded in their historical contexts.

In his essay "Teaching Nineteenth-Century American Women Writers," Paul Lauter challenges the formal and conceptual standards we apply to canonical literary works and explains the way nineteenth-century women's literature has been traditionally devalued:

If we accept the definitions of literary excellence constructed in significant measure from the canonical works and used to perpetuate their status, we will inevitably place most of the fiction by nineteenth-century white women and black writers at a discount, and view them as at best elegaic local colorists, at worst, domestic sentimentalists. Indeed, we will not see what these writers are attempting to accomplish, much less how well or poorly they do what Jane Tompkins calls their "cultural work."[10]

For Lauter, looking from the standpoint of a classic, a work that by definition has transcended the time in which it was written, prevents us from appreciating the qualities that make nineteenth-century women's writing distinctive. Viewing texts as historical agents, Lauter argues that they encode and transmit ideas pervading the literary works and culture of their time. If we accept only the standards of self-containment, metaphysical ambiguity, and irony extolled by the New Critics, we will appreciate neither the stated nor implicit intentions of the author, nor their relative success or failure, much less their ability to effect social change. According to the New Critics, discerning the motives of the author to justify her aesthetic achievement is fallacious. Yet ignoring the limiting topics applied to women's verse and the circumstances of its writing threatens to make us underrate their work.

Both Tompkins and Lauter make compelling arguments for including nineteenth-century American women writers in the canon based on their intellectual and historical contribution to our culture, and they separately combat innumerable obstacles raised by other critics as to the reasons why women's literature should be kept outside the classroom, including what Lauter terms "the problem of standards" (114). Even while acknowledging Dickinson's linguistic superiority to the other female poets of her era, I wish to question the definition of "greatness" that has operated so long in academic scholarship and in the classroom and has prevented us from fully awarding their due to previously neglected and long-maligned poets.

Nineteenth-century American women's poetry conforms to the dominant narratives concerning women's lives and the generic tropes and structure of women's verse. Whenever they published, these poets spoke covertly and under the shelter of initials or anonymity. Nevertheless, their poems promote a sense of social cohesion and create a forum from which to address issues of national importance, such as slavery, alcohol abuse, animal rights, children's education, women's suffrage, and the forcible removal and divestment of Indians from their lands.[11] Furthermore, ambiguity, double-voicing, common imagistic patterns, and dialect are some literary techniques that appear in both women's fiction and poetry. We might classify the speakerly voices of many women's poems as mimetic: as Mary Jacobus explains, mimetism contains a voice that imitates a traditional view of the lives of women who, unable to write outside of the patriarchal literary tradition, must even in representing a literary heroine adopt the vocabulary and stylistic techniques of the tradition in order to undo it.[12] For Osgood, Sigourney, and Jackson, the pressures to conform to a way of speaking led them frequently to adopt, sometimes posing, the voices of docile women. Yet these poets wore a mask of servility, as did Dickinson, through which they questioned, mocked, and cajoled the reader. Lydia Sigourney often promoted the interests of women in her poems on infant death, albeit sentimentally, by displacing the father and erecting the mother as her children's sole caretaker and primary teacher. Frances Sargent Osgood used floral poems, a popular feminine discourse, as a covert means to portray erotic feelings. Only Helen Hunt Jackson, who wrote many sonnets in addition to lyrics perhaps because they afforded her greater flexibility to voice a number of opinions that respectable women could not espouse, did not meld the voice of rebellion with that of subservience—she chose instead to portray a female speaker who comments on the misspent lives of women while employing a traditional verse form. Nineteenth-century American female poets chose to use a rhetoric of secrets, silence, and deferral rather than overt expression to bypass the era's norms of expression and involve the reader actively in issues of national importance.

While Dickinson rejected the manipulation, constriction, and bowdlerizing of women's verse in print culture, she also was thoroughly imbued in and shaped by it. An early lyric sent to Higginson in 1862 describes the process by which she comes to recognize great poetry from experimenting with lesser and perhaps worthless materials:

> We play at Paste—
> Till qualified, for Pearl—
> Then, drop the Paste—
> And deem ourself a fool—

The Shapes—though—were similar—
And our new Hands
Learned *Gem*-Tactics—
Practicing *Sands*—

(J, 320)

Dickinson was undoubtedly responding in this poem to Higginson's essay "Letter to a Young Contributor," published in the April 1862 *Atlantic Monthly* (which she took as an open invitation to send him her poetry), and especially to his emphasis on accepting the perpetual deferral of fame, as expressed in lines from the concluding paragraph: "we may learn humility, without learning to despair, from earth's evanescent glories. Who cannot bear a few disappointments, if the vista be so wide that the mute inglorious Miltons of this sphere may in some other sing their Paradise as Found?"[13] Sewall observes that "'We play at Paste' agreed, on one level, with his emphasis on the necessity of constant revision, or practice, in literary composition and, on a higher level, echoed the idea in his final paragraph that the whole human exercise was merely preparation for the divine" (Sewall 2, 545). Equally important to understanding Dickinson's process of composition, however, is that through these repeated efforts of trial and error she developed "*Gem*-Tactics," almost as if her poems represented near military encounters or skirmishes with an enemy. Indeed, as a woman and as a poet, Dickinson must have been aware of the restrictions placed on her verse, and her choice of "Pearl" as a metaphor for poetry confirms her familiarity with the common description of women's lyrics as gems. "*Sands*," too, not only puns on the paste commonly used to make nineteenth-century costume jewelry but also may allude to the fact that women's topics were limited, as implied in the French word *sans*, "without." Whereas the first stanza describes the actual process of writing, the second comments on the method by which she recognizes "Pearl" from dross. "*Gem*-Tactics" thus underscores her self-conscious adaptation of poetic methods her contemporaries used, while she acknowledges the tactical nature of her own poetry.

Teaching nineteenth-century American women's poetry provides thematic and formal insight into the shapes that taught "*Gem*-Tactics." Nineteenth-century female poets modify the predominant characterizations of women and subvert language from within. Like any substantial body of poetry, women's verse has its own formal intricacies and irregularities, its original lights, but even a cursory glance at a variety of women poets suggests that they possess artistic value and insight complementary and equivalent to men's. By taking into account a larger literary landscape that includes nineteenth-century women's poetry, students can both appreciate a neglected group of poets and begin to interrogate the limitations of conventional notions of greatness. Commonly exposed to only a handful of major texts, they find their presuppositions about women's weepy poetry questioned once they read more than a few central poets. Furthermore, the emphasis placed on emotion rather than intellect in many nineteenth-century women's poems may lead students to expand their sense of the range and intensity of emotions poetry can represent and allow for useful cross-referencing between male and female writers. Regularly taught to discount their emotions in college classrooms, students find that reading sentimental poetry often validates their own emotional responses to works of literature. Among the many uses of women's poetry is consolation—the public exhibition of sympathy—which promoted a sense of cohesion among members of a nineteenth-century reading community often afflicted by the deaths of relatives and friends. Indeed, its emphasis on emotion over intellect may lead us to reevaluate not only the poetry but the very way we teach. As Jane Tompkins has argued, the focus on a narrow range of intellectual pursuits in college classrooms has created a sterile and even paranoid environment in which students betray "a divided state of consciousness, a hypertrophy of the intellect and will, an undernourished heart."[14] Cultivating a balanced emotional and intellectual response, or perhaps simply taking account of our still strong affective response to many texts, might lead us to reevaluate this poetry.

Dickinson adapted the verse genres already popular among other women poets and transformed them. Her life story is in many respects a classic example of the nineteenth-century American woman writer, since it both publicly maintains and privately undermines adherence to the so-called doctrine of "True Womanhood." Nineteenth-century American women's poetry connects with their audience and repairs divisions between people. To contend that nineteenth-century American women's writing is worth reading—is, in fact, readable—we need to acknowledge its very different criteria for judging value, which are based on a desire to bridge the gap between alienated selves. Freed from the constraints on the topics of women's verse, Emily Dickinson adapts these norms to her own uses and creates poetry that transcends her age and ours. Until we examine the poetry of other nineteenth-century women as seriously as Dickinson's, it will be long before we appreciate the interrelation of both.

Notes

1. Introduction (pp. 1–18)

1. Marianne Moore, "Emily Dickinson," *Poetry* 41, no. 4 (January 1933): 222.
2. Joanne Dobson, *Dickinson and the Strategies of Reticence: The Woman Writer in Nineteenth-Century America* (Bloomington and Indianapolis: Indiana University Press, 1989), xii.
3. Jane Donahue Eberwein, *Dickinson: Strategies of Limitation* (Amherst: University of Massachusetts Press, 1985). According to Eberwein, Dickinson employed strategies, including role playing and imaginative identification with more powerful figures, in order to make her religious quest: "If she were to grow, she would do so by pressing in upon limitations and then devising those strategies for expansion that poetry encouraged" (19). Like both Dobson and Eberwein, who contend that Dickinson's linguistic habits and techniques allowed her to bypass limitations applying to women in particular, I argue that Dickinson's adaptation of specifically female poetic genres, such as the child elegy and the flower poem, responded to the condition of women's lives in nineteenth-century America.
4. See, for instance, Jane Tompkins, *Sensational Designs: The Cultural Work of American Fiction, 1790–1860* (New York: Oxford University Press, 1985); Judith Fetterley, ed., *Provisions: A Reader from 19th-Century American Women* (Bloomington: Indiana University Press, 1985); and Sandra A. Zagarell, "Expanding 'America': Lydia Sigourney's Sketch of Connecticut, Catharine Sedgwick's Hope Leslie," *Tulsa Studies in Women's Literature* 6, no. 2 (Fall 1987): 225–45.
5. For discussion of Jackson's submission to publishing dictates and Dickinson's refusal to conform, see Erkkila, "Going to Market: Helen Hunt Jackson," *The Wicked Sisters: Women Poets, Literary History & Discord* (New York: Oxford University Press, 1992), 86–98.
6. See Barton Levi St. Armand, *Emily Dickinson and Her Culture: The Soul's Society* (Cambridge: Cambridge University Press, 1984), and Judith Farr, *The Passion of Emily Dickinson* (Cambridge, Mass.: Harvard University Press, 1992).
7. See Ann Douglas, *The Feminization of American Culture* (1977; New York: Anchor Press, 1988); St. Armand, *Emily Dickinson and Her Culture*; Lawrence Buell, *New England Literary Culture: From Revolution Through Renaissance* (Cambridge: Cambridge University Press, 1986); and David S. Reynolds, *Beneath the American Renaissance: The Subversive Imagination in the Age of Emerson and Melville* (Cambridge, Mass.: Harvard University Press, 1989).
8. Sandra M. Gilbert and Susan Gubar, *The Madwoman in the Attic: The Woman Writer and the Nineteenth-Century Literary Imagination* (New Haven: Yale University Press, 1979), 583.
9. Phillips argues that Dickinson's "histrionic imagination" is represented in poems that "reveal as they enact in words situations that she thought significant or interesting. The monologues are not necessarily masks for Dickinson herself; they are

often performances that reflect the lives of people whose voices she 'supposed'" (85). See Elizabeth Phillips, *Emily Dickinson: Personae and Performance* (University Park, Penn.: The Pennsylvania State University Press, 1988).

10. Other influential Dickinson critics either approach her poetry from a feminist perspective or describe a psycho-biographical background for appreciating her work. See Margaret Homans, *Women Writers and Poetic Identity: Dorothy Wordsworth, Emily Brontë, and Emily Dickinson* (Princeton: Princeton University Press, 1980); Vivian R. Pollak, *Dickinson: The Anxiety of Gender* (Ithaca: Cornell University Press, 1984); Susan Juhasz, ed., *Feminist Critics Read Emily Dickinson* (Bloomington: Indiana University Press, 1983); and Cynthia G. Wolff, *Emily Dickinson* (Reading, Mass.: Addison-Wesley, 1986).

11. Alicia Suskin Ostriker, *Stealing the Language: The Emergence of Women's Poetry in America* (Boston: Beacon Books, 1986), 40 and *passim*.

12. Henry Wadsworth Longfellow, *Selected Poems*, ed. Lawrence Buell (New York: Penguin Books, 1988), 83.

13. For discussion of these types of poems, as well as others describing the "burden of beauty," and the experienced woman, see Cheryl Walker, *The Nightingale's Burden: Women Poets and American Culture before 1900* (Bloomington: Indiana University Press, 1982), *passim*.

14. Emily Stipes Watts, *The Poetry of American Women from 1632 to 1945* (Austin and London: University of Texas Press, 1977), 4–7.

15. Paula Bennett, *Emily Dickinson: Woman Poet* (Iowa City: University of Iowa Press, 1990), 18.

16. See, for instance, Dobson, *Dickinson and the Strategies of Reticence*. Dobson proposes that women's writing at mid-century "shows characteristics of . . . an expressive community—constituting a discourse distinctively and discernibly patterned by cultural assumptions regarding the nature of womanhood and her 'divine reticence'" (9). Although Dobson correctly defines this "community of expression" as a prescriptive and constraining set of conventions against which women defined themselves, their discomfort with these norms, I would argue, more often appears in the occasional breaks, fissures, and omissions within their texts, rather than in any strategic and conscious subversion.

17. *The Springfield Daily Republican* 17, no. 160, whole no. 4981 (July 7, 1860), 4; quoted in David S. Reynolds, *Beneath the American Renaissance: The Subversive Imagination in the Age of Emerson and Melville* (Cambridge and London: Harvard University Press, 1989), 395.

18. Walker, *Nightingale's Burden*, 88.

19. Donald Hall, ed., *The Oxford Book of Children's Verse in America* (New York and Oxford: Oxford University Press, 1985), 21, ll. 13–20.

20. Mary Kelley, *Private Woman, Public Stage: Literary Domesticity in Nineteenth-Century America* (New York and Oxford: Oxford University Press, 1984).

21. In a very influential article, Barbara Welter has argued for the existence of a "Cult of True Womanhood." Welter defines the feminine ideal during this period as pious, loyal, submissive, and, ideally, married with children. Welter, "The Cult of True Womanhood: 1820–1860," *American Quarterly* 18 (Summer 1966): 151–74. For another early and instrumental discussion of "woman's sphere," see Nancy F.

Cott, *The Bonds of Womanhood: "Woman's Sphere" in New England, 1780–1835* (New Haven: Yale University Press, 1977). For a summary of noteworthy research about the domestic lives of nineteenth-century women, see Mary P. Ryan, "In Domestic Captivity: A Decade in the Historiography of Women," in *The Empire of the Mother: American Writing about Domesticity, 1830 to 1860*, Women & History, nos. 2 and 3 (New York: The Institute for Research in History and the Haworth Press, 1982), 1–18.

22. Barbara Ehrenreich and Deirdre English, eds., *For Her Own Good: 150 Years of the Medical Profession's Advice to Women* (Garden City, N.J.: Anchor Press, 1978), esp. 5–13.

23. Nina Baym, *Women's Fiction: A Guide to Novels by and about Women in America, 1820–70* (1978; reprint: Urbana and Chicago: University of Illinois Press, 1993), 26.

24. Shirley Samuels, "Introduction," *The Culture of Sentiment: Race, Gender, and Sentimentality in Nineteenth-Century America* (New York and Oxford: Oxford University Press, 1992), 4.

25. Harriet Beecher Stowe, *Uncle Tom's Cabin* (New York: Bantam, 1981), 281.

26. Rufus Wilmot Griswold, ed., *The Female Poets of America* (New York: P. F. Collier, 1870), 322, ll. 1–18, 25–34. All further references to this poem are to the version in this edition.

27. Griswold, *Female Poets*, 187.

28. See, for example, representative arguments made by Margaret Homans, "'Oh, Vision of Language!': Dickinson's Poems of Love and Death," in Juhasz, *Feminist Critics Read Emily Dickinson*, 114–33; and Mary Loeffelholz, *Dickinson and the Boundaries of Feminist Theory* (Urbana and Chicago: University of Illinois Press, 1991).

2. "This—Was a Poet" (pp. 19–48)

1. William Carlos Williams, *In the American Grain* (1925; reprint: New York: New Directions, 1956), 178–79.

2. Quoted in Gordon S. Haight, *Mrs. Sigourney: The Sweet Singer of Hartford* (New Haven: Yale University Press, 1930), 77; quoted from Edgar Allan Poe, *Complete Works*, ed. James A. Harrison, 17 vols. (New York: Thomas Y. Crowell & Co., 1902), 16: 117.

3. Quoted in Haight, *Mrs. Sigourney*, 99; quoted from Poe, *Complete Works*, 16:12.

4. Thomas Wentworth Higginson, "An Open Portfolio," *The Christian Union* 42 (September 25, 1890): 393.

5. Quoted by Mary Clemmer Ames in a letter to *The Springfield Republican* on the death of Adelaide Procter. Leyda 2: 88.

6. There is a strong field of criticism related to Dickinson's scribal publishing that provides possible explanations as to how the poet composed and circulated manuscripts in various states of completion. For representative debates concerning the significance of the fascicles, see Sharon Cameron, *Choosing Not Choosing: Dickinson's Fascicles* (Chicago: University of Chicago Press, 1992), and Dorothy Huff Oberhaus, *Emily Dickinson's Fascicles: Method & Meaning* (University Park: The

Pennsylvania State University Press, 1995). For a discussion of the relation of the poet's handwriting to the actual page, see Susan Howe, "Some Notes on Visual Intentionality in Emily Dickinson," *HOW(ever)* 3, no. 4 (1986): 11–13; "These Flames and Generosities of the Heart: Emily Dickinson and the Illogic of Sumptuary Values," *Sulfur* 28 (1991): 134–55; and Paul Crumbley, *Inflections of the Pen: Dash and Voice in Emily Dickinson* (Lexington: The University Press of Kentucky, 1997). For a discussion of the poet's late prose fragments, including their script and relation to her canon, see Marta L. Werner, *Emily Dickinson's Open Folios: Scenes of Reading, Surfaces of Writing* (Ann Arbor: The University of Michigan Press, 1995). McGann has also argued that one should consider the poet's script as evidence of her aesthetic vision: "Her surviving manuscript texts urge us to take them at face value, to treat all her scriptural forms as potentially significant *at the aesthetic or expressive level*" (38; emphasis original). See Jerome McGann, *Black Riders: The Visible Language of Modernism* (Princeton: Princeton University Press, 1993).

7. Smith has most forcefully made this argument in *Rowing in Eden: Rereading Emily Dickinson* (Austin: The University of Texas Press, 1992). Other critics argue that the poet's relationship with Susan Gilbert Dickinson was a formative, editorial one and postulate that Sue constituted her ideal audience. See Ellen Louise Hart, "The Encoding of Homoerotic Desire: Emily Dickinson's Letters and Poems to Susan Dickinson, 1850–1886," *Tulsa Studies in Women's Literature* 9, no. 2 (1990): 251–72; and Smith, "To Fill a Gap," *San José Studies* 13 (1987): 3–25.

8. Karen Dandurand, "Dickinson and the Public," *Dickinson and Audience*, ed. Martin Orzeck and Robert Weisbuch (Ann Arbor: The University of Michigan Press, 1996), 257–58.

9. David S. Reynolds, *Beneath the American Renaissance: The Subversive Imagination in the Age of Emerson and Melville*, 414.

10. For a fuller discussion of women's and men's magazine publication, see William Charvat, *Literary Publishing in America, 1790–1850* (Philadelphia: University of Pennsylvania, 1959).

11. Other authors, however, like Longfellow, used the widespread marketing of literature to their advantage. Deemed by common readers since the Romantic era to be intellectual, artistic, and effete, poetry had fallen into disrepute by the middle part of the century. Longfellow redeemed its value by portraying the poet as a sublime prophet, philosopher, and actor in the political and social worlds, much as Emerson in "The American Scholar" called upon the scholar to shape his society. Once he established an audience for his works, Longfellow allowed cheap pamphlet and broadside editions to be published for much reduced rates in order to increase his readership. Authors could thus skillfully turn the demands of the publishing world to their advantage. In contrast, Emerson chose to be published in Boston, where publishers relied for their revenues on an extremely concentrated book-buying public. Partly as a result of his decision to be known by a regional audience, and partly because he wrote essays rather than novels or short stories, Emerson had smaller distribution of his work and arguably less impact on many authors, except for some of the most notable ones, than he otherwise might have had. See Charvat, *The Profession of Authorship in America, 1800–1870* (1968; reprint: New York: Columbia University Press, 1992), 155–67.

12. Review by Poe, *Complete Works*, 16: 118.

13. Charvat, *The Profession of Authorship in America, 1800–1870*, 24.

14. My reading of the publishing milieu has been informed by Coultrap-McQuin's argument. See Susan Coultrap-McQuin, *Doing Literary Business: American Women Writers in the Nineteenth Century* (Chapel Hill: The University of North Carolina Press, 1990), esp. 28–48.

15. Rufus W. Griswold, ed., *The Female Poets of America* (1848; reprint: Philadelphia: Moss, 1863), 7.

16. Caroline May, ed., *The American Female Poets* (Philadelphia: Lindsay & Blakiston, 1848), v.

17. Review of *The Female Poets of America, Scribner's Monthly* 8, no. 1 (May 1874): 120.

18. Poe, *Complete Works*, 8: 122.

19. Review of Alice Carey's [*sic*] *Lyra and Other Poems, Harper's New Montly Magazine* 5, no. 25 (June 1852): 138.

20. For a discussion of women's writing as more ornamental, pious, and "natural" than men's, see Ann Douglas [Wood], "The 'Scribbling Women' and Fanny Fern: Why Women Wrote," *American Quarterly* 23 (Spring 1971): 3–24.

21. "H.H.," *The Nation* 13, no. 298 (March 16, 1871): 183–84.

22. Edgar Allan Poe, *Essays and Reviews*, ed. G. R. Thompson (New York: [Literary Classics of the United States/Distributed by Viking Press] Library of America, 1984), 759.

23. Keese, Preface to Elizabeth Oakes Smith's *The Sinless Child, and Other Poems* (New York and Boston: Wiley & Putnam and W. D. Ticknor, 1843), viii.

24. Walker, *The Nightingale's Burden: Women Poets and American Culture before 1900* (Bloomington: Indiana University Press, 1982), 89.

25. Alicia Suskin Ostriker, *Stealing the Language: The Emergence of Women's Poetry in America* (Boston: Beacon Books, 1986), 40–41.

26. Lydia Sigourney, *Poems* (Philadelphia: Key & Biddle, 1834), v.

27. *Verses* [By "H.H."] (1870; reprint: Boston: Roberts Brothers & Company, 1875), iii.

28. Ralph Waldo Emerson, *Essays and Lectures*, ed. Joel Porte (New York: [Literary Classics of the United States/Distributed by the Viking Press] The Library of America, 1983), 1170. F eferences to Emerson's essays will be abbreviated *E&L* and conform to this edition.

29. Ralph Waldo Emerson, ed., *Parnassus* (Boston: Houghton Mifflin Co., 1874), iii.

30. Emily Dickinson, *Poems*, ed. Thomas W. Higginson and Mabel Loomis Todd (1890; reprint: Boston: Little, Brown, and Company, 1902), iii.

31. Thomas W. Higginson, *Carlyle's Laugh and Other Surprises* (Boston and New York: Houghton Mifflin Co., 1909), 250.

32. Howe, "Some Notes on Visual Intentionality in Emily Dickinson," 13.

33. Barton Levi St. Armand, *Emily Dickinson and Her Culture: The Soul's Society* (Cambridge: Cambridge University Press, 1984), 213.

34. Henry Wadsworth Longfellow, *Kavanagh: A Tale* (Boston: Ticknor, Reed, and Fields, 1849); rpt. ed. Jean Downey (New Haven: College & University Press, 1965), 90.

35. I am building here on the discussion of Dickinson's professional and personal re-
lationship with Higginson by other critics. See St. Armand, *Emily Dickinson and
Her Culture*, esp. 207–16; Raymond A. Mazurek, "'I Have no Monarch in My
Life': Feminism, Poetry, and Politics in Dickinson and Higginson," in *Patrons and
Protégées*, 122–40; Tilden G. Edelstein, "Emily Dickinson and Her Mentor in
Feminist Perspective," and Anna Mary Wells, "The Soul's Society: Emily Dickin-
son and Colonel Higginson," in *Nineteenth-Century Women Writers of the English
Speaking World*, ed. Rhoda B. Nathan, Contributions in Women's Studies, 69
(Westport, Conn.: Greenwood Press, 1986), 37–43; 221–30; and Elizabeth
Phillips, "Duplicities and Desires," *Emily Dickinson: Personae and Performance*
(University Park, Penn.: The Pennsylvania State University Press, 1988), 27–41.
36. St. Armand, *Emily Dickinson and Her Culture*, 215.
37. Cristanne Miller, *Emily Dickinson: A Poet's Grammar* (Cambridge: Harvard University Press, 1987), 4–5.
38. Nathaniel Hawthorne, *The Scarlet Letter* (New York: Norton, 1988), 51.
39. For a fuller summary of the resonance of the color white among female literary
characters, see Sandra M. Gilbert and Susan Gubar, *The Madwoman in the Attic:
The Woman Writer and the Nineteenth-Century Literary Imagination* (New Haven:
Yale University Press, 1979), 617–21.
40. Galway Kinnell, "The Deconstruction of Emily Dickinson," *American Poetry Review* 23 (1994): 40.

3. "Feet So Precious Charged" (pp. 53–93)

1. Lydia Sigourney, *The Faded Hope* (New York, 1853), 12–13.
2. Elizabeth Oakes Smith, *The Sinless Child, and Other Poems*, ed. John Keese (New
York: Wiley & Putnam; and Boston: W. D. Ticknor, 1843), 52.
3. Betsy Erkkila, "Emily Dickinson and Class," *American Literary History* 4, no. 1
(Spring 1992): 4 and *passim*.
4. Sigourney, *The Faded Hope*, 11.
5. Smith, *The Sinless Child*, 40–41.
6. A suggestive reading might be that Andrew engages in an Oedipal conflict with
his father: he assumes a degree of paternal authority by slaying his father's possessions and, symbolically, clearing the way for his mother's love. Whether or not
Sigourney was expressing Andrew's deep-seated attachment to her in this passage,
her depiction suggests that, like flowers, Andrew is subject to being cut down himself without explanation.

     Studies of the elegy have only recently begun to reinterpret this genre as har-
boring the author's response to his or her poetic precursors. Peter M. Sacks's *The
English Elegy: Studies in the Genre from Spenser to Yeats* (Baltimore: The Johns
Hopkins University Press, 1985) contends that an elegy actually effects the "work
of mourning," rather than simply describing the poet's experience of loss. Other
critics have pointed specifically to ways in which women poets have appropriated
and revised the elegy, often considered to be a patriarchal genre. Both Celeste M.
Schenck in "Feminism and Deconstruction: Re-Constructing the Elegy" [*Tulsa*

Studies in Women's Literature 5 (1) (Spring 1986): 13–27] and Joanne Feit Diehl in "'Come Slowly—Eden': An Exploration of Women Poets and Their Muse" [*Signs: Journal of Women in Culture and Society* 3, no. 3 (Spring 1978): 572–87] explore the use of the elegy by women poets who refigure their relation to female precursors in an effort to escape the imposing presence of a male authority figure or poetic tradition. Like these critics, I want to suggest that Sigourney revises the infant elegy by privileging the bond between a mother and her son, while she genuinely works through the loss of her own son in her poems.

7. For examples of this genre among American women writers in the two centuries prior to Emily Dickinson's, one might consider Anne Bradstreet's "In Memory of My Dear Grandchild Elizabeth Bradstreet, Who Deceased August, 1665, Being a Year and a Half Old" and "In Memory of My Dear Grandchild Anne Bradstreet, Who Deceased June 20, 1669, Being Three Years and Seven Months Old"; and Phillis Wheatley's "On the Death of a Young Lady of Five Years of Age." While Bradstreet's poems consider the child's death a lesson for its relatives in the transience of earthly relationships, Wheatley's elegy depicts a child who praises God in heaven while her parents listen from earth. Both poems offer normative Christian consolation that assured the child salvation in heaven, yet Wheatley's elegy looks forward to nineteenth-century poems in which the infant plays a central role in teaching its parents an exemplary lesson in resigning their fates to God.

8. This comparison of infants and adolescents (especially male ones, like Sigourney's son) to flowers derives from the legends of antiquity. In Greek mythology, the death of a young man was considered an affront to the culture's aesthetic sense. The gods regularly take pity on dead or dying youths by turning them into flowers. Hyacinth, for example, was struck by Apollo's discus, and the god was so grieved at the sight of the young man's injury that he transformed him into a flower. Narcissus, too, after pining away at the reflection of his own image in a pool of water, takes the shape of a flower. For the Greeks, early death is a disfigurement and travesty of the beauty of youth, the destruction of which is redressed in their myths with an image of equal beauty. See Edith Hamilton, *Mythology* (New York and Scarborough, Ontario: Mentor Books/New American Library, 1969), 87–91.

9. For an overview of parental attitudes toward infant mortality, including the common myth that dying children had the power to redeem others, see Sylvia D. Hoffert, "'A Very Peculiar Sorrow': Attitudes Toward Infant Death in the Urban Northeast, 1800–1860," *American Quarterly* 39, no. 4 (Winter 1987): 601–16. For a study of attitudes toward death and actual levels of mortality in early America, see Maris A. Vinovskis, "Angel's Heads and Weeping Willows: Death in Early America," *Proceedings of the American Antiquarian Society* 86 (1976) (Part 2): 273–302. Although Vinovskis argues that the overall rate of mortality was dropping in the seventeenth and eighteenth centuries, he nevertheless points out that infant mortality remained very high from the Puritan era through the nineteenth century.

10. Donald Hall, ed., *The Oxford Book of Children's Verse in America* (New York: Oxford University Press, 1985), 21, ll. 9–12.

11. In Cheryl Walker, ed., *American Women Poets of the Nineteenth Century: An Anthology* (New Brunswick: Rutgers University Press, 1992), 280–81.

12. For other examples of popular mourning artifacts, see Mary Lynn Stevens Heininger, et al., eds., *A Century of Childhood: 1820–1920* (Rochester, N.Y.: The Margaret Woodbury Strong Museum, 1984); A. Bruce MacLeish, "Paintings in the New York State Historical Association," *The Magazine Antiques* 126, no. 3 (September 1984): 590–600; Harvey Green, "A Home in Heaven: Religion, Death, and Mourning," *The Light of the Home: An Intimate View of the Lives of Women in Victorian America* (New York: Pantheon Books, 1983), 163–79; and Kenneth L. Ames, *Death in the Dining Room and Other Tales of Victorian Culture* (Philadelphia: Temple University Press, 1992).

13. Originally appeared in *The Flag of Our Union* 21, no. 37 (Sept. 15, 1866); reprinted in Hall, *The Oxford Book of Children's Verse in America*, 117, ll. 37–40.

14. William Wordsworth, "Ode: Intimations of Immortality from Recollections of Early Childhood," *Selected Poems and Prefaces*, ed. Jack Stillinger (Boston: Houghton Mifflin Co., 1965), 190, ll. 78. Other references will be noted parenthetically in the text.

15. For a discussion of Johnson's career, especially his choice of subject matter, see Carolyn J. Weekley and Stiles Tuttle Colwill, *Joshua Johnson: Freeman and Early American Portrait Painter* (Baltimore: Abby Aldrich Rockefeller Folk Art Center and the Maryland Historical Society, 1988).

16. For a discussion of *Emma Van Name*, see Anita Schorsch, *Images of Childhood: An Illustrated Social History* (New York: Mayflower Books, Inc., 1979), 66.

17. See Karin Calvert, "Cradle to Crib: The Revolution in Nineteenth-Century Children's Furniture," in *A Century of Childhood: 1820–1920*, ed. Mary Lynn Stevens Heininger (Rochester, N.Y.: Margaret Woodbury Strong Musuem, 1984), 38.

18. Jackson, *Verses*, 105–6.

19. This poem appears in Mrs. M. L. Rayne, ed., *What Can A Woman Do?; Or, Her Position in the Business and Literary World* (Detroit: F. B. Dickerson & Co., 1885), 349–51. Rayne's book is a collection of essays on occupations for women and includes a short anthology of poems. By the last two decades of the nineteenth century, professional options for women had increased dramatically. Among the careers open to women that Rayne lists are law, medicine, journalism, music, and—of course—literature.

20. For the conventions of epitaphic inscriptions, see Debra Fried, "Repetition, Refrain, and Epitaph," *ELH* 53, no. 3 (Fall 1986): 615–32; Karen Mills Campbell, "Poetry as Epitaph," *Journal of Popular Culture* 14, no. 4 (Spring 1981): 657–68; Karen Mills-Courts, *Poetry as Epitaph: Representation and Poetic Language* (Baton Rouge: Louisiana State University Press, 1990); Tarah Sage Somers, "Relict, Consort, Wife: The Use of Connecticut Valley Gravestones to Understand Concepts of Gender in the Late Eighteenth and Early Nineteenth Centuries," *Association for Gravestone Studies Newsletter* 19, no. 4 (1995): 3–4; Diana Ross McCain, "Graveyards and Gravestones," *Early American Life* 23, no. 5 (1992): 14–18; Cynthia Chase, "Reading Epitaphs," *Deconstruction Is/in America: A New Sense of the Political*, ed. Anselm Haverkamp (New York: New York University Press, 1995), 52–59; Henry Hart, "Graven Images," in *Postmodern Culture: An Electronic Journal of Interdisciplinary Criticism* 1, no 2 (1991): 7 paragraphs; and Deborah A. Smith, "'Safe in the Arms of Jesus': Consolation on Delaware Chil-

dren's Gravestones, 1840–99," *Markers: The Journal of the Association for Gravestone Studies* 4 (1987): 85–106.

21. For a discussion on the historical importance of the education that mothers gave to their children, see Nancy F. Cott, *The Bonds of Womanhood: "Woman's Sphere" in New England, 1780–1835* (New Haven: Yale University Press, 1977), 64–86 *passim*; Linda K. Kerber, "Why Should Girls Be Learnd or Wise?: Education and Intellect in the Early Republic," *Women of the Republic: Intellect and Ideology in Revolutionary America* (New York and London: W. W. Norton, 1986), 185–231; Carroll Smith-Rosenberg, "Bourgeois Discourse and the Progressive Era: An Introduction," *Disorderly Conduct: Visions of Gender in Victorian America* (New York: Oxford University Press, 1985), esp. 167–176; Mary P. Ryan, "Tying the Maternal Knot: 1830–1850," in *The Empire of the Mother: American Writing About Domesticity: 1830 to 1860*, Women & History, nos. 2 and 3 (The Institute for Research in History and the Haworth Press, 1982), 45–70; and Susan K. Harris, "Responding to the Text(s): Women Readers and the Quest for Higher Education," in *Readers in History: Nineteenth-Century American Literature and the Contexts of Response*, ed. James L. Machor (Baltimore: Johns Hopkins University Press, 1993), 259–82.

22. Sigourney's biographer, Gordon S. Haight, makes this observation in *Mrs. Sigourney: The Sweet Singer of Hartford* (New Haven: Yale University Press, 1930), 163.

23. Mary Kelley, *Private Woman, Public Stage: Literary Domesticity in Nineteenth-Century America* (Oxford: Oxford University Press, 1984), viii.

24. Haight, *Mrs. Sigourney*, 15.

25. Haight, *Mrs. Sigourney*, 44.

26. See Cheryl Walker, "A Composite Biography: Early Nineteenth-Century Women Poets," *The Nightingale's Burden: Women Poets and American Culture before 1900* (Bloomington: Indiana University Press, 1982), 67–86. In discussing the lives of professional women writers, Walker describes Sigourney as the most successful of a number of women poets publishing in this period. She portrays the poet as having a keen business sense which brought her substantial monetary success, although her pursuit of a career created serious tensions in her marriage.

27. Haight, *Mrs. Sigourney*, 45.

28. As Philip Judd Brockway notes, Judd interestingly chooses a woman as the primary source of the town's spiritual regeneration. Philip Judd Brockway, "Sylvester Judd (1813–1853): Novelist of Transcendentalism," *University of Maine Studies* 2nd ser., no. 53 (April 1941): 78. For a contemporary nineteenth-century perspective of Judd's life and times, see Arethusa Hall, *Life and Character of Sylvester Judd* (Boston: Crosby, Nichols, and Company, 1854).

29. Sigourney relates that, at the age of eighteen, Andrew returned home from college to announce that he would become a soldier. A lifelong pacifist, Sigourney was shocked by her son's intention; after long arguments, she eventually agreed to use her influence among friends to get him admitted to West Point. Despite her efforts, however, his application came too late, leaving her temporarily satisfied that she had been able to keep her son at her side a little longer. Haight, *Mrs. Sigourney*, 148–49.

30. Haight, *Mrs. Sigourney*, 150–51.

31. Haight provides this statistic and alludes to the "pale maidens who languish and die so meekly in Victorian novels" on p. 158. Sigourney wrote, of course, at a time of high infant as well as adolescent mortality. Haight also notes that one half of all children born in the nineteenth century died before reaching five years of age.

32. Harriet B. Stowe, *Uncle Tom's Cabin* (New York: Bantam Books, 1981), 286.

33. See also Ann Douglas [Wood], "Mrs. Sigourney and the Sensibility of Inner Space," *New England Quarterly* 45 (1972): 163–181. Douglas contends that Sigourney believed that women composed poetry according to a natural and spontaneous creative process that excluded men and sublimated their own sexuality. Her argument lends further support to the claim that Sigourney preferred in her poems the desexualized, less threatening male child to the man. Nina Baym has argued that although Sigourney has been noted, when she is mentioned at all, for her elegies, she also wrote a number of historical poems which should cause us to reevaluate our perception of her as a wholly private and domestic poet. See Nina Baym, "Reinventing Lydia Sigourney," *American Literature* 62, no. 3 (Sept. 1990): 385–404. In addition, Annie Finch has argued that sentimental poets, like Sigourney, who were typically allied with nature, lack the privileged central lyric self of male writers. Regularly objectified and naturalized herself as a figure, the woman poet turns to God as the ultimate lyric subject, structurally similar to concepts like nature, beauty, truth, or the beloved, against which she could prop her own lyric subjectivity: "In Sigourney's nature poems, the speaker frequently addresses, describes, or meditates alone on nature, thus providing the poetess ample opportunity to develop subjective romantic lyric 'insight' and to describe nature's transformations in relation to a central poet-self" (6). See Annie Finch, "The Sentimental Poetess in the World: Metaphor and Subjectivity in Lydia Sigourney's Nature Poetry," *Legacy* 8, no. 2 (1988): 3–18.

34. I am indebted to Shannon Minter for impressing on me the importance of this observation.

35. Even the few poems that do contain a male speaker portray the influence a mother has over her children's lives. In Sigourney's "A Father to His Motherless Children," for example, a man consoles his children on their mother's death—only to encourage them to follow her holy and virtuous example.

36. Lydia Sigourney, *Poems* (Philadelphia: Key & Biddle, 1834), 138. All further poems will be referred to by line number only within the text.

37. Joanne Dobson, "Reclaiming Sentimental Literature," *American Literature* 69, no. 2 (1997): 272.

38. For an account of the dangers that accompanied pregnancy in the nineteenth century, see "Marriage and Maternity: Introduction," *Women from Birth to Death: The Female Life Cycle in Britain, 1830–1914*, ed. Dr. Pat Jalland and Dr. John Hooper (Atlantic Highlands, N.J.: Humanities Press International, 1986), 117–23.

39. Lydia H. Sigourney, *Letters to Young Ladies* (New York: Harper Brothers, 1838), 11–12.

40. Sigourney's belief in the mother's power to educate the young appears in poems of hers that articulate a missionary zeal intended to convert the unregenerate. For Sigourney, as well as for Elizabeth Barrett Browning and for other both British and American women writers, the Greek Revolution against the Ottoman Empire

(c. 1821–31) offered an opportunity to proselytize an undereducated and needy population. In her "Intellectual Wants of Greece," Sigourney appeals directly to the generosity of all American "Sisters" and "Mothers," encouraging them to answer the "cry for knowledge" abroad with the "angel food" of their intellect. In making the desire to "feed" the mind a purely feminine task, Sigourney, as she frequently does in her poems of infant death, aligns the substantial bodily nourishment which only a mother can give to her child with the intellectual training that produces a lasting effect on children.

41. John Milton, *Paradise Lost*, Book 4, lines 269–71; in *Complete Poems and Major Prose*, ed. Merritt Y. Hughes (Indianapolis, Indiana: The Odyssey Press, 1957), 284.

42. Other poems in which children or women resemble flowers include the following: Sigourney's "Flora's Party" and "The Boy's Last Bequest"; and Frances Sargent Osgood's "'Ashes of Roses.'" Memorial sculptures of the period also frequently featured bouquets, twining wreaths of ivy, and cut lilies over the graves of women and children. One tombstone at Mt. Auburn depicts an overflowing basket of flowers and twining leaves with an inscription that reads: "My Wife & Child."

43. See Mary Lynn Stevens Heininger, "Children, Childhood, and Change in America, 1820–1920," *A Century of Childhood*, esp. 2–3, 10–11.

44. Barton Levi St. Armand, *Emily Dickinson and Her Culture: The Soul's Society* (Cambridge: Cambridge University Press, 1984), 45.

45. St. Armand, *Emily Dickinson and Her Culture*, 73.

46. Gilbert's cry to be allowed into heaven closely echoes the deathbed scenes of infants as depicted by other nineteenth-century American women poets. In "Request of a Dying Child," Sigourney records in an epigraph a dying child's plea that strikingly parallels Dickinson's own recollection of her nephew's death. She relates that a four-year-old boy "in his last moments spoke of fair green fields, and beautiful groves" (as does the dying Falstaff who "babbled of green fields" in Shakespeare's *Henry V* [II.iii.16]). Sigourney then quotes his last words: "'Let me go to them. Open the door, and let me go. Oh, *do* let me go home.'" The motif of the open door in heaven originally appears in the Book of Revelations: "behold, I have set before thee an open door, and no man can shut it" (3:8).

47. In discussing ED's use of a child's voice, I am building on previous criticism in this area, especially by feminist critics, who view her use of child speakers as a way to overturn accepted doctrines concerning women's place. See Barbara Antonina Clarke Mossberg, "Emily Dickinson's Nursery Rhymes," in *Feminist Critics Read Emily Dickinson*, ed. Suzanne Juhasz (Bloomington: Indiana University Press, 1983), 45–66; Cynthia Griffin Wolff, "The Voice of the Child," *Emily Dickinson* (Reading, Mass.: Addison-Wesley Publishing Company, 1988), 178–200; and Sandra M. Gilbert and Susan Gubar, "'A Woman—White': Emily Dickinson's Yarn of Pearl," *The Madwoman in the Attic: The Woman Writer and the Nineteenth-Century Literary Imagination* (New Haven: Yale University Press, 1979), esp. 587–94. For a discussion of Dickinson's use of the trope of the posthumous voice, see April Selley, "Satisfied Shivering: Emily Dickinson's Deceased Speakers," *ESQ: A Journal of the American Renaissance* 37, 2nd and 3rd Quarters (1991): 215–33.

48. I thank Francesca Sawaya for suggesting an alternate reading of these lines.
49. Many of Dickinson's poems image a spiritual or emotional lack as an economic deprivation. For a poem that ranks an intangible "name of Gold" over the actual, precious metal, see "It was given to me by the Gods—" (J, 454).
50. Hall, *The Oxford Book of Children's Verse in America*, 37; originally appeared in Anna Maria Wells, *Poems and Juvenile Sketches* (Boston: Carter, Hendee & Babcock, 1830).
51. Dobson, "Reclaiming Sentimental Literature," 270.

4. "Alabaster Chambers" (pp. 96–124)

1. Sylvester Judd, Jr., *Margaret: A Tale of the Real and the Ideal, Blight and Bloom; Including Sketches of a Place Not Before Described, Called Mons Christi*, 2 vols. (1845; rpt.: Boston: Philips, Sampson, and Company, 1851), 1: 269–70.
2. Reprinted in Karen L. Kilcup, ed., *Nineteenth-Century American Women Writers: An Anthology* (Oxford: Blackwell Publishers, 1997), 7.
3. Malcolm A. Nelson and Diana Hume George, "Grinning Skulls, Smiling Cherubs, Bitter Words," *Journal of Popular Culture* 15, no. 4 (Spring 1982): 171.
4. H.H. (Helen Hunt Jackson), *Bits of Travel at Home* (1878; rpt.: Boston: Roberts Brothers, 1882), 201.
5. Sylvester Judd, Jr., *Margaret*, 1, 269. Judd's novel first appeared as a one-volume edition in 1845; thus, Hawthorne may have been familiar with the work when he wrote *The Scarlet Letter* (1850), a consideration which becomes significant later in this chapter.
6. For the history of the "rural cemetery" movement, see Blanche Linden-Ward, "Putting the Past in Place: The Making of Mount Auburn Cemetery," *Cambridge Historical Society Proceedings, 1976–1979* (Rpt. 1985) 44: 171–96; Linden-Ward, *Silent City on a Hill: Landscapes of Memory & Boston's Mount Auburn Cemetery*, Urban Life & Landscapes Series (Columbus: Ohio State University Press, 1989); Stanley French, "The Cemetery as Cultural Institution: The Establishment of Mount Auburn and the 'Rural Cemetery' Movement," in *Death in America*, ed. David E. Stannard (Philadelphia: University of Pennsylvania Press, 1975), esp. 74–76; and Ann Douglas, "The Domestication of Death," *The Feminization of American Culture* (New York: Doubleday, 1988), 200–26.
7. Douglas, *Feminization*, 210.
8. Douglas, *Feminization*, 373, n.30.
9. Douglas, *Feminization*, 212.
10. See Lewis O. Saum, "Death in the Popular Mind of Pre-Civil War America," in Stannard, *Death in America*, 38.
11. William Wordsworth, "Essays Upon Epitaphs," *Literary Criticism of William Wordsworth*, ed. Paul M. Zall (Lincoln: University of Nebraska Press, 1966), 96.
12. As Ellen Louise Hart argues, Dickinson may have fantasized a relationship between herself and Susan Gilbert Dickinson that could persist beyond the grave. Rather than accept death as a stark and inevitable reality, as did their Puritan forebears, nineteenth-century writers came to view the grave increasingly as a continuation of

a bodily existence. See Ellen Louise Hart, "The Encoding of Homoerotic Desire: Emily Dickinson's Letters and Poems to Susan Dickinson, 1850–1886," *Tulsa Studies in Women's Literature* 9, no. 2 (1990): 251–72.

13. Lawrence Buell has also noted the importance and rare qualities of Allen's poem. He places her lyric in the context of others like them, including those by Whittier, Tuckerman, and Longfellow, that exemplify the fear of experience and psychological regression common in the period. See Buell, "New England Poetics: Emerson, Dickinson, and Others," *New England Literary Culture: From Revolution through Renaissance* (New York: Cambridge University Press, 1986), 124.

14. Donald Hall, ed., *Oxford Book of Children's Verse in America* (New York: Oxford University Press, 1985), 119.

15. Cheryl Walker, ed., *American Women Poets of the Nineteenth Century: An Anthology* (New Brunswick, N.J.: Rutgers University Press, 1992), 72.

16. Fried, "Repetition, Refrain, and Epitaph," *ELH* 53, no. 3 (1986): 617.

17. Jonathan Culler, "Apostrophe," *The Pursuit of Signs: Semiotics, Literature, Deconstruction* (Ithaca: Cornell University Press, 1981), 142.

18. For another poem of Dickinson's that invokes the consolatory fiction of the dead's ability to speak, see the lyric beginning "I died for Beauty—but was scarce" (J, 449).

19. Barton Levi St. Armand, *Emily Dickinson and Her Culture: The Soul's Society* (Cambridge: Cambridge University Press, 1984), 45.

20. John Calvin, *Institutes of the Christian Religion* (Edinburgh, 1845), 560; quoted in Allan I. Ludwig, *Graven Images: New England Stonecarving and its Symbols, 1650–1815* (Middletown, Conn.: Wesleyan University Press, 1966), 121.

21. Millicent Todd Bingham, *Ancestors' Brocades: The Literary Debut of Emily Dickinson* (New York: Harper & Brothers Publishers, 1945), 130.

22. Thomas H. Johnson, ed., *The Poetical Works of Edward Taylor* (Princeton: Princeton University Press, 1966), 140.

23. My interpretation of the weeping willow motif relies heavily on St. Armand's discussion in "Dark Parade: Dickinson, Sigourney, and the Victorian Way of Death," *Emily Dickinson and Her Culture*, esp. 42–46.

24. *The Poems of Herman Melville*, ed. Douglas Robillard (Albany, N.Y.: New College and University Press, 1976), 116.

25. Karen Mills Campbell, "Poetry as Epitaph," *Journal of Popular Culture* 14, no. 4 (Spring 1981): 660.

26. For a fuller discussion of cosmological symbols on gravestones and funerary iconography from the Puritans to the Victorians, see Ludwig, *Graven Images*, 187–97.

27. For a discussion of Dickinson's use of emblems and pictorial representations, especially in relation to the poem beginning "She laid her docile Crescent down" (J, 1396), see Barton Levi St. Armand and George Monteiro, "The Experienced Emblem: A Study of the Poetry of Emily Dickinson," *Prospects: An Annual Journal of American Cultural Studies* 6 (1981), esp. 197–200.

28. For the significance of Dickinson's handwriting and use of visual space, see Jerome McGann, *Black Riders: The Visible Language of Modernism* (Princeton: Princeton University Press, 1993). In addition, Susan Howe has described the typographic

ideal, so familiar to nineteenth-century audiences, that Dickinson manipulates in the presentation of her lyrics. See "These Flames and Generosities of the Heart: Emily Dickinson and the Illogic of Sumptuary Values," *Sulfur* 28 (1991): 151–52n.

29. See St. Armand, "Appendix C: Dickinson's Mystic Day," *Emily Dickinson and Her Culture*, 317.

30. Martha Nell Smith provides a full discussion of the lyric's domestic and cosmic metaphors. Reading Dickinson's poem as a prominent example of her "poetry workshop," she contends that the poet's exchanges with Susan Gilbert Dickinson about this poem's five versions alter our understanding of her reclusive writing habits. Rather than write in isolation, the poet actively sought advice and editorial criticism from her sister-in-law, whose participation leads Smith to conclude that some of her important poems are not the product of a single author but collaborative efforts. See Martha Nell Smith, "To Be Susan Is Imagination: Dickinson's Poetry Workshop," *Rowing In Eden*, esp. 180–97.

5. "Paradise Persuaded" (pp. 129–158)

1. Frances Sargent Osgood, *The Poetry of Flowers, and Flowers of Poetry, To Which Are Added, A Simple Treatise on Botany, With Familiar Examples, And A Copious Floral Dictionary* (New York: J. C. Riker, 1841), 23.

2. James Joyce, *Ulysses* (New York: Vintage Books, 1961), 78. Originally published: 1921.

3. Thomas Wentworth Higginson, "The Procession of the Flowers," *Out-Door Papers* (Boston: Ticknor and Fields, 1863), 320. All further references will be abbreviated *ODP* and appear parenthetically in the text.

4. Edward Hitchcock, "Prefatory," *Catalogue of Plants Growing Without Cultivation in the Vicinity of Amherst College* (Amherst: J. S. and C. Adams, and Co., 1829), iii.

5. Mrs. C. M. Badger, *Wild Flowers Drawn and Colored From Nature*, introduction by L. H. Sigourney (New York: Charles Scribner, 1859), 2.

6. Paula Bennett, *Emily Dickinson: Woman Poet* (Iowa City: University of Iowa, 1990), 100.

7. Nathaniel Hawthorne, *The Scarlet Letter* (New York: W. W. Norton & Co., 1988), 36. Originally published: 1850.

8. For examples of floral dictionaries that begin with lengthy synopses of European floral legends, see "Revised by the editor of 'Forget me not'" (possibly Frederic Shoberl, based on text by Louise Cortembert), *The Language of Flowers With Illustrative Poetry: To Which Is Now First Added The Calendar Of Flowers* (Philadelphia: Lea and Blanchard, 1843); and Dorothea Dix, *The Garland of Flora* (Boston: S. G. Goodrich and Co. and Carter and Hendee, 1829).

9. Jack Goody, *The Culture of Flowers* (Cambridge: Cambridge University Press, 1993). Much of my discussion of the history of floral rhetoric derives from Goody's assessment.

10. For a discussion of the language of flowers, its history, and its importance as a

cultural system, both in France and in England, see Sabine Haass, "'Speaking Flowers and Floral Emblems': The Victorian Language of Flowers," *Word and Visual Imagination: Studies in the Interaction of English and the Visual Arts*, ed. Karl Josef Höltgen, Peter M. Daly, and Wolfgang Lottes (Erlangen: Universitatsbibliothek Erlangen Nurnberg, 1988), 241–67; Brent Elliott, "The Victorian Language of Flowers," *Plant-Lore Studies: Papers Read at a Joint Conference of the Botanical Society of the British Isles and the Folklore Society Held at the University of Sussex, April 1983*, ed. Roy Vickery (London: The Folklore Society, University College of London, 1984), 61–65; Claudette Sartiliot, *Herbarium Verbarium: The Discourse of Flowers* (Lincoln: University of Nebraska Press, 1993); Beverly Seaton, "French Flower Books of the Early Nineteenth Century," *Nineteenth-Century French Studies* 11, nos. 1–2 (Fall-Winter 1982): 60–71; and Jack Goody, "The Secret Language of Flowers," *The Yale Journal of Criticism* 3, no. 2 (1990): 133–52.

11. The floral dictionaries dating from this period are numerous. Among many examples of dictionaries published both in America and England, I have consulted the following: *The Language of Flowers; With Illustrative Poetry: To Which Is Now First Added, The Calendar of Flowers*, 6th ed. (Philadelphia: Lee and Blanchard, 1843); Anna Elizabeth, ed., *The Vase of Flowers* (Boston: J. Buffum, 1851); Robert Tyas, *The Language of Flowers; or, Floral Emblems of Thoughts, Feelings, and Sentiments* (London and New York: George Routledge and Sons, 1869); J. Stevenson Bushnan, *Flowers and Their Poetry* (London: W. S. Orr & Company, 1851); M. A. (Mary Ann) Bacon, *Flowers and Their Kindred Thoughts* (London: Longman & Company, 1848); H. G. (Henry Gardiner) Adams, *Oriental Text Book and Language of Flowers* (London: Dean & Son, 1851?); *The Flowers of Shakespeare*, Plates drawn by J. E. G. (Jane Elizabeth Giraud) (London: Day & Haghe, 1845); *The Flowers of Milton*, Plates drawn by J. E. G. (Jane Elizabeth Giraud) (London: Day & Haghe, 1846); and *How to Grow Fruit and Vegetables; and The Language of Flowers* (New York: Norman L. Monro Publishers, n.d.). Osgood published several floral dictionaries that included her own floral poetry. Two examples are Frances Sargent (Locke) Osgood, *A Wreath of Wildflowers* (London: Edward Churton, 1838); and Frances Sargent Osgood, ed., *The Floral Offering, A Token of Friendship* (Philadelphia: Carey and Hart, 1847). Among the floral dictionaries available in modern reprints are Kathleen M. Gips, *The Language of Flowers: A Book of Victorian Floral Sentiments* (Chagrin Falls, Ohio: Pine Creek Press, 1990); F.W.L., *The Language of Flowers* (England: Michael Joseph, Ltd., 1968); and Sheila Pickles, ed., *The Language of Flowers* (New York: Harmony Books, 1990).

12. Almira H. Lincoln (Phelps), "Section VI. Symbolical Language of Flowers," *Familiar Lectures on Botany, Practical, Elementary, and Physiological: With an Appendix, Containing Descriptions of The Plants of the United States and Exotics, &c. For the Use of Seminaries and Private Students*, 7th ed. (New York: F. J. Huntington & Co., 1838), 171–74.

13. Dix, *The Garland of Flora*, 4.

14. Sarah Josepha Hale, *Flora's Interpreter, and Fortuna Flora* (Boston: Benjamin B. Massey and Company, 1850), iv.

15. Goody, *The Culture of Flowers*, 269–70.

16. *The Language of Flowers* (Philadelphia: Lea and Blanchard, 1843), 33.

17. [Anonymous.] Review of Alice Cary's *Lyra and Other Poems*, *Harpers New Monthly Magazine* 5, no. 25 (June 1852): 138.

18. Higginson, "Preface," *Poems of Emily Dickinson* (Boston: Roberts Brothers, 1890), v–vi.

19. "Who Is Saxe Holm?" *The Springfield Republican* (25 May 1878); rpt. *The Colorado Prospector* 15, no. 4 (April 1984): 7.

20. I am indebted to Jerome McGann for this observation.

21. For an assemblage of meanings, I consulted F. W. L., *The Language of Flowers*. According to Beverly Seaton, "there was no agreed-upon set of meanings. Instead of a universal symbolic language, the language of flowers was a vocabulary list, matching flowers with meanings, differing from book to book." See Seaton, *The Language of Flowers: A History* (Charlottesville: University of Virginia Press, 1995), 1–2. For a discussion of Dickinson's adaptation of features of floral discourse, see Elizabeth C. Stevens, "Dickinson's Language of Flowers," *Legacy* 2, no. 2 (Nov/Dec 1990), 3, 5.

22. *The Language of Flowers*, 5–6.

23. Osgood, *The Poetry of Flowers, and Flowers of Poetry*, 4.

24. Cheryl Walker, "Legacy Profile: Frances Osgood: 1811–1850," *Legacy* 1, no. 2 (Fall 1984): 5.

25. Cheryl Walker ed., *American Women Poets of the Nineteenth Century: An Anthology* (New Brunswick: Rutgers University Press, 1992), 107.

26. Watts, *The Poetry of American Women from 1632 to 1945* (Austin: University of Texas Press, 1977), 83.

27. Among the recent work by scholars concerned with recovering Osgood's fame and reputation for contemporary readers, see Dobson, "Sex, Wit, and Sentiment: Frances Osgood and the Poetry of Love," *American Literature* 65, no. 4 (December 1993): 631–50; Mary G. De Jong, "Her Fair Fame: The Reputation of Frances Sargent Osgood, Woman Poet," *Studies in the American Renaissance*, ed. Joel Myerson (Charlottesville: The University Press of Virginia, 1987), 265–84; and Paula Bennett, "'The Descent of the Angel': Interrogating Domestic Ideology in American Women's Poetry, 1858–1890," *American Literary History* 7, no. 4 (1995): 591–610. In particular, Bennett's most recent work attempts to delineate a new American women's poetic tradition which shows the protomodernism of their lyrics and disproves the belief that women's poems were written from a wholly sentimental aesthetic. See Bennett, "Late Nineteenth-Century American Women's Nature Poetry and the Evolution of the Imagist Poem," *Legacy* 9, no. 2 (1992): 89–103.

28. See Dobson, "Sex, Wit, and Sentiment," 632.

29. Dobson, "Sex, Wit, and Sentiment," 635.

30. Frances Sargent Osgood, *Poems* (New York: Clark & Austin, 1846), 67–68.

31. See Mary G. DeJong, "Lines from a Partly Published Drama: The Romance of Frances Sargent Osgood and Edgar Allan Poe," in *Patrons and Protégées: Gender, Friendship, and Writing in Nineteenth-Century America*, ed. Shirley Marchalonis (New Brunswick: Rutgers University Press, 1988), 41–42.

32. Frances Sargent Osgood, *Poems* (Philadelphia: Carey & Hart, 1850), 212, ll. 1–8.

33. Part of the poem reads:

> Ah! Thus the child of Genius pours,
>   In solitude and tears,
> On one poor fleeting page, the light,
>   The love of long, long years;
> And the gay world receives the ray
>   Without a thought of all
> The clouds of fear and grief, through which
>   Its prism'd glories fall!
>   (*Poems* [1850], 109–10, ll. 17–24)

34. Patterson has tabulated the number of times jewels appear in Dickinson's work. The three most common are the pearl (thirty-one times), amber (twenty-three times), and the diamond (fourteen times). For a discussion of image clusters in Dickinson's poems and letters, see Rebecca Patterson, "The Jewel Imagery," *Emily Dickinson's Imagery* (Amherst: University of Massachusetts Press, 1979), esp. 74–93.
35. "Diamonds and Pearls," *The Atlantic Monthly*, 7, no. 41 (March 1861): 369.
36. For a discussion of erotic relations between women in nineteenth-century America, see Lillian Faderman, *Surpassing the Love of Men: Romantic Friendship and Love Between Women From the Sixteenth Century to the Present* (New York: Morrow, 1981); and Carroll Smith-Rosenberg, "The Female World of Love and Ritual: Relations Between Women in Nineteenth-Century America," *Disorderly Conduct: Visions of Gender in Victorian America* (New York: Oxford University Press, 1985), 53–76.
37. Although Smith-Rosenberg contends that a woman's letters "were but an example of the romantic rhetoric with which the nineteenth century surrounded the concept of friendship" (59), she also argues that female friendships revealed true passion and allowed women to share their pains and joys apart from men (63 *passim*).
38. Martha Nell Smith, *Rowing in Eden: Rereading Emily Dickinson* (Austin: The University of Texas Press, 1992), 143.
39. Rebecca Patterson, *Emily Dickinson's Imagery*, 83.
40. Paula Bennett, *Emily Dickinson: Woman Poet* (Iowa City: University of Iowa, 1900), 168.
41. Cherly Walker, *The Nightingale's Burden: Woman Poets and American Culture before 1900* (Bloomington: Indiana University Press, 1982), 94.
42. Osgood, *The Poetry of Flowers*, 261, 262.
43. Rebecca Patterson, *Emily Dickinson's Imagery* (Amherst: The University of Massachusetts Press, 1979), 35.
44. Patterson notes that "the pearl figures clearly and consciously as the outer defense works of virginity" (87).
45. Osgood, *The Poetry of Flowers*, 262.
46. Gips, *The Language of Flowers*, 109.
47. According to Charles R. Anderson, *Emily Dickinson's Poetry: A Stairway of Surprise* (New York: Holt, Rinehart and Winston, 1960), the poet's use of traditional subjects drawn from nature, like flowers, never fully escaped "the sentimental and

the fanciful" (98). Although for him the poem "makes a fine beginning, with its precise notations," it loses its detachment and objectivity at approximately line 5. I would argue that it is precisely the association with emotion and women's lives embedded in floral images that make them fit conveyers of her critique of stereotypical female behavior. Nevertheless, Anderson notes the centrality of the arbutus to Dickinson's circle as youths, noting that it was considered "emblematic" in men's and women's love relations, and a sprig of the same flower was pinned to Austin's earliest surviving letter to his future fiancée in 1850.

48. Osgood, *The Poetry of Flowers*, 84–85.
49. Lincoln, *Familiar Lectures on Botany*, 102.
50. Martha Dickinson Bianchi, "Emily Dickinson's Garden," *Emily Dickinson International Society Bulletin* 2, no. 2 (Nov/Dec 1990): 1.
51. Margaret Homans, "'Oh, Vision of Language!': Dickinson's Poems of Love and Death," in *Feminist Critics Read Emily Dickinson*, ed. Suzanne Juhasz (Bloomington: Indiana University Press, 1983), 118.

6. "Fame of Myself" (pp. 161–200)

1. "Who Is Saxe Holm?," *The Springfield Republican* (25 May 1878); rpt.: *The Colorado Prospector* 15, no. 4 (April 1984): 7.
2. Review from *The Boston Courier* (n.d.); rpt.: Helen Hunt Jackson [H.H.], *Bits of Travel at Home* (Boston: Roberts Brothers, 1884), n.p.
3. Several critics have condemned Jackson's verse, and few have considered it worth investigating. Michael Dorris condemns her work for being too sentimental: "Much of Mrs. Jackson's verse seems by contemporary standards overly sentimental and even saccharine. Fond of addressing the seasons, religious themes, the 'higher emotions,' and particular aspects of the landscape, her language was high Victorian, her style, arch," Dorris, "Introduction," *Ramona: A Story* (New York: Signet, 1988), vii. Other noteworthy critics, such as Richard Chase, Denis Donahue, and even one of Jackson's biographers, Evelyn Banning, have similarly disparaged her verse or have explained away ED's taste. See Michael E. Staub, "White Moth and Ox: The Friendship of ED and H. H. Jackson," *Dickinson Studies: Emily Dickinson (1830–86), U.S. Poet* 68 (1988): 19.

Nevertheless, many critics have begun to investigate Jackson's relationship with Dickinson as an index to the aesthetic standards of her age. Cheryl Walker makes the case for Jackson's importance most forcefully in "Tradition and the Individual Talent: Helen Hunt Jackson and Emily Dickinson," in *The Nightingale's Burden: Women Poets and American Culture before 1900* (Bloomington: Indiana University Press, 1982), 87–116. Walker writes: "The puzzle of Emily Dickinson's work is finally not a question of the identity of the Master or the extent of her real experience, but one of tradition and the individual talent. Although the concern with intense feeling, the ambivalence toward power, the fascination with death, the forbidden lover and secret sorrow all belong to this woman's tradition, Emily Dickinson's best work so far surpasses anything that a logical extension of that tradition's codes could have produced that the only way to explain it is by the single word, genius" (116). For a discussion of Dickinson's friendship with Jackson and its impact on her decision not to publish, see Betsy Erkkila, "Dickinson, Women Writers, and the Marketplace," *Wicked Sisters: Women Poets, Literary History & Discord* (New York: Oxford University Press, 1992), esp. 86–98; Richard B. Sewall, "Helen Hunt Jackson," *The Life of Emily Dickinson* (New York: Farrar, Straus and Giroux, 1974), 2, 577–92; and Susan Coultrap-McQuin, "'Very Serious Literary Labor': The Career of Helen Hunt Jackson," *Doing Literary Business: American Women Writers in the Nineteenth Century* (Chapel Hill: The University of North Carolina Press, 1990), 137–66. For a discussion of the differences in style and language between the two poets, see Staub; and Joanne Dobson, "'The Grieved—are Many—I am Told—': The Woman Writer and Public Discourse," *Dickinson and the Strategies of Reticence*, esp. 96–98.

4. Betsy Erkkila, *Wicked Sisters*, 98.

5. Unpublished correspondence of Jackson will be identified by date, collection, and assigned number. Manuscripts from the Thomas Baily Aldrich Papers appear courtesy of the Houghton Library, Harvard University. Manuscripts from the Abigail May-Goddard Papers appear courtesy of the Schlesinger Library, Radcliffe College. This letter is A-134, of the May-Goddard Collection.

6. Susan Coultrap-McQuin argues that Jackson's reluctance to speak out on public issues except by pleading the desire to help individuals parallels a new type of woman writer who seeks to achieve fame "by the application of individual efforts, not by advocating social change" (150). No longer wholly dependent on the Gentleman Publisher, she advocates her professional abilities "in the dress of a True Woman but with the drive of an individualistic worker" (150–51). I would agree that Jackson's desire to advance herself is accomplished through hard work, but her social advocacy, even though it is performed under the guise of feminine helpfulness, is well documented and genuinely felt. Most articles and books on Jackson focus on her Indian activism. See, for example, William Oandasan, "*Ramona*: Reflected through Indigenous Eyes," *California Courier* (Feb.–Mar. 1986): 7; Karl Keller, "Helen Hunt Jackson: Pioneer Activist of Southern California," *Seacoast* 2 (Mar. 1981): 60–65; and Michael T. Marsden, "Helen Hunt Jackson: Docudramatist of the American Indian," *Markham Review* 10 (Fall 1980–Winter 1981): 15–19.

7. "Father Junípero and His Work," by "H.H.," *Century Magazine* (May 1883); "The Present Condition of the Mission Indians in Southern California," by "H.H.," *Century Magazine* (August 1883).

8. Carroll Smith-Rosenberg *Disorderly Conduct: Visions of Gender in Victorian America* (New York and Oxford: Oxford University Press, 1985), 130–31.

9. Ralph Waldo Emerson, *Parnassus*, ed. Ralph Waldo Emerson (Boston: Houghton Mifflin, 1874), x.

10. Emerson, *Journals*, 10 vols. (Boston and New York: Houghton Mifflin Company, 1909–1914), 10: 252.

11. Quoted by Emily Pierce, "Helen Hunt Jackson (H.H.): What She Wrote, How She Lived, and Where She is Buried," *Frank Leslie's Illustrated Newspaper* (1887): 314. Courtesy of the Jones Library, Amherst, Massachusetts.

12. *Verses* [By "H.H."] (1870; rpt.: Boston: Roberts Brothers, 1875), 190, ll. 1–8. All further references are abbreviated *Verses* and included parenthetically.

13. Richard Ellmann, ed., *The New Oxford Book of American Verse* (New York: Oxford University Press, 1976), 74, ll. 1–5.

14. Thomas Wentworth Higginson, Review of *Verses* [by "H.H."], *The Atlantic Monthly*, 26, no. 161 (1871): 400.

15. *The Nation* 13, no. 298 (16 March 1871): 184.

16. Quoted in Pierce, 315; and in "Mrs. Helen Jackson ('H.H.')," attributed to Thomas W. Higginson, *Century Magazine* 31 (November 1885–April 1886): 256.

17. Helen Jackson, *Poems* (Boston: Little, Brown, and Company, 1910).

18. Ellmann, *The New Oxford Book of American Verse*, 84, l. 2.

19. See Antoinette May, *Helen Hunt Jackson: A Lonely Voice of Conscience* (San Francisco: Chronicle Books, 1987), 27. This remark of Jackson's has been quoted frequently by her biographers as well as the popular press. From the nineteenth through the early twentieth centuries, critics and editors were interested by Jackson's businesslike attitude toward publishing. For instance, the caption to a cartoon in the *New York Times Book Review* for 3 August 1930 reads as follows: "'H.H.' Neatly Splits a Hair. Helen Hunt Jackson Makes a Nice Distinction. She Began to Write Because She Needed Money. Later She Remarked, 'I Do Not Write for Money, But I Print for Money.'" Rather than explain her remark as emanating from an ethos of privacy, these editors promoted the common image of nineteenth-century women writers as hacks, an impression that has continued until today.

20. Ralph Waldo Emerson, *Essay and Lectures*, ed. Joel Porte (New York: Library of America, 1983), 262–63.

21. Barton Levi St. Armand, *Emily Dickinson and Her Culture: The Soul's Society* (Cambridge: Cambridge University Press, 1984), 63.

22. See May, *Helen Hunt Jackson*, 26.

23. "Mrs. Helen Jackson ('H.H.')," 253.

24. Sigourney poignantly acknowledged late in life that writing too much had made her a literary jack-of-all-trades: "If there is any kitchen in Parnassus, my Muse has surely officiated there as a woman of all work, and an aproned waiter." Gordon S. Haight, *Mrs. Sigourney: The Sweet Singer of Hartford* (New Haven: Yale University Press, 1930), 46; originally in Lydia H. Sigourney, *Letters of Life* (New York, 1866), 376.

25. For another of Dickinson's bluebird poems, see the lyric beginning "After all Birds have been investigated and laid aside—" (J, 1395).

26. Reprinted in *The Colorado Prospector: Historical Highlights From Early Day Newspapers* 15, no. 4 (April 1984): 6. Courtesy of the Jones Library, Amherst, Massachusetts. Page numbers correspond to this reprint and are included parenthetically in the text.

27. Reprinted in *The Colorado Prospector: Historical Highlights from Early Day Newspapers* 15, no. 4 (April 1984): 4. Courtesy of the Jones Library, Amherst, Massachusetts. Page numbers correspond to this reprint and are included parenthetically in the text.

28. Alistair Fowler, *Kinds of Literature* (Cambridge, Mass.: Harvard University Press, 1982), 31. Quoted in Michael R. G. Spiller, *The Development of the Sonnet: An Introduction* (London and New York: Routledge, 1992), 2.

29. For similar lyrics by Jackson in which a woman is abandoned or injured within the home, see "Exile" and "A Woman's Death-Wound."
30. Spiller, *Development of the Sonnet*, 43–44.
31. See Johnson, ed., *The Poems of Emily Dickinson*, 3 vols. (Cambridge, Mass.: Harvard University Press, 1955), 1, 151–55; and Sewall 2, 491.
32. St. Armand, *Emily Dickinson and Her Culture*, 317.
33. Patterson, *Emily Dickinson's Imagery* (Amherst: University of Massachusetts, 1979), 141.
34. Adrienne Rich, "Vesuvius at Home: The Power of Emily Dickinson," *On Lies, Secrets, and Silence: Selected Prose 1966–1978* (New York: W. W. Norton & Company, 1979), esp. 166–74.
35. Ellmann, *The New Oxford Book of American Verse*, 211, l. 106.
36. Joanne Dobson, *Dickinson and the Strategies of Reticence: The Woman Writer in Nineteenth-Century America* (Bloomington and Indianapolis: Indiana University Press, 1989), 96.
37. Ellmann, *The New Oxford Book of American Verse*, 310, l. 31.
38. See "When the Baby Died" and "Just Out of Sight," *Poems*, 91–92, 240–41.

7. Seeing "New Englandly" (pp. 201–210)

1. Gilles Deleuze and Félix Guattari, *Kafka: Toward a Minor Literature*, trans. Dana Polan, Theory and History of Literature (Minneapolis: University of Minnesota Press, 1986), 30: 16.
2. George Monteiro and Barton Levi St. Armand, "The Experienced Emblem: A Study of the Poetry of Emily Dickinson," *Prospects: A Journal of American Cultural Studies* 6 (1981): 187.
3. For recent critiques of sentimental literature designed to reclaim nineteenth-century American women's literature, see Joanne Dobson, "Reclaiming Sentimental Literature," *American Literature* 69, no. 2 (June 1997): 263–88; Paula Bennett, "Not Just Filler and Not Just Sentimental: Women's Poetry in American Victorian Periodicals, 1860–1900," *Periodical Literature in Nineteenth-Century America*, ed. Kenneth M. Price and Susan Belasco Smith (Charlottesville: The University Press of Virginia, 1995); and Susan K. Harris, *19th-Century American Women's Novels: Interpretive Strategies* (Cambridge: Cambridge University Press, 1990).
4. Dobson, "Reclaiming Sentimental Literature," 266.
5. Judith Fetterley, "Commentary: Nineteenth-Century American Women Writers and the Politics of Recovery," *American Literary History* 6, no. 3 (Fall 1994): 603.
6. See Paula Bennett, "Late Nineteenth-Century American Women's Nature Poetry and the Evolution of the Imagist Poem," *Legacy: A Journal of American Women Writers* 9, no. 2 (1992): 92.
7. Louise Bogan, *Achievement in American Poetry, 1900–1950* (Chicago: Henry Regnery Company, 1951), 21.
8. Fetterley, "Commentary," 600.
9. Jane Tompkins, *Sensational Designs: The Cultural Work of American Fiction, 1790–1860* (New York: Oxford University Press, 1985), 126.

10. Paul Lauter, "Teaching Nineteenth-Century American Women Writers," *Canons and Contexts* (New York: Oxford University Press, 1991), 128.

11. Often describing the setting of primeval America, in which Native-Americans figure prominently and whose dispossession and effacement from history is recounted, Sigourney, for example, undertook to address the relentless genocide in nineteenth-century America in *Zinzendorff and Other Poems* (New York and Boston, 1833) and *Pocahontas and Other Poems* (London, 1841). For a discussion of Sigourney's political and historical activism, see Nina Baym, "Reinventing Lydia Sigourney," *American Literature* 62, no. 3 (Sept. 1990): 385–404.

12. Mary Jacobus, "The Question of Language: Men of Maxims and *The Mill on the Floss*," *Critical Inquiry* 8, no. 2 (Winter 1981): 210.

13. See Sewall 2, 539. Originally appeared as Thomas Wentworth Higginson, "Letter to a Young Contributor," *The Atlantic Monthly* 9, no. 54 (April 1862): 410.

14. Jane Tompkins, *A Life in School: What the Teacher Learned* (Reading, Mass.: Addison-Wesley Publishing Company, Inc., 1996), 212.

Index

University Press of New England publishes books under its own imprint and is the publisher for Brandeis University Press, Dartmouth College, Middlebury College Press, University of New Hampshire, Tufts University, and Wesleyan University Press.

Library of Congress Cataloging-in-Publication Data
Petrino, Elizabeth A., 1962–
Emily Dickinson and her contemporaries : women's verse in America, 1820–1885 / Elizabeth A. Petrino.
    p.   cm.
  Includes bibliographical references and index.
  ISBN 0–87451–838–5 (alk. paper)
    1. Dickinson, Emily, 1830–1886—Criticism and interpretation.
2. Women and literature—United States—History—19th century.
3. American poetry—Women authors—History and criticism.
4. American poetry—19th century—History and criticism.
5. Dickinson, Emily, 1830–1886—Contemporaries.
PS1541.Z5P44   1998
811'.3099287'09034—dc21   97–44600

DATE DUE

#47-0108 Peel Off Pressure Sensitive